Comparative Law Yearbook of International Business

Comparative Law Yearbook of International Business

Volume 42A, 2021

General Editor

Christian Campbell

Wolters Kluwer

Published by:
Kluwer Law International B.V.
PO Box 316
2400 AH Alphen aan den Rijn
The Netherlands
E-mail: international-sales@wolterskluwer.com
Website: lrus.wolterskluwer.com

Sold and distributed by:
Wolters Kluwer Legal & Regulatory U.S.
7201 McKinney Circle
Frederick, MD 21704
United States of America
Email: customer.service@wolterskluwer.com

Printed on acid-free paper.

ISBN 978-94-035-3163-2

e-Book: ISBN 978-94-035-3164-9
web-PDF: ISBN 978-94-035-3165-6

Printed and bound by CPI Group (UK) Ltd, Croydon, CR0 4YY

The Center for International Legal Studies

The Center for International Legal Studies is a non-profit research and publications institute established and operating under Austrian law, with its international headquarters in Salzburg, Austria.

The Center has operated since 1976 in Salzburg, and it has close cooperation with the faculties of law of the University of Salzburg, Boston University and Suffolk University in the United States, Lazarski University in Poland, Eötvös Loránd University in Hungary, and numerous other universities and educational institutions in Europe.

The Comparative Law Yearbook of International Business prints matter it deems worthy of publication. Views expressed in material appearing herein are those of the authors and do not necessarily reflect the policies or opinions of the Comparative Law Yearbook of International Business, its editors, or the Center for International Legal Studies.

Manuscripts proposed for publication may be sent by email to:

The Editor

Comparative Law Yearbook of International Business
christian.campbell@cils.org

Summary of Contents

Table of Contents

Editor's Note

Climate change and the COVID-19 pandemic have brought into focus how vulnerable our "normal" lives are. More than ever, there is a need to regulate the competition for and exploitation of increasingly scare natural resources. But how are the competing interests to be balanced? And who is to undertake the regulation? The air, the climate, and the seas escape national boundaries. And while the reset of the pandemic may have alleviated some of the pressure, it has also highlighted how health and hygiene regimes are of global importance.

The present volume does not capture the breadth or depth of current concerns of international environmental law. However, it does offer seven *amuse-bouches* to whet readers' intellectual appetites: EU perspectives on habitat protection and risk management in times of climate change and health crises; WTO perspectives on the renewable energy sector and the protection of marine habitats; a discourse on how international law imposes environmental responsibilities with regard to disputed maritime areas; a comparison of national regulations against each other and the international framework for dealing with plastic waste; a look at Kuwait's evolving approach to waste disposal and management; an examination of Brazil's legal framework for dam safety in the wake of recent catastrophic events; and finally, a pioneering Third World Approaches to International Law (TWAIL) in regard to destruction of the Amazon.

Acknowledgments

Interpretation of Article 6(3) of the Habitats Directive in Light of Recent ECJ Case Law

Kim Trenskow, Mads U. Østergaard & Mikkel Vindfeldt
Rådhuspladsen 3
8000, Aarhus C,
Denmark
Phone number: +45 38 77 43 99
Email address: kt@kromannreumert.com
mvi@kromannreumert.com
mtg@kromannreumert.com

Climate Change and Pandemics: The Need for a Renewed EU Risk-Management Strategy

Alessandra Donati
18/A, Rue de Mamer
8081 Bertrange,
Luxembourg
Email address: adonati4so@gmail.com
alessandra.donati@mpi.lu

Domestic Content Requirements in the Renewable Energy Sector: What Policy Space Exists under WTO Rules?

Nathan Jin Bao
Gowling WLG LLP
160 Elgin Street, Ottawa, Canada
K1P 1C3
Ottawa
Canada
Phone number: 6469159737
Email address: china_icsid_bao@yahoo.com

WTO Panel and Appellate Body Jurisprudence on Environmental Protection of Marine Living Resources: Considerations for the Maritime Silk Road Shipping Policies

Henrik Andersen
CBS Law – Copenhagen Business School
Porcelænshaven 18/B
2000
Frederiksberg
Denamrk
Phone number: +4531404145
Email address: ha.law@cbs.dk

States' Environmental Obligations in Disputed Maritime Areas and the Limits of International Law

Constantinos Yiallourides & Natalia Ermolina
British Institute of International and Comparative Law
Charles Clore House, 17 Russell Square
WC1B 5JP
London
United Kingdom
Phone number: +44-7716066021
Email address: c.yiallourides@biicl.org

Grappling with Plastic: An Increasingly Inflexible Legal Issue

Adam R. Fox, Chassica Soo & Jonathan S. King
Squire Patton Boggs
1801 California Street, Ste 4900 Denver,
CO 80202
Phone number: 970 309 4314
Email address: jonathan.king@squirepb.com

Environmental Degradation: Waste Disposal and Management in Kuwait

Ralph Palliam & Sara Al-Othman
American University of Kuwait
3423, Kuwait City
Kuwait
Phone number: +965 670 40 237
Email Address: rpalliam@cwk.edu.kw

Brazil's Comprehensive Regulations on Large Dams Safety

Leonardo Lamego
Azevedo Sette Advogados
R. Paraíba, 1000, Savasi, Belo Horizonte
Minas Gerais, Brazil, 30130145
Email Address: llamego@zazevedosette.com.br

The Collapsing of the Earth's Lungs: Could "Third World Approaches to International Law" Breathe Air into the Amazonian Crisis?

Warona Jolomba
King's Collge, London
WC2R 2LS
London
United Kingdom
Phone number: +44 7575 201 569
Email address: waronajolomba@hotmail.co.uk

Interpretation of Article 6(3) of the Habitats Directive in Light of Recent ECJ Case Law

Kim Trenskow
Partner (Aarhus), Kromann Reumert, Denmark

Mads U. Østergaard
Senior Attorney (Aarhus), Kromann Reumert, Denmark

Mikkel Vindfeldt
Assistant Attorney (Aarhus), Kromann Reumert, Denmark

Introduction

Since the EU passed Directive 92/43/EEC on the Conservation of Natural Habitats and of Wild Fauna and Flora (the 'Habitats Directive') on 21 May 1992, screenings and assessments of environmental implications on NATURA 2000 sites have been an essential component in national authorities' permitting regimes.[1]

Before issuing the necessary permits for a wide variety of projects, e.g., the establishment or expansion of production facilities, raw materials extraction, and almost every other industrial activity, the national authority must conduct a screening and, in some cases, an appropriate assessment examining the project's implications for NATURA 2000 sites.[2] However, it is important to stress that not only will these obligations under the

---

1 NATURA 2000 sites are locations designated in accordance with the Habitats Directive and Directive 2009/147/EC on the Conservation of Wild Birds (the 'Birds Directive'), *see* EU FAQ.

2 This chapter focuses on the regime defined in Article 6(3) of the Habitats Directive which applies to specific circumstances. However, the Habitats Directive also contains in Article 6(1) and 6(2) a general regime described by the European Commission as follows: 'Article 6(1) deals with the establishment of the necessary conservation measures, and focuses on positive and proactive measures to maintain or restore the natural habitats and the populations of species of wild fauna and flora at a favorable status. Article 6(2) makes provision for avoidance of habitat deterioration and significant species disturbance. Its emphasis is therefore preventive', cf. the European Commission, *Managing Natura 2000 Sites – The Provisions of Article 6 of the 'Habitats' Directive 92/43/EEC* (2018), pp. 7-8.

Habitats Directive be relevant to traditional industrial activities causing material pollution and the like, but their reach is also wider and extends even to 'projects' with no – apparent – measurable adverse effect on the environment. In recent years, we have seen case law on, e.g., coastal protection and deforestation with the aim of preserving forests, in which permitted measures were deemed inconsistent with the Habitats Directive.

The obligation to screen and assess is derived from Article 6(3) of the Habitats Directive, according to which national authorities shall agree to the project only after having ascertained that it will not adversely affect the integrity of a NATURA 2000 site.

The effective implementation and application of Article 6(3) of the Habitats Directive in national permitting procedures has been supported by extensive case law from the European Court of Justice (the 'ECJ' or the 'Court'), in which the ECJ interprets and clarifies the various criteria of Article 6(3), and by the fact that the Habitats Directive has direct effect in the Member States, cf. Case C-127/02, *Waddenzee*, paragraphs 69-70.

Due to the requirements laid down in Article 6(3) of the Habitats Directive, the implementation of the Habitats Directive in the Danish law has had a huge impact on Danish companies and the ability to establish and conduct projects and industrial activities.[3] In some cases, the appropriate assessment has rejected the establishment of the project, and, in other cases, Danish appeals bodies have revoked or invalidated companies' newly issued permits due to lack of or errors in the assessment. To our knowledge, similar consequences of the Habitats Directive are seen in other Member States, although awareness of recent ECJ case law varies throughout the Member States.

Therefore, it is important – especially for legal advisors on environmental matters – to be aware of the procedures and requirements laid down in Article 6(3) of the Habitats Directive. Disregard for those procedures and requirements, ultimately, could lead to the annulment of a permit necessary for conducting a legal and ongoing activity.

The purpose of this chapter is to examine – in light of recent case law from the ECJ – selected criteria of Article 6(3) of the Habitats Directive that are essential for national authorities, legal advisors and companies to be aware of when interpreting and understanding the requirements of the Habitats Directive. These are:

(1)   What is a 'project' for the purposes of Article 6(3)?

---

3 Jacob Brandt & Mark Walters, *Miljøret* (9th edn, 2018), p. 232.

(2) When is a project not 'likely to have a significant effect' on a NATURA 2000 site?
(3) What is meant by an 'appropriate' assessment?
(4) When will a project 'not adversely affect the integrity' of a NATURA 2000 site?
(5) Who is responsible for conducting the appropriate assessment?

Article 6(3) of the Habitats Directive

The full wording of Article 6 of the Habitats Directive is as follows:

1. For special areas of conservation, Member States shall establish the necessary conservation measures involving, if need be, appropriate management plans specifically designed for the sites or integrated into other development plans, and appropriate statutory, administrative or contractual measures which correspond to the ecological requirements of the natural habitat types in Annex I and the species in Annex II present on the sites.
2. Member States shall take appropriate steps to avoid, in the special areas of conservation, the deterioration of natural habitats and the habitats of species as well as disturbance of the species for which the areas have been designated, in so far as such disturbance could be significant in relation to the objectives of this Directive.
3. *Any plan or project not directly connected with or necessary to the management of the site but likely to have a significant effect thereon, either individually or in combination with other plans or projects, shall be subject to appropriate assessment of its implications for the site in view of the site's conservation objectives. In the light of the conclusions of the assessment of the implications for the site and subject to the provisions of paragraph 4, the competent national authorities shall agree to the plan or project only after having ascertained that it will not adversely affect the integrity of the site concerned and, if appropriate, after having obtained the opinion of the general public.* (emphasis added)

4. If, in spite of a negative assessment of the implications for the site and in the absence of alternative solutions, a plan or project must nevertheless be carried out for imperative reasons of overriding public interest, including those of a social or economic nature, the Member State shall take all compensatory measures necessary to ensure that the overall coherence of Natura 2000 is protected. It shall inform the Commission of the compensatory measures adopted.

Where the site concerned hosts a priority natural habitat type and/or a priority species, the only considerations which may be raised are those relating to human health or public safety, to beneficial consequences of primary importance for the environment or, further to an opinion from the Commission, to other imperative reasons of overriding public interest.

The European Commission has stated:

'Article 6 [of the Habitats Directive] is one of the most important of the 24 articles of the Directive, being the one which most determines the relationship between conservation and other socioeconomic activities' and that '[t]he provisions of Article 6(3) and (4) constitute a form of permitting regime, setting out the circumstances within which plans and projects with likely significant negative effects on Natura 2000 sites may or may not be allowed'.[4]

Article 6(3) of the Habitats Directive contains both procedural and substantive aspects.

The procedural aspect lies in the obligation to conduct a screening and, in some cases, an appropriate assessment of the project. For example, when companies apply for establishment or expansion of, e.g., a plant, the national authority is, first, obliged to conduct a screening to establish if the project is 'likely to have a significant effect' on one or more NATURA 2000 sites. Second, if the project is likely to have significant effect, the project 'shall be subject to appropriate assessment of its implications for the site in view of the site's conservation objectives'.

---

4 The European Commission, *Managing Natura 2000 Sites – The Provisions of Article 6 of the 'Habitats' Directive 92/43/EEC* (2018), pp. 7 and 33.

The substantive aspect lies primarily in the second sentence of Article 6(3), which states that the national authority may issue the necessary permits to the project 'only after having ascertained that it will not adversely affect the integrity of the [NATURA 2000] site concerned'. Also, the necessary permit may only be issued if the project is not likely to have a significant effect on NATURA 2000 sites.

A step-by-step guide on the procedural and substantive aspects of Article 6(3) has been summarized by the European Commission in this figure.[5]

---

5 The figure is found in the European Commission, *Managing Natura 2000 Sites – The Provisions of Article 6 of the 'Habitats' Directive 92/43/EEC* (2018), p. 78.

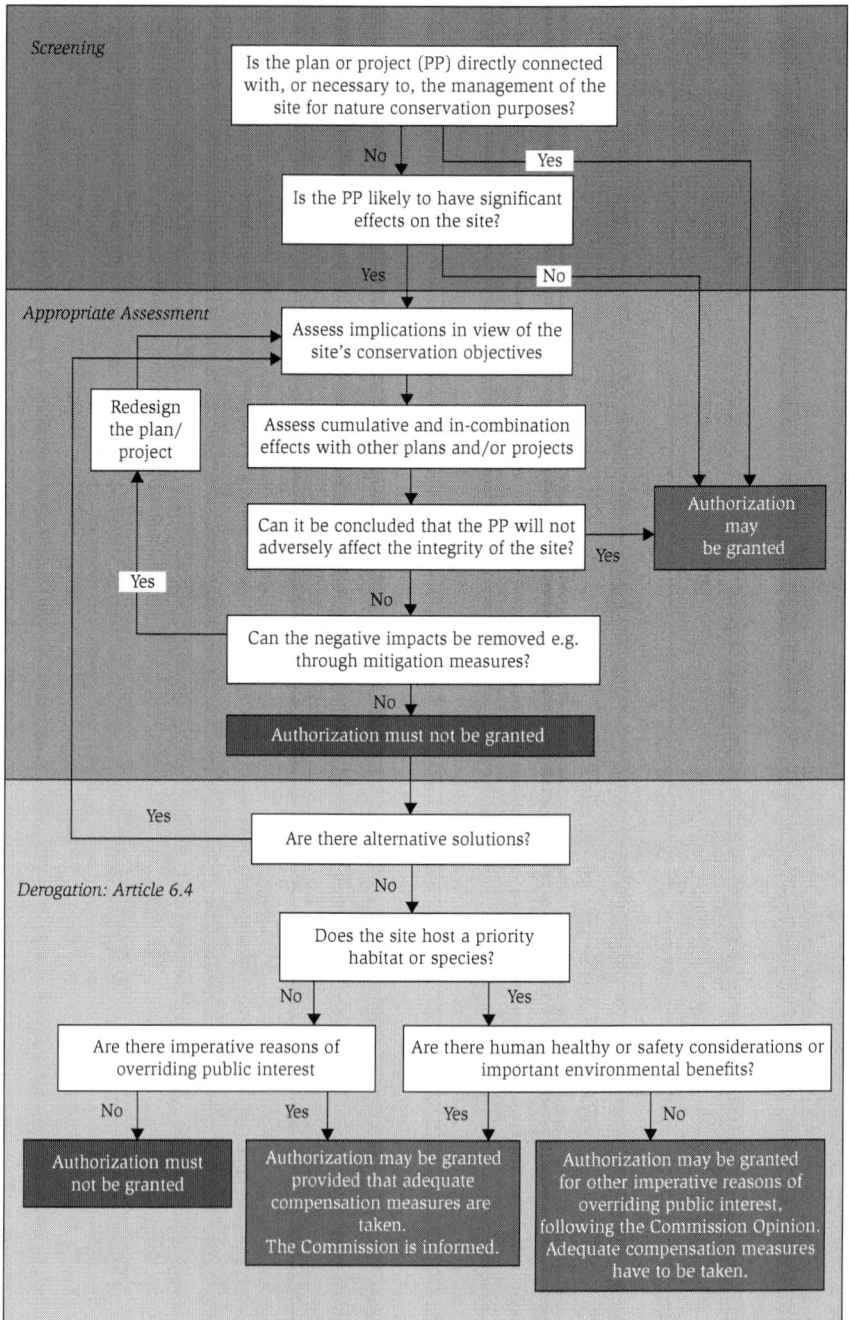

Screening

Is the plan or project (PP) directly connected with, or necessary to, the management of the site for nature conservation purposes?

No → | Yes →

Is the PP likely to have significant effects on the site?

Yes ↓ | No →

Appropriate Assessment

Assess implications in view of the site's conservation objectives

Redesign the plan/project

Assess cumulative and in-combination effects with other plans and/or projects

Can it be concluded that the PP will not adversely affect the integrity of the site? — Yes →

Authorization may be granted

Yes

No ↓

Can the negative impacts be removed e.g. through mitigation measures?

No ↓

Authorization must not be granted

Yes

Are there alternative solutions?

Derogation: Article 6.4

No ↓

Does the site host a priority habitat or species?

No ↓ | Yes ↓

Are there imperative reasons of overriding public interest | Are there human healthy or safety considerations or important environmental benefits?

No ↓ | Yes ↓ | Yes ↓ | No ↓

Authorization must not be granted | Authorization may be granted provided that adequate compensation measures are taken. The Commission is informed. | Authorization may be granted for other imperative reasons of overriding public interest, following the Commission Opinion. Adequate compensation measures have to be taken.

The figure shows the large number of steps and assessments that must be completed prior to the national authorities' authorization of a company's project, indicating by extension that the procedure can be protracted.

On these grounds, the Habitats Directive might be an obstacle to companies' business plans, preventing the establishment or expansion of necessary plants or setting a time frame that is too long to be commercially feasible from a business perspective. These obstacles can be prevented or mitigated only if the company's legal advisor knows about the different criteria of Article 6(3) of the Habitats Directive and their application.

In the following, therefore, we will examine those of the listed criteria of Article 6(3) which an environmental legal advisor to companies should, in our opinion, be aware of:

(1) What is a 'project' for the purposes of Article 6(3)?
(2) When is a project not 'likely to have a significant effect' on a NATURA 2000 site?
(3) What is meant by an 'appropriate' assessment?
(4) When will a project 'not adversely affect the integrity' of a NATURA 2000 site?
(5) Who is responsible for conducting the appropriate assessment?

Before looking into these questions, the leading ECJ case on the interpretation of Article 6(3) will be presented.

Case Law from the ECJ and the Leading Case

There is extensive ECJ case law on the Habitats Directive, in which the Court has interpreted and – to a certain degree – clarified the different criteria in Article 6(3). The leading case in this regard is Case C-127/02, *Waddenzee*, which the ECJ still refers to in its newest decisions. As we will be referring to this case when examining the questions listed above, the factual background to the case will be presented here.

In 1999 and 2000, the Dutch Secretary of State licensed Coöperatieve Producentenorganisatie van de Nederlandse Kokkelvisserij UA (Cooperative Producers' Association of Netherlands Cockle Fisheries) to engage in mechanical cockle fishing in the Waddenzee. At the time of the issuing of the licences, the Waddenzee was designated as a national natural site.

Two nature protection associations challenged the decisions of the Secretary of State before the Raad van State (Council of State), claiming in essence:

[C]ockle fishing, as authorised by the decisions at issue in the main action, causes permanent damage to the geomorphology, flora and fauna of the Waddenzee's seabed. They also submitted that such fishing reduces the food stocks of birds which feed on shellfish, causing a decline in their populations, in particular for oystercatchers and eider ducks. [The two nature protection associations] also claimed that those decisions were contrary to the Habitats and Birds Directives.[6]

The Council of State submitted five questions (and a number of sub-questions) regarding the interpretation of Article 6(3) of the Habitats Directive, which the ECJ answered in its decision. The Court's answers to these fundamental questions will be presented in the following sections.

What Is a 'Project' for the Purposes of Article 6(3)?

The Habitats Directive contains no definition of the term 'project', the understanding of which must be derived from ECJ case law.

In Case C-127/02, *Waddenzee*, paragraphs 21-30, the ECJ interpreted the term 'project' of the Habitats Directive in accordance with the definition of 'project' in Directive 85/337/EEC on the Assessment of the Effects of Certain Public and Private Projects on the Environment (the 'EIA Directive').[7] The Court stated:

> 23. The Habitats Directive does not define the terms 'plan' and 'project'.
> 24. By contrast, Council Directive 85/337/EEC of 27 June 1985 on the assessment of the effects of certain public and private projects on the environment (OJ 1985 L 175, p. 40), (...), defines 'project' as follows in Article 1(2):
> '– the execution of construction works or of other installations or schemes,
> – other interventions in the natural surroundings and landscape including those involving the extraction of mineral resources.'

---

6 Cf. Case C-127/02, *Waddenzee*, paragraph 13.
7 The EIA Directive was amended in 2011 by the new EIA Directive (Directive 2011/92/EU) which contains the same definition of 'project' as the previous EIA Directive.

25. An activity such as mechanical cockle fishing is within the concept of 'project' as defined in the second indent of Article 1(2) of Directive 85/337.

26. *Such a definition of 'project' is relevant to defining the concept of plan or project as provided for in the Habitats Directive* (emphasis added), which, as is clear from the foregoing, seeks, as does Directive 85/337, to prevent activities which are likely to damage the environment from being authorised without prior assessment of their impact on the environment.

27. Therefore, an activity such as mechanical cockle fishing is covered by the concept of plan or project set out in Article 6(3) of the Habitats Directive.

As mentioned in *Waddenzee*, Article 1(2)(a) of the EIA Directive defines a 'project' as 'the execution of construction works or of other installations or schemes, [or] other interventions in the natural surroundings and landscape including those involving the extraction of mineral resources'.

Elaborating on this definition, the European Commission has stated that '[t]his is a very broad definition ... which is not limited to physical construction but also covers other interventions in the natural environment including regular activities aimed at utilising natural resources. For example, a significant intensification of agriculture which threatens to damage or destroy the semi-natural character of a site may be covered.'[8]

Therefore, when deciding whether, e.g., a company's establishment or expansion of a plant constitutes a 'project' for the purposes of the Habitats Directive, it is relevant to examine the definition of 'project' in the EIA Directive and case law in relation to both the Habitats Directive and the EIA Directive.

However, a recent decision from the ECJ shows that the Habitats Directive adopts a broader definition of a 'project' than does Article 1(2)(a) of the EIA Directive. In Joined Cases C-293/17 and C-294/17, *Coöperatie Mobilisation for the Environment*, paragraphs 59-73, the Court stated:

59. By the first question in Case C-293/17, the referring court asks, in essence, whether Article 6(3) of the Habitats Directive must be interpreted as meaning that the grazing of cattle and the application of fertilisers on the surface of land or below its surface in the vicinity of Natura 2000 sites may be classified as a 'project' within

---

8   The European Commission, *Managing Natura 2000 Sites – The Provisions of Article 6 of the 'Habitats' Directive 92/43/EEC* (2018), p. 36.

the meaning of that provision, on the ground that they are likely to have significant consequences for those sites, even if those activities, in so far as they are not a physical intervention in the natural surroundings, do not constitute a 'project' within the meaning of Article 1(2)(a) of the EIA Directive.

60. In the first place, it must be noted that, while the Habitats Directive does not define the concept of 'project', it is apparent from the Court's case-law that the definition of 'project' within the meaning of Article 1(2)(a) of the EIA Directive is relevant to defining the concept of project as provided for in the Habitats Directive … .

…

63. It must be noted that the requirements relating to 'works' or 'interventions involving alterations to the physical aspect' or even an 'intervention in the natural surroundings' are not to be found in Article 6(3) of the Habitats Directive, that provision requiring an appropriate assessment, inter alia where a project is likely to have a 'significant' effect on a site.

64. Thus, Article 1(2)(a) of the EIA Directive defines the concept of 'project' for the proposes of that provision, attaching to it conditions that are not specified in the equivalent provision of the Habitats Directive.

65. In the same vein, it follows from the Court's case-law that, in so far as the definition of the concept of 'project' stemming from Directive 85/337 is more restrictive than that stemming from the Habitats Directive, if an activity is covered by Directive 85/337, it must, a fortiori, be covered the Habitats Directive … .

66. *It follows that, if an activity is regarded as a 'project' within the meaning of the EIA Directive, it may constitute a 'project' within the meaning of the Habitats Directive. However, the mere fact that an activity may not be classified as a 'project' within the meaning of the EIA Directive does not suffice, in itself, to infer therefrom that the activity may not be covered by the concept of 'project' within the meaning of the Habitats Directive.* (emphasis added)

67. In the second place, in order to determine whether the grazing of cattle and the application of fertilisers on the surface of land or below its surface may be classified as a 'project' within the meaning of Article 6(3) of the Habitats Directive, it is important to examine whether such activities are likely to have a significant effect on a protected site.

68. The 10th recital of the Habitats Directive states that an appropriate assessment must be made of any plan or programme likely to have a significant effect on the conservation objectives of a site which has been designated or is designated in future. That recital finds expression in Article 6(3) of the directive, which provides, inter alia, that a plan or project likely to have a significant effect on the site concerned cannot be authorised without a prior assessment of its implications for that site … .

…

73. *In the light of the foregoing, the answer to the first question in Case C-293/17 is that Article 6(3) of the Habitats Directive must be interpreted as meaning that the grazing of cattle and the application of fertilisers on the surface of land or below its surface in the vicinity of Natura 2000 sites may be classified as a 'project' within the meaning of that provision, even if those activities, in so far as they are not a physical intervention in the natural surroundings, do not constitute a 'project' within the meaning of Article 1(2)(a) of the EIA Directive.* (emphasis added)

Based on this case, legal advisors and national authorities cannot rely entirely on the definition of a 'project' in the EIA Directive and related case law. Even though the definition of 'project' in the EIA Directive offers a guideline, a 'project' for the purposes of the Habitats Directive must be understood in a broader perspective, and the decisive factor in the interpretation of a 'project' rather seems to be whether the activity is likely to have a significant effect on a protected site.

The term 'project' does not indicate whether the national authorities must conduct a screening and, if necessary, an appropriate assessment according to Article 6(3) when renewing or reissuing companies' environmental permit or other permits that were issued prior to the Habitats Directive coming into force.[9]

Some clarification to this question was provided in Case C-127/02, *Waddenzee*, paragraphs 29-30, in which the Court stated:

---

9 In Case C-226/08, *Stadt Papenburg*, and Joined Cases C-293/17 and C-294/17, *Coöperatie Mobilisation for the Environment*, the Court considered whether recurring activities authorized under national law before the entry into force of the Habitats Directive may be regarded as one and the same project for the purposes of Article 6(3), and found that such activities do not fall within the scope of said provision.

28. The fact that the activity has been carried on periodically for several years on the site concerned and that a licence has to be obtained for it every year, each new issuance of *which requires an assessment both of the possibility of carrying on that activity and of the site where it may be carried on* (emphasis added), does not in itself constitute an obstacle to considering it, at the time of each application, as a distinct plan or project within the meaning of the Habitats Directive.

29. The answer ... must therefore be that mechanical cockle fishing *which has been carried on for many years but for which a licence is granted annually for a limited period, with each licence entailing a new assessment both of the possibility of carrying on that activity and of the site where it may be carried on, falls within the concept of 'plan' or 'project' within the meaning of Article 6(3) of the Habitats Directive.* (emphasis added)

However, many permits are not granted for a limited period. Further, if the company has not increased or expanded its activities, a renewal or reissue of the permit does not necessarily entail new assessments of the company's possibility of carrying on the activities or the site where the activities may be carried on. The *Waddenzee* case does not address the applicability of Article 6(3) in these situations.

It is still not clarified in ECJ case law whether Article 6(3) is applicable in these situations. An indication to the answer might be found in Case C-275/09, *Brussels Airport*, regarding the interpretation of the term 'project' in the EIA Directive. In paragraphs 20-24, the Court stated:

20. ..., it is apparent from the very wording of Article 1(2) of Directive 85/337 that the term 'project' refers to works or physical interventions.

21. It is expressly stated in the order for reference that *the measure at issue in the main proceedings is limited to the renewal of the existing consent to operate Bruxelles National Airport* and does not entail works or interventions which alter the physical aspect of the site. (emphasis added)

...

24. It follows that *the renewal of an existing permit to operate an airport cannot, in the absence of any works or interventions involving alterations to the physical aspect of the site, be classified as a 'project'* (emphasis added) within the meaning of the second indent of Article 1(2) of Directive 85/337.

In Case C-121/11, *Pro Braine*, paragraphs 31-32, the Court similarly stated:

> 31. As has been established by the Court, the term 'project' refers to works or interventions involving alterations to the physical aspect of the site … .
> 32. *Thus, the mere renewal of an existing permit to operate a landfill site cannot, in the absence of any works or interventions involving alterations to the physical aspect of the site, be classified as a 'project'* (emphasis added) within the meaning of Article 1(2) of Directive 85/337.

Therefore, relevant case law related to the EIA Directive could indicate that such renewals and reissues do not fall within the scope of 'project' in Article 6(3) of the Habitats Directive, either, but the ECJ has not yet, as mentioned, clarified these situations.

In light of the case law related to the EIA Directive, we are currently conducting a case in which the relation between renewal of permits issued prior to the Habitats Directive coming into force and the term 'project' in Article 6(3) becomes relevant and which will be referred to the ECJ for a preliminary ruling. Presumably, this preliminary ruling will clarify the scope of the term 'project' in Article 6(3) in relation to renewal and reissue of such permits.

When Is a Project Not 'Likely to Have a Significant Effect' on a NATURA 2000 Site?

According to the first sentence of Article 6(3), any project likely to have a significant effect on a NATURA 2000 site should be subject to an appropriate assessment.

From the wording of the Article, it is not clear if it should be substantiated that the project might have a significant effect on a NATURA 2000 site, or if an appropriate assessment will be necessary in every case where it cannot be excluded that the project would have such an effect.

This question was clarified in Case C-127/02, *Waddenzee*, paragraphs 39-45, in which the Court found:

> 39. According to the first sentence of Article 6(3) of the Habitats Directive, any plan or project not directly connected with or necessary to the management of the site but likely to have a significant effect thereon, either individually or in combination with other plans

or projects, is to be subject to appropriate assessment of its implications for the site in view of the site's conservation objectives.

40. The requirement for an appropriate assessment of the implications of a plan or project is thus conditional on its being likely to
have a significant effect on the site.

41. Therefore, the triggering of the environmental protection
mechanism provided for in Article 6(3) of the Habitats Directive
does not presume – ... – that the plan or project considered
definitely has significant effects on the site concerned *but follows
from the mere probability that such an effect attaches to that plan or
project* (emphasis added).

...

43. It follows that the first sentence of Article 6(3) of the Habitats
Directive subordinates the requirement for an appropriate assessment of the implications of a plan or project to the condition that
there be a probability or a risk that the latter will have significant
effects on the site concerned.

44. In the light, in particular, of the precautionary principle, ... , and
by reference to which the Habitats Directive must be interpreted,
*such a risk exists if it cannot be excluded on the basis of objective
information that the plan or project will have significant effects on
the site concerned* (emphasis added) .... Such an interpretation of
the condition to which the assessment of the implications of a plan
or project for a specific site is subject, which implies *that in case of
doubt as to the absence of significant effects such an assessment
must be carried out* (emphasis added), makes it possible to ensure
effectively that plans or projects which adversely affect the integrity
of the site concerned are not authorised, ...

45. In the light of the foregoing, the answer ... must be that the first
sentence of Article 6(3) of the Habitats Directive must be interpreted as meaning that any plan or project not directly connected
with or necessary to the management of the site is to be subject to an
appropriate assessment of its implications for the site in view of the
site's conservation objectives *if it cannot be excluded, on the basis of
objective information, that it will have a significant effect on that
site* (emphasis added), either individually or in combination with
other plans or projects.

In the case, the ECJ established the general presumption in Article 6(3)
that all projects are likely to have a significant effect on a NATURA 2000

site and, therefore, should be subject to an appropriate assessment. Consequently, an appropriate assessment can only be omitted if it can be excluded, based on objective information, that the project will have a significant effect on a NATURA 2000 site.

The ECJ has considered in a number of cases whether it can be excluded, on the basis of objective information, that a project will have a significant effect and, as a result thereof, a screening being sufficient according to Article 6(3).

It does not necessarily exclude a project from having significant effect on a NATURA 2000 site that the project is located outside NATURA 2000 sites or the proximity hereof.[10] In some cases, even very large distances between the project and the NATURA 2000 site will not be enough to exclude a significant effect on the site concerned. For an illustrative example of this, Case C-142/16, *The European Commission v. Germany,* the so-called *Moorburg case*, will be useful.

In this case, the European Commission had brought an action against Germany for failure to fulfilling obligations under Article 6(3) of the Habitats Directive. The action concerned a coal-fired power plant in Hamburg and the migratory route for certain fish species to NATURA 2000 sites. A description of the plant and its location in relation to the migratory route is given in paragraph 6 of the judgment:

6. The Moorburg coal-fired power plant is situated within the port of Hamburg, on the south bank of the southern section of *the Elbe river which, as a migratory route for certain fish species listed in Annex II to the Habitats Directive, namely river lamprey (Lampetra fluviatilis), sea lamprey (Petromyzon marinus) and salmon (Salmo salar), plays an important role in a number of Natura 2000 areas situated upstream of the Geesthacht weir* (emphasis added) (Germany) whose conservation objectives cover those species. Those areas are situated in the Länder of Lower Saxony, Mecklenburg-Vorpommern, Saxony-Anhalt, Brandenburg, and Saxony, up to a distance of 600 km from the plant. The Geesthacht weir is situated on the Elbe corridor, in between the Moorburg power plant and the Natura 2000 areas.

10 *See also* the European Commission, *Managing Natura 2000 Sites – The Provisions of Article 6 of the 'Habitats' Directive 92/43/EEC* (2018), p. 41.

In the judgment, the Court considered the significance of the large distance between the plant and the relevant NATURA 2000 sites and stated in paragraphs 29-32:

> 29. It should be noted at the outset that the fact that the project to which the environmental assessment being challenged relates *is not situated in the Natura 2000 areas concerned, but rather at a considerable distance from them, upstream of the Elbe, in no way precludes the applicability of the requirements laid down in Article 6(3) of the Habitats Directive.* (emphasis added) It is clear from the wording of that provision that 'any plan or project not directly connected with or necessary to the management of the site but likely to have a significant effect thereon' is subject to the environmental protection mechanism it prescribes.
>
> 30. In the present case, it is apparent from the file submitted to the Court that *the cooling mechanism of the Moorburg plant is likely to have a significant effect* (emphasis added)on certain fish species listed in Annex II to the Habitats Directive and protected in the Natura 2000 areas concerned.
>
> 31. The impact assessment carried out by the German authorities showed that the death of fish pertaining to three species listed in Annex II to the Habitats Directive, *on account of the Moorburg plant drawing cooling water from their migratory corridor, would affect the reproduction of those species in the relevant protected areas* (emphasis added). In particular, that assessment indicated a high risk for highly migratory species such as river lamprey, sea lamprey and salmon.
>
> 32. In the light of that impact assessment, the German authorities could not, pursuant to the second sentence of Article 6(3) of the Habitats Directive, agree to the construction of the Moorburg power station until they had 'ascertained that it [would] not adversely affect the integrity of the site[s] concerned'.

Even though the proposed project is not in itself likely to have a significant effect on NATURA 2000 sites, it is necessary in the screening to consider existing projects in the vicinity of the proposed project. In this regard, it does not matter whether the existing projects were approved prior to the passing of the Habitats Directive. The European Commission has summarized the relevance of existing projects as follows:

In addition to the effects of those plans or projects which are the main subject of the assessment, it may be appropriate *to consider the effects of already completed plans and projects* (emphasis added) in this 'second level' of assessment, including those preceding the date of transposition of the Directive or the date of designation of the site (*see, for example*, C142/16, paragraphs 61 and 63). Although already completed plans and projects are themselves excluded from the assessment requirements of Article 6(3), *it is still important to take them into consideration when assessing the impacts of the current plan or project in order to determine whether there are any potential cumulative effects arising from the current project in combination with other already completed plans and projects.* (emphasis added).[11]

In Case C-323/17, *People over Wind*, the Court considered whether mitigation measures can be taken into consideration in the screening stage of the process, stating in paragraphs 31-40:

31. In the present instance, as the parties to the main proceedings and the Commission agree, the uncertainty of the referring court concerns only the screening stage. More specifically, the referring court asks *whether measures intended to avoid or reduce the harmful effects of a plan or project on the site concerned can be taken into consideration at the screening stage, in order to determine whether it is necessary to carry out an appropriate assessment of the implications, for the site, of that plan or project* (emphasis added).
32. Article 6(3) of the Habitats Directive sets out clearly that the obligation to carry out an assessment is dependent on both of the following conditions being met: the plan or project in question must not be connected with or necessary to the management of the site, and it must be likely to have a significant effect on the site.
...
35. As the applicants in the main proceedings and the Commission submit, the fact that, as the referring court has observed, measures intended to avoid or reduce the harmful effects of a plan or project on the site concerned are taken into consideration when determining whether it is necessary to carry out an appropriate assessment *presupposes that it is likely that the site is affected significantly and*

11 The European Commission, *Managing Natura 2000 Sites – The Provisions of Article 6 of the 'Habitats' Directive 92/43/EEC* (2018), p. 43.

that, consequently, such an assessment should be carried out (emphasis added).

36. That conclusion is supported by the fact that a full and precise analysis of the measures capable of avoiding or reducing any significant effects on the site concerned must be carried out not at the screening stage, but specifically at the stage of the appropriate assessment.

37. Taking account of such measures at the screening stage would be liable to compromise the practical effect of the Habitats Directive in general, and the assessment stage in particular, as the latter stage would be deprived of its purpose and there would be a risk of circumvention of that stage, which constitutes, however, an essential safeguard provided for by the directive.

38. In that regard, the Court's case-law emphasises the fact that the assessment carried out under Article 6(3) of the Habitats Directive may not have lacunae and must contain complete, precise and definitive findings and conclusions capable of removing all reasonable scientific doubt as to the effects of the proposed works on the protected site concerned ... .

...

40. *In the light of all the foregoing considerations, the answer to the question referred is that Article 6(3) of the Habitats Directive must be interpreted as meaning that, in order to determine whether it is necessary to carry out, subsequently, an appropriate assessment of the implications, for a site concerned, of a plan or project, it is not appropriate, at the screening stage, to take account of the measures intended to avoid or reduce the harmful effects of the plan or project on that site* (emphasis added).

The case shows that mitigation measures cannot be taken into consideration in the screening stage of the process. However, these measures might be relevant when conducting the appropriate assessment after having conducted the screening.

On the basis of the case law examined in this section, legal advisors and national authorities should be aware that projects – as a general presumption – are likely to have a significant effect on NATURA 2000 sites and therefore should be subject to an appropriate assessment. The appropriate assessment can only be omitted if it can be excluded, based on objective information, that the project will have a significant effect on a NATURA 2000 site.

When determining whether it can be excluded that the project will have significant effect on NATURA 2000 sites, other projects in the vicinity of the proposed project must be taken into consideration and, in some cases, even very large distances between the proposed project and NATURA 2000 will not suffice to exclude a 'significant effect'. If mitigation measures are incorporated in the project to avoid or reduce negative effects, these cannot be considered in the screening stage.

What Is Meant by an 'Appropriate' Assessment?

If it cannot be excluded, on the basis of objective information, that a project will have a significant effect on a NATURA 2000 site, an appropriate assessment must be conducted.

While the Habitats Directive does not define specific methods or factors that should be applied in the assessment process, ECJ case law offers some clarification.

In Case C-127/02, *Waddenzee*, paragraph 54, the Court found that:

> [s]uch an assessment therefore implies that all the aspects of the plan or project which can, either individually or in combination with other plans or projects, affect [the site's conservation] objectives must be identified in the light of the best scientific knowledge in the field. Those objectives may, …, be established on the basis, inter alia, of the importance of the sites for the maintenance or restoration at a favourable conservation status of a natural habitat type in Annex I to that directive or a species in Annex II thereto and for the coherence of Natura 2000, and of the threats of degradation or destruction to which they are exposed.

Since *Waddenzee*, the term 'appropriate' has been subject to several preliminary questions before the Court, and in recent case law, the Court has elaborated further on the interpretation of the term. In Case C-461/17, *Holohan*, paragraphs 32-40, the Court found:

> 32. By its first three questions, which can be examined together, the referring court seeks, in essence, to ascertain whether Article 6(3) of the Habitats Directive must be interpreted as meaning that an 'appropriate assessment' must, on the one hand, catalogue all the habitat types and species for which a site is protected, and, on the other, identify and examine both the effects of the proposed project on the species present on the site, but for which that site has not been

listed, and the effects on habitat types and species to be found outside the boundaries of that site.

...

36. Taking account of those conservation objectives, the Court must determine the extent of the obligation to carry out an appropriate assessment of the implications of a plan or project for a site in question.

37. Since, ... , all aspects which might affect those [conservation] objectives must be identified and since the assessment carried out must contain complete, precise and definitive findings in that regard, it must be held that *all the habitats and species for which the site is protected must be catalogued.* A failure, in that assessment, *to identify the entirety of the habitats and species for which the site has been listed would be to disregard the abovementioned requirements* and, therefore, as observed, in essence, by the Advocate General in point 31 of her Opinion, would not be sufficient to dispel all reasonable scientific doubt as to the absence of adverse effects on the integrity of the protected site (emphasis added).

38. It must also be added that, since the assessment must clearly demonstrate why the protected habitat types and species are not affected, it may be sufficient to establish, as observed by the Advocate General in point 30 of her Opinion, that only certain protected habitat types and species are present in the part of the protected area that is affected by the project and that the other protected habitat types and species present on the site are not liable to be affected.

39. As regards other habitat types or species, which are present on the site, but for which that site has not been listed, and with respect to habitat types and species located outside that site, it must be recalled that the Habitats Directive, as follows from the wording of Article 6(3) of that directive, subjects '[a]ny plan or project not directly connected with or necessary to the management of the site but likely to have a significant effect thereon' to the environmental protection mechanism of that provision. In that regard, ... , the conservation objective pursued by the Habitats Directive, ... , entails that typical habitats or species must be included in the appropriate assessment, if they are necessary to the conservation of the habitat types and species listed for the protected area.

40. In the light of the foregoing, *the answer to the first three questions is that Article 6(3) of the Habitats Directive must be interpreted as meaning that an 'appropriate assessment' must, on the one hand, catalogue the entirety of habitat types and species for*

which a site is protected, and, on the other, identify and examine both the implications of the proposed project for the species present on that site, and for which that site has not been listed, and the implications for habitat types and species to be found outside the boundaries of that site, provided that those implications are liable to affect the conservation objectives of the site (emphasis added).

The case illustrates the extensive examination requirement that follows from the 'appropriate' assessment according to Article 6(3).[12] Also, the requirements to the 'appropriate' assessment intensify if a recommendation to obtain additional information is made in a scientific expert opinion, but is rejected by the national authority, cf. Case C-461/17, *Holohan*, paragraph 52, in which the Court found:

In the light of the foregoing, ... Article 6(3) of the Habitats Directive must be interpreted as meaning that, where the competent authority rejects the findings in a scientific expert opinion recommending that additional information be obtained, *the 'appropriate assessment' must include an explicit and detailed statement of reasons, capable of dispelling all reasonable scientific doubt concerning the effects of the work envisaged on the site concerned* (emphasis added).

One of the consequences associated with this extensive assessment process is the time frame. Depending on the scale of the proposed project, these examinations and assessments might take years, which can be a decisive obstacle for a company's business plan. It is imperative, therefore, that legal advisors are aware of this potential time frame for the appropriate assessment stage and consider initiating the screening and appropriate assessment stages as early in the project process as possible.

When Will a Project 'Not Adversely Affect the Integrity' of a NATURA 2000 Site?

According to Article 6(3), a national authority may agree to a project '*only after having ascertained that it will not adversely affect the integrity of the site concerned*'. In Case C-127/02, *Waddenzee*, paragraphs 55-61, the Court interpreted this criterion as follows:

12 *See also* the European Commission, *Managing Natura 2000 Sites – The Provisions of Article 6 of the 'Habitats' Directive 92/43/EEC* (2018), pp. 46-57.

55. ... , it lies with the competent national authorities, in the light of the conclusions of the assessment of the implications of a plan or project for the site concerned, to approve the plan or project *only after having made sure that it will not adversely affect the integrity of that site* (emphasis added).

56. It is therefore apparent that the plan or project in question may be granted authorisation only on the condition that the competent national authorities are convinced that it will not adversely affect the integrity of the site concerned.

57. So, *where doubt remains as to the absence of adverse effects on the integrity of the site linked to the plan or project being considered, the competent authority will have to refuse authorization* (emphasis added).

58. In this respect, it is clear that the authorisation criterion laid down in the second sentence of Article 6(3) of the Habitats Directive integrates the precautionary principle ... and makes it possible effectively to prevent adverse effects on the integrity of protected sites as the result of the plans or projects being considered. A less stringent authorisation criterion than that in question could not as effectively ensure the fulfilment of the objective of site protection intended under that provision.

59. Therefore, pursuant to Article 6(3) of the Habitats Directive, the competent national authorities, taking account of the conclusions of the appropriate assessment of the implications of mechanical cockle fishing for the site concerned, in the light of the site's conservation objectives, *are to authorise such activity only if they have made certain that it will not adversely affect the integrity of that site. That is the case where no reasonable scientific doubt remains as to the absence of such effects* (emphasis added).

According to this case, the requirement for certainty that the project will have no negative effect on the NATURA 2000 site is high; there should be no reasonable scientific doubt as to the absence of the project having negative effects on the NATURA 2000 site. In case of doubt, authorization should not be granted.[13]

This strict requirement of the second sentence of Article 6(3) is supported by the fact that the Court does not seem to operate with a lower threshold in relation to a project's negative effects on a NATURA 2000 site.

---

13 *See also* the European Commission, *Managing Natura 2000 Sites – The Provisions of Article 6 of the 'Habitats' Directive 92/43/EEC* (2018), p. 54.

This is illustrated in Case C-258/11, *Sweetman*, regarding a permanent loss of a priority habitat type (limestone pavement) due to an outer bypass road scheme. The facts about the permanent loss of limestone pavement are described in paragraph 12 of the case:

12. The road scheme involves *the permanent loss within the Lough Corrib SCI of approximately 1.47 hectares of that limestone pavement*. Those 1.47 hectares will be lost from an area which was described by An Bord Pleanála's inspector as constituting a 'distinct sub-area and an area having the particular characteristic of possessing substantial areas of a priority habitat', and which contains a total of 85 hectares of limestone pavement. That surface of 85 hectares itself forms part of *a total of 270 hectares of such limestone pavement* – which constitutes a priority habitat type referred to in Annex I to the Habitats Directive – in the entire SCI (emphasis added).

The permanent loss of limestone pavement amounted to approximately 0.5% of the total NATURA 2000 site, but the Court seems to have attached little or no importance to this fact. In paragraphs 39-48, the Court found:

39. Consequently, it should be inferred that in order for the integrity of a site as a natural habitat not to be adversely affected for the purposes of the second sentence of Article 6(3) of the Habitats Directive the site needs to be preserved at a favourable conservation status; this entails, … , *the lasting preservation of the constitutive characteristics of the site concerned that are connected to the presence of a natural habitat type whose preservation was the objective justifying the designation of that site in the list of SCIs, in accordance with the directive* (emphasis added).

…

43. The competent national authorities cannot therefore authorise interventions where there is a risk of lasting harm to the ecological characteristics of sites which host priority natural habitat types. That would particularly be so where *there is a risk* that an intervention of a particular kind will bring about the disappearance or *the partial and irreparable destruction of a priority natural habitat type present on the site concerned* (emphasis added).

44. So far as concerns the assessment carried out under Article 6(3) of the Habitats Directive, it should be pointed out that it cannot have lacunae and must contain complete, precise and definitive findings

and conclusions capable of removing all reasonable scientific doubt as to the effects of the works proposed on the protected site concerned .... It is for the national court to establish whether the assessment of the implications for the site meets these requirements.
45. In the main proceedings, the Lough Corrib SCI was designated as a site hosting a priority habitat type because, in particular, of the presence in that site of limestone pavement, a natural resource which, once destroyed, cannot be replaced. *Having regard to the criteria referred to above, the conservation objective thus corresponds to maintenance at a favourable conservation status of that site's constitutive characteristics, namely the presence of limestone pavement* (emphasis added).
46. Consequently, if, after an appropriate assessment of a plan or project's implications for a site, carried out on the basis of the first sentence of Article 6(3) of the Habitats Directive, the competent national authority concludes that that plan or project will lead to *the lasting and irreparable loss of the whole or part of a priority natural habitat type* whose conservation was the objective that justified the designation of the site concerned as an SCI, *the view should be taken that such a plan or project will adversely affect the integrity of that site* (emphasis added).
47. *In those circumstances, that plan or project cannot be authorised on the basis of Article 6(3) of the Habitats Directive.* Nevertheless, in such a situation, the competent national authority could, where appropriate, grant authorisation under Article 6(4) of the directive, provided that the conditions set out therein are satisfied (emphasis added).

The Court concluded that the project could not be authorized – even though the permanent loss of limestone pavement amounted to only 0.5% of the total NATURA 2000 site – unless the exemption in Article 6(4) was applicable.

As mentioned above, mitigation measures might be relevant for purposes of obtaining project authorization under Article 6(3). The relevance of mitigation measures is described by the European Commission as follows:

[i]f adverse impacts on the site's integrity have been identified during the appropriate assessment or cannot be ruled out, the plan or project in question cannot be approved. However, depending on the degree of impact identified, it may be possible to introduce certain

mitigation measures that will avoid these impacts or reduce them to a level where they will no longer adversely affect the integrity of the site.[14]

If mitigation measures are sufficient to avoid or reduce the impact of the project on NATURA 2000 sites, the national authorities will implement the mitigation measures as a condition for the authorization of the project.

It is important to appreciate the distinction between mitigation measures and compensatory measures. The Court has in previous decisions construed that mitigation measures might be covered by Article 6(3), while compensatory measures are only relevant according to the exemption in Article 6(4).

In Case C-164/17, *Edel Grace*, paragraph 47, the Court described the distinction in this way:

> it follows from Article 6(3) and (4) of the Habitats Directive and the Court's related case-law that there is a distinction to be drawn between *protective measures* forming part of a project and intended avoid or reduce any direct adverse effects that may be caused by the project in order to ensure that the project does not adversely affect the integrity of the area, which are covered by Article 6(3), and *measures* which, in accordance with Article 6(4), are aimed at compensating for the negative effects of the project on a protected area and cannot be taken into account in the assessment of the implications of the project (emphasis added).

Based on the cited case law, it is relevant for legal advisors to consider whether mitigation measures can be implemented in the project to avoid or reduce the impact on NATURA 2000 sites. If it is possible to introduce such mitigation measures, the project will only be subject to the assessments prescribed in Article 6(3).

If the measures are not sufficient to ensure that the project will not adversely affect the integrity of the NATURA 2000 site, the project cannot be authorized by the national authorities unless the exemption in Article 6(4) is applicable. As stated in Case C-258/11, *Sweetman*, the assessment of '*adversely affect the integrity*' is strict.

---

14 The European Commission, *Managing Natura 2000 Sites – The Provisions of Article 6 of the 'Habitats' Directive 92/43/EEC* (2018), p. 51.

Who Is Responsible for Conducting the Appropriate Assessment?

The wording of Article 6(3) does not specify who is responsible for conducting the appropriate assessment as described in the Article. In Case C-461/17, *Holohan*, paragraph 43-45, the Court considered this question and stated:

> 43. ... , an appropriate assessment of the implications of a plan or project for a protected site entails, first, that, before that plan or project is approved, all aspects of that plan or project that might affect the conservation objectives of that site are identified. Second, such an assessment cannot be considered to be appropriate if it contains lacunae and does not contain complete, precise and definitive findings and conclusions capable of dispelling all reasonable scientific doubt as to the effects of the plan or project on that site. Third, all aspects of the plan or project in question which may, either individually or in combination with other plans or projects, affect the conservation objectives of that site must be identified, in the light of the best scientific knowledge in the field.
>
> 44. Those obligations, in accordance with the wording of Article 6(3) of the Habitats Directive, *are borne not by the developer*, even if the developer is, as in this case, a public authority, *but by the competent authority, namely the authority that the Member States designate as responsible for performing the duties arising from that directive* (emphasis added).
>
> 45. It follows that *that provision requires the competent authority* to catalogue and assess all aspects of a plan or project that might affect the conservation objectives of the protected site before granting the development consent at issue (emphasis added).

Based on this case, the obligation under Article 6(3) to conduct an appropriate assessment lies with the national authorities. The associated cost to conduct an appropriate assessment must also be defrayed by the relevant authority.

Conclusion

Our examination of recent, relevant ECJ case law shows that screenings and habitat assessments are an essential part of national authorities' permitting regimes when it comes to companies that might have an environmental impact.

The requirements in Article 6(3) – as interpreted by the ECJ – are detailed and extensive and might lead to long time frames for issuing final permits. Therefore, mistakes are easily made in the permitting process if the national authorities and the companies' legal advisors are not aware of and up to date with recent ECJ decisions.

Climate Change and Pandemics: The Need for a Renewed EU Risk-Management Strategy

Alessandra Donati
Senior Research Fellow at the Max Planck Institute for Procedural Law, Luxembourg

Introduction

"An absent dog does not bark, says an African proverb."[1] One can hardly accuse the media of being absent during the coronavirus pandemic; many outlets have run stories about little else. But focusing on the virus has distracted the media from its watchdog function on other matters of public importance, including the climate crisis. The same conclusion can be reached at the political level: the spreading of COVID-19 seems to have taken EU decision-makers away from pursuing the roadmap aimed at tackling the climate emergency.[2] Yet, not only does climate change seem to have disappeared from the media and political discourse, but also some of the milestones in the fight against climate change may have been undermined by the coronavirus outbreak. As an example, hydro-alcoholic gel flasks, plastic-packaged food, and other single-use plastic products, which were yesterday pointed at by zero-waste advocates and European regulators, are now massively used. The situation is particularly striking with regard to polypropylene protective masks. Research shows that to support the lifting of containment measures in the coming months, in Italy alone more than 1 billion single masks may be used every month and very few of them will be recycled.[3] The use of polymers, 99% of which are produced

---

1   Covering Climate Now, *Silence of the Climate Watchdogs*, Apr. 8, 2020, https://www. coveringclimatenow.org/climate-beat/silence-of-the-climate-watchdogs.

2   N. De Sadeleer, J. Godfroid, *COVID-19 Is an Environmental Crisis Too*, Apr. 6, 2020, http://www.internationalaffairs.org.au/australianoutlook/covid-19-is-an-environmental-crisis-too/.

3   La Repubblica, *Coronavirus, allarme smaltimento mascherine: "Non è sostenibile, serve filiera per il riciclo,"* May 7, 2020, https://www.repubblica.it/ambiente/2020/05/ 07/news/coronavirus_allarme_smaltimento_mascherine_non_e_sostenibile_serve_fi liera_per_il_riciclo_-255932095/?ref=fbpa&fbclid=IwAR1Q7Rhi6lGtH0Pew7vKT Yn96hN_C9tI4mggDxeuPPUPmSXHRIJOqqr6bI8.

from oil, gas, or coal, is now spreading along with coronavirus. This represents a strong comeback that the plastic industry intends to exploit by promoting the slogan that plastic bags save lives and that plastic bags would be the ultimate guarantee of hygiene, unlike reusable cloth bags, which are accused of being breeding grounds for viruses. This is despite the fact that scientific studies agree that plastic is, along with steel, the surface on which the coronavirus is most stable.[4] Against this backdrop, the lobby of European plastic companies, in a letter to the EU Commission on April 8, called on the Commission to postpone for at least one year the implementation of Directive (EU) 2019/904 of the European Parliament and of the Council of June 5, 2019 on the reduction of the impact of certain plastic products on the environment.[5] In this context, the Italian Government decided to postpone until January 2021 the plastic tax of EUR 0.45 per kilo, which was due to come into force in July 2020.

Despite the tendency to focus on the coronavirus crisis and to neglect the climate crisis, these two crises are intertwined. Coronavirus and climate change are not two different crises. They represent two sides of the same significant turmoil relating to the progressive degradation of our environmental and health ecosystems. In this regard, the French High Council for Climate underlined that most of the structural causes of the COVID-19 pandemic are also at the origin of climate change and, thus, it is necessary to accelerate the green transition to strengthen our resilience to both climate risks and health crises stemming from the pandemic.[6] The correlations between climate change and the COVID-19 crisis are, at least, twofold. First, people generally think that viruses have always existed, that epidemics have nothing to do with the state of biodiversity or climate change. Yet, in recent decades, they have been on the rise. According to the World Health Organization (WHO), 60% of new human infectious diseases are of zoonotic origin, i.e., they are transmitted by animals: Rift Valley Fever, SARS, H1N1, yellow fever, avian influenza H5N1, H7N9, MERS-CoV, and now very likely COVID-19.[7] Even if its origin is still

---

4 N. Van Doremalen, T. Bushmaker, D.H. Morris, *Aerosol and Surface Stability of SARS-CoV-2 as Compared with SARS-CoV-1* in *The New England Journal of Medicine*, Apr. 16, 2020, https://www.nejm.org/doi/full/10.1056/NEJMc2004973.
5 Directive (EU) 2019/904 of the European Parliament and of the Council of Jun. 5, 2019 on the reduction of the impact of certain plastic products on the environment, OJ L 155, 2019, pp. 1-19.
6 Haut Conseil pour le Climat, *Climat, Santé: mieux prévenir, mieux guérir*, https://www.hautconseilclimat.fr/publications/climat-sante-mieux-prevenir-mieux-guerir/.
7 Le Monde, *Coronavirus: "Les animaux qui nous ont infectés ne sont pas venus à nous; nous sommes allés les chercher,"* Mar. 29, 2020, https://www.lemonde.fr/idees/

uncertain, several virological, epidemiological, and ethnographic arguments suggest that coronavirus has a zoonotic origin. The pangolin, a
species on the verge of extinction, is now suspected of having facilitated
the transmission to humans of a virus that probably originated in a species
of bat. Human predation "of wild fauna and the reduction in habitats have
thus ended up creating new interfaces that allow the passage of pathogens,
mainly viruses, to humans."[8] The emergence of these infectious diseases is,
therefore, a consequence of our increasing attempts to control the natural
environment. We are deforesting and bringing wild animals hounded from
their natural habitat into contact with domestic livestock in unbalanced
ecosystems close to urban areas. In this way, we are offering infectious
agents new chains of transmission that benefit from the vast network of
diffusion opened up by the interconnections between their potential hosts,
humans.[9] As has been clearly stated by some scientists, there is no doubt
that by destroying biodiversity and deforesting, we are in the process of
unearthing powerful monsters, of opening a Pandora's Box, which has
always existed, but which is now releasing a flood of ever-increasing
microorganisms. Second, it appears that there might be a link between air
pollution and coronavirus. On the one hand, some studies indicate that
coronavirus causes a higher death toll among patients in areas—like the
north of Italy—with slightly increased levels of a particularly dangerous
form of air pollution. A study from Harvard University links an increase in
fine particle exposure levels of just 1 microgram per cubic meter of air with
a 15% higher death rate from COVID-19.[10] On the other hand, a sharp
reduction in the concentration of nitrogen dioxide—a pollutant mainly
emitted from motor vehicle emissions and produced as a result of road
traffic—can be seen in Northern Italy during the coronavirus lockdown,

article/2020/03/29/coronavirus-la-pandemie-demande-que-nous-re-definissions-un-co
ntrat-naturel-et-social-entre-l-homme-et-la-nature_6034804_3232.html?utm_term=Au
tofeed&utm_medium=Social&utm_source=Twitter#Echobox=1585462267.

8 N. De Sadeleer, J. Godfroid, *COVID-19 Is an Environmental Crisis Too*, Apr. 6, 2020,
http://www.internationalaffairs.org.au/australianoutlook/covid-19-is-an-environment
al-crisis-too/.

9 Libération, *La prochaine pandémie est prévisible, rompons avec le déni de la crise
écologique*, Apr. 8, 2020, https://www.liberation.fr/debats/2020/04/08/la-prochaine-
pandemie-est-previsible-rompons-avec-le-deni-de-la-crise-ecologique_1784471?utm
_medium=Social&utm_source=Facebook#Echobox=1586329478.

10 X. Wu, R.C. Nethery, *Exposure to Air pollution and COVID-19 Mortality in the United
States*, Harvard T.H. Chan School of Public Health, Apr. 5, 2020.

which led to dramatically reduced traffic and industrial activities.[11] Data from the European Environmental Agency confirms this trend by stating that also in other EU Member States concentrations of nitrogen dioxide have significantly decreased where lockdown measures have been implemented.[12] These data corroborate the existence of a relationship between human activities and climate change. Specifically, they suggest that the continuous degradation of the environment is not neutral for humans, but is an aggravating phenomenon that, in the context of future predictable pandemics, may play a major role in increasing the level of harm to the environment and our health.

Notwithstanding the interdependences between climate change and pandemics, when a danger appears, "we first try not to see it."[13] Even if the tremendous risks linked to climate change have been known since the 1970s, the actions taken to fight what can be considered as "the most urgent story of our time"[14] have so far failed to address such risks.[15] Likewise, even if the emergence of zoonotic pandemics was predictable and the outbreak of COVID-19 in China in January 2020 should have alerted EU Member States to the risks of rapid contagion, they delayed taking protective measures until the spread of coronavirus was already significant in their territories, thus exacerbating the consequences (sanitary, social, and economic) of the pandemic.[16]

In this scenario, given the cyclical timing of pandemics—indeed, according to the WHO, pandemics may cause several waves of severe

---

11 N. De Sadeleer, J. Godfroid, *COVID-19 Is an Environmental Crisis Too*, Apr. 6, 2020, http://www.internationalaffairs.org.au/australianoutlook/covid-19-is-an-environmental-crisis-too/.

12 European Environment Agency, *Air Quality and COVID-19*, Apr. 4, 2020, https://www.eea.europa.eu/themes/air/air-quality-and-covid19.

13 J. Delumeau, *La peur en Occident (XIVe-XVIIIe siècles). Une cité assiégée*, in *Annales*, pp. 1262-1266.

14 M. Hertsgaard, K. Pope, *Transforming the Media's Coverage of the Climate Crisis*, in *Columbia Journalism Review*, May 22, 2019, https://www.cjr.org/watchdog/climate-crisis-media.php.

15 Intergovernmental Panel on Climate Change ("IPCC"), *Global warming of 1.5° C., Summary for policy-making*, 2018, https://www.ipcc.ch/2018/10/08/summary-for-policymakers-of-ipcc-special-report-on-global-warming-of-1-5c-approved-by-govern ments/.

16 A. Donati, *The Coronavirus Crisis in Europe: Is This the Time of the Precautionary Principle*, in *EU Law Live, in* D. Utrilla, A. Shabbir (eds.), *EU Law in Times of Pandemic, The EU's Legal Response to Covid-19*, EU Law Live press, 2020, pp. 184-189.

epidemics after the first outbreak[17]—and the predictable occurrence of a new pandemic associated with the worsening of the climate crisis,[18] what should EU law do to prevent and better manage the occurrence of such risks? To answer this question, the core claim of this chapter is that the EU should implement a common, coordinated, and consistent risk-management strategy.

A Common Risk-Management Strategy

First, EU institutions and Member States should implement a common risk-management strategy that encompasses both climate change and pandemics. The existence of a strict connection between health and environmental risks is not new. Article 191 paragraph 1 TFEU provides that the protection of human health is an objective of EU environmental policy. This means—as stated by the Court of Justice of the European Union ("CJ")—that when taking actions to preserve the environment, decision-makers must also ensure that human health is protected.[19] Moreover, under the Seventh Action Program for the environment covering the horizon 2013-2020 it is clearly stated that environmental problems and impacts continue to pose significant risks for human health (whereas Article 25) and that the goal of EU action is to safeguard the Union's citizens from environment-related pressures and risks to health and well-being (Article 2).[20] If the connections between environmental and human health risks are recognized, what about the interrelations between environmental risks and those incurred by animals and plant health, which, in turn, can significantly affect human health? As the COVID-19 crisis shows, most pandemics have a zoonotic origin, and the loss of biodiversity, as well as the strong human

---

17 World Health Organization, *Guide to Revision of National Pandemic Influenza Preparedness plans*, 2017, http://www.euro.who.int/en/health-topics/communicable-dis eases/influenza/publications/2017/guide-to-revision-of-national-pandemic-influenza-preparedness-plans-2017.

18 A. Renda, R.J. Castro, *Chronicle of a Pandemic Foretold*, in *CEPS Policy Insights*, Mar. 5, 2020.

19 Court of Justice, Judgment of May 5, 1998, Case C-157/96, *National Farmers' Union*, EU:C:1998:191, paragraphs 63 and 64; Court of Justice, Judgment of May 5, 1998, Case C-180/96, *United Kingdom v. European Commission*, EU:C:1998:192, paragraphs 99 and 100.

20 Decision 1386/2013/EU of the European Parliament and of the Council of Nov. 20, 2013 on a General Union Environment Action Programme to 2020 "Living well, within the limits of our planet," OJ L 354, 2013, pp. 171-200.

impact on the environment, has made the transmission of pathogens from plants and animals to humans more likely. In this context, a new evaluation and regulation of the connections between environmental risks, on the one hand, and plant, animal, and human health risks on the other should be undertaken to foster the implementation of a more systemic and integrated approach for the prevention and management of such risks.[21]

Furthermore, as the climate and coronavirus crises demonstrate, environmental and health risks can also trigger significant social, economic, and political risks. From this perspective, the management of such crises requires the adoption of a holistic and interdisciplinary approach that enables EU decision-makers to tackle transversally both the environmental and health dimensions of such risks and their consequences on the social, economic, and political level. In particular, this means that the definition and implementation of environmental and health objectives and requirements cannot be separated from the setting-up of the political, social, and economic roadmap that will guide the EU in the coming months and years. Therefore, the ultimate goal of the *EU Green Deal* should be to link the achievements of economic objectives with the management of health and the environmental risks caused by climate change and the new predictable waves of pandemics, while mitigating the social impacts of the protective measures to be taken.[22]

A Coordinated Risk-Management Strategy

Second, the EU should implement a coordinated risk-management strategy based both on better articulation of the relationship between EU institutions and Member States and a stronger partnership between public institutions and private stakeholders.

Coordination Between EU Institutions and Member States

The ongoing climate and coronavirus crises show the intense degree of interdependence achieved by our societies because of globalization, where

---

21 ECDC, *Towards One Health Preparedness*, *Technical Report*, Expert consultation Dec. 11-12, 2017.
22 Communication from the Commission to the European Parliament, the European Council, the Council, the European Economic, and Social Committee and the Committee of the Regions, the European Green Deal, COM/2019/640 final.

not only the production-transportation-consumption chain is extended, but also the risks are global. In such a scenario, there is a need to enhance the coordination of risk strategy by combining timely national and EU strategies. This is even more necessary as EU competences in the field of public health are limited. On the one hand, under Articles 6(a) and 168 TFEU, the Union's competence is restricted to taking action to support, coordinate, or supplement the action of the Member States and to adopt incentive measures designed, in particular, to combat major cross-border health scourges and threats to health. On the other hand, according to Article 4(k), the Union has shared competence with the Member States to adopt measures relating to common safety concerns in public health matters, for the aspects defined in the Treaty. In this framework, in 2013, the EU adopted Decision 1082/2013/EU of the European Parliament and of the Council of October 22, 2013 on serious cross-border threats to health.[23] This is the main legal document coordinating EU action related to crisis preparedness and responses to cross-border health threats. Yet, as the European Court of Auditors stated, significant gaps remain in the implementation of this measure,[24] and the EU legislative framework remains extremely limited by the need to respect the competences of the Member States.[25] In an attempt to strengthen Europe's response capability and to provide technical support to the Member States, a dedicated agency—the European Centre for Disease Prevention and Control ("ECDC") was set up. The ECDC is in charge of the surveillance, detection, and risk assessment of threats, epidemiological surveillance, and the operation of the Early Warning and Response System ("EWRS")—a web-based platform linking the European Commission, ECDC and public health authorities of the Member States which is responsible for measures to control serious cross-border threats to health.[26] A recent external evaluation highlighted some significant weaknesses in the activities of the ECDC, including the fact that it has not been able to adequately cover its staff costs and hire additional staff (the agency is currently understaffed and under-budgeted), and it has not been

---

23 Decision 1082/2013/EU of the European Parliament and of the Council of Oct. 22, 2013 on serious cross-border threats to health and repealing, OJ L 293, 2013, pp. 1-15.

24 European Court of Auditors, *Special Report No 28. Dealing with Serious Cross-Border Threats to Health in the EU, Important Steps Taken but More Needs to Be Done*, 2016, https://www.eca.europa.eu/en/Pages/DocItem.aspx?did=40126.

25 A. Renda, R. Castro, *Towards Stronger EU Governance of Health Threats after the COVID-19 Pandemic*, in *EJRR Special Issue, Taming Covid-19 by Regulation*, April 2020, p. 5.

26 ECDC, *Early Warning and Response System (EWRS)*, https://www.ecdc.europa.eu/en/early-warning-and-response-system-ewrs.

able to establish efficient cooperation with the Member States.[27] As an example of its weakness and limited powers, during the current coronavirus outbreak the ECDC has issued several recommendations, including on the criteria for social distancing[28] and contact tracing.[29] However, these recommendations are not binding on the EU Member States, and national authorities—by disregarding these recommendations and the request for coordination put forward by the agency—adopted their own decisions on testing, trace contacts, and social distancing.

Against this backdrop, and to foster the full implementation of the principle of subsidiarity, it would be worth considering an expansion of the scope of application of Article 4(k) and, more generally, strengthening EU health governance by ensuring more efficient equipment and operation of the ECDC. Indeed, as the coronavirus crisis has shown, it is mainly at the European level that public health policy can be efficiently adopted to prevent, coordinate, and control the adoption of consistent protective measures in all EU Member States.[30] Yet, "in spite of having a legally binding instrument (the Decision 1082/2013/EU) and a dedicated agency (the ECDC), the EU governance framework remains a work in progress."[31] This is critical for cross-border health threats—like pandemics and climate change—, which require harmonization and coordinated action that supersedes national borders.

---

27 ECDC, *Third Independent External Evaluation of the ECDC in Accordance with Its Founding Regulation*, September 2019, https://www.ecdc.europa.eu/sites/default/files/documents/third-independent-external-evaluation-of-ECDC-report.pdf.

28 ECDC, *Considerations Relating to Social Distancing Measures in Response to COVID-19—Second Update*, Mar. 23, 2020, https://www.ecdc.europa.eu/en/publications-data/considerations-relating-social-distancing-measures-response-covid-19-second.

29 ECDC, *Contact Tracing: Public Health Management of Persons, Including Healthcare Workers, Having Had Contact with COVID-19 Cases in the European Union—First Update*, Mar. 31, 2020, https://www.ecdc.europa.eu/sites/default/files/documents/Public-health-management-persons-contact-novel-coronavirus-cases-2020-03-31.pdf.

30 S. Rodrigues, *Les chantiers de l'Europe post-Covid-19*, in *blogdroiteuropéen*, May 9, 2020, https://blogdroiteuropeen.com/2020/05/09/les-chantiers-de-leurope-post-covid19-par-stephane-rodrigues/.

31 A. Renda, R. Castro, *Towards Stronger EU Governance of Health Threats after the Covid-19 Pandemic*, in *EJRR Special Issue, Taming Covid-19 by Regulation*, April 2020, p. 5.

Coordination Between Public Institutions and Private Stakeholders

While the management of environmental and health risks has been long perceived as the sole responsibility of public authorities, it is now conceived more as a collective work. Private stakeholders are also called upon to participate actively in risk management. Indeed, faced with the multiplication and increasing complexity of these risks, private decision-makers are often in a better position to control them since they are often at the origin of the risks.[32] The unprecedented change required by the International Panel on Climate Change ("IPCC")[33] to cope with climate change, and in similar terms with pandemics, will only be possible if it takes place simultaneously across a range of sectors, and if it is carefully coordinated within an overall strategy that allows the implementation of pluralist and sustainable governance based on a partnership between public institutions and private actors. According to the UN's Sustainable Development Goals 17, "these inclusive partnerships, built upon principles and values, a shared vision, and shared goals that place people and the planet at the center, are needed to allow the great transformation of our systems."[34]

From this perspective, the *EU Green Deal* explicitly recognizes the need to ensure wider involvement and commitment of both public and private stakeholders in the fight against climate change.[35] To do so, three main measures have been announced by the EU Commission. First, partnerships with industry and the Member States will be encouraged to support research and innovation on transportation, clean hydrogen, low-carbon steel making, circular bio-based sectors, and the built environment.[36] Second, while the EU and its Member States remain the world's leading donors of development assistance and provide over 40% of the world's public climate finance, the EU and its Member States will

32 M.A. Hermitte, *Introduction générale*, in F. Rousseau, K. Foucher, *Les réponses du droit aux crises sanitaires*, Paris: L'Harmattan, 2016, pp. 13-14.
33 IPCC, *Global warming of 1.5° C., Summary for Policy-Making*, 2018, https://www.ipcc.ch/2018/10/08/summary-for-policymakers-of-ipcc-special-report-on-global-warming-of-1-5c-approved-by-governments/.
34 United Nations, *Sustainable Development Goals, Goal n° 17, Strengthen the Means of Implementation and Revitalize the Global Partnership for Sustainable Development*, https://sustainabledevelopment.un.org/sdg17.
35 Communication from the Commission to the European Parliament, the European Council, the Council, the European Economic, and Social Committee and the Committee of the Regions, the European Green Deal, COM/2019/640 final, p. 22.
36 Communication from the Commission to the European Parliament, the European Council, the Council, the European Economic, and Social Committee and the Committee of the Regions, the European Green Deal, COM/2019/640 final, p. 18.

coordinate their support to engage with partners to bridge the funding gap by mobilizing private finance.[37] Third, a *European Climate Pact* will be adopted to inform, inspire, and foster cooperation between public institutions, citizens and other private stakeholders to accompany the transition toward a climate-neutral society.[38] To reinforce its commitment to bridge the gap between public institutions and private stakeholders, on March 11, 2020 the EU Commission presented its new *Industrial Strategy* to accompany Europe's industry in their transition toward climate neutrality.[39]

A Consistent Risk-Management Strategy

Lastly, the EU institutions and the Member States should implement a consistent risk-management strategy that considers the need to anticipate the occurrence of risks. This might be achieved by applying the precautionary principle and fostering the adoption of a new approach to nature based on the acknowledgment of the principle of non-regression.

Application of the Precautionary Principle

As recently affirmed by the German philosopher Habermas, *"il nous faut agir dans le savoir explicite de notre non-savoir"* (we must act in the explicit knowledge of our non-knowledge).[40] This statement translates the idea that the solution to both the climate and coronavirus crises requires a "transition to the era of precaution."[41] To tackle climate change and pandemics, it is necessary to prevent their occurrence as far as is possible

---

37 Communication from the Commission to the European Parliament, the European Council, the Council, the European Economic, and Social Committee and the Committee of the Regions, the European Green Deal, COM/2019/640 final, p. 22.
38 EU Commission, *European Climate Pact*, https://ec.europa.eu/clima/policies/eu-climate-action/pact_en.
39 Communication from the Commission to the European Parliament, the European Council, the Council, the European Economic and Social Committee and the Committee of the Regions, a new Industrial Strategy for Europe, COM/2020/102 final.
40 Le Monde, *Jürgen Habermas: "Dans cette crise, il nous faut agir dans le savoir explicite de notre non-savoir,"* Apr. 10, 2020, https://www.lemonde.fr/idees/article/2020/04/10/jurgen-habermas-dans-cette-crise-il-nous-faut-agir-dans-le-savoir-explicite-de-notre-non-savoir_6036178_3232.html.
41 Le Monde, *Pascal Lamy: "Le Covid-19 va accélérer le passage du protectionnisme au précautionnisme,"* Apr. 9, 2020, https://www.lemonde.fr/economie/article/2020/04/09/pascal-lamy-le-covid-19-va-accelerer-le-passage-du-protectionnisme-au-precautionnisme_6036080_3234.html.

by anticipating the time of action on the basis of the precautionary principle. This principle, laid down in Article 191(2) TFEU and taken up by a multitude of directives and regulations, can be defined as a principle of anticipated action which, in the context of risk and uncertainty for the environment and public health, requires the competent authorities to take protective measures without waiting for certain scientific proof of the existence and extent of the risk in question.[42] As both climate change and coronavirus crises show, if the precautionary principle is not applied in a timely manner and no preventive measures are adopted, it will be too late to act when the risk materializes. Consequently, decision-makers would be bound to act in the context of an emergency, where the need to mitigate (as much as possible) the risk's effects would take over the need to prevent the very materialization of the (already occurred) risk.[43] Yet, if EU decision-makers are already struggling to mitigate the health and economic consequences of COVID-19, what will happen when the risk at stake is severe flooding, droughts, higher temperatures, and the rising sea levels as a consequence of climate change? If amid a health crisis, it seems essential to legislate in an emergency, EU law will *"need to take its time"* afterward.[44] To avoid constructing a society commanded by subsequent "states of emergency"—which would undermine the very notion of democracy—precaution should be the guiding principle of an EU risk-management strategy aimed at anticipating more than mitigating the risks stemming from climate change and pandemics.

A New Approach to Nature and the Principle of Non-regression

The implementation of a consistent risk-management strategy requires reexamining our relationship with nature. Similar pandemics and even more severe climate change events will occur in the near future if the logic of current interactions between human populations and nature is not fundamentally challenged.[45] Humans are omnivores that have become super-predators, degrading the equivalent of half of the EU's arable land

42 A. Donati, *Le principe de précaution en droit de l'Union européenne*, Bruxelles, Bruylant, forthcoming 2021.
43 A. Donati, *Le principe de précaution: un outil de gestion des crises en droit de l'Union européenne ?*, in *JTDE*, n° 10, 2020, pp. 430-436.
44 M. Torre-Schaub, *Post-Covid: les outils du droit contre la régression environnementale*, in *The Conversation*, May 6, 2020, https://theconversation.com/post-covid-les-outils-du-droit-contre-la-regression-environnementale-137638.
45 Le Monde, *Coronavirus: "L'origine de l'épidémie de Covid-19 est liée aux bouleversements que nous imposons à la biodiversité*, Apr. 4, 2020, https://www.lemonde.fr/

every year. To fight epidemics and climate change, the necessary changes required are at the level of civilization. As in the symbolism of yin and yang, we must accept the dual nature of what surrounds us. We need to completely reconsider our relationship with the living world, natural eco-systems, and their biological diversity, which are both the guarantors of great balances and the source of many dangers.[46] From this perspective, a UN General Assembly resolution suggested incorporating in our legal systems the right to live in harmony with nature.[47] This concept epitomizes the need for an epistemological shift in our relationship to nature, moving from a human-centered approach to an Earth-centered approach, which should ensure that human governance systems are consistent with natural systems. Another proposal worthy of consideration is the inclusion by Ecuador and Bolivia of references to the rights of nature in their constitutional texts.[48] In Ecuador, nature is recognized as a legal entity. All persons, communities, and nations can call upon public authorities to enforce the rights of nature. In Bolivia, nature has not been recognized as a legal entity; however, the concept of harmony with nature is embedded in the Constitution, and it is considered as an ethical and moral principle to which the State adheres. Likewise, the Inter-American Court of Human Rights[49] and the Council of Europe[50]—by stressing the existence of a link between human rights and the right to a healthy environment—are starting to promote the idea that the environment is a common space of interaction between humans and nature. What all these proposals have in common is the acknowledgment that the vulnerability of humankind depends on the vulnerability of nature and that consequently the protection of humans against climate change and pandemics requires effective protection of nature. This means that nature can no longer simply be an "object" of

---

    sciences/article/2020/04/04/pandemies-nous-offrons-a-des-agents-infectieux-de-nou velles-chaines-de-transmission_6035590_1650684.html.

46 Le Monde, *Si nous ne changeons pas nos modes de vie, nous subirons des monstres autrement plus violents que ce coronavirus*, Apr. 17, 2020, https://www.lemonde.fr/ idees/article/2020/04/17/jean-francois-guegan-en-supprimant-les-forets-primaires-no us-sommes-en-train-de-debusquer-des-monstres_6036871_3232.html.

47 UN General Assembly, Harmony with Nature, Jan. 17, 2020, A/RES/74/224.

48 A. Acosta, E. Martinez (eds), *La naturaleza con derechos: de la filosofía a la política*, Quito: Ediciones Abya-Yala, 2011.

49 Inter-American Court of Human Rights, opinion of Nov. 15, 2017, case OC 23/17, paragraphs 56-68.

50 E. Lambert, *The Environment and Human Rights. Introductory Report to the High-Level Conference, Environmental Protection and Human Rights*, Strasbourg, Feb. 27, 2020.

human domination but needs to progressively shift toward its consecration as a "subject" granted, like humans, rights, and prerogatives.[51]

The promotion of a new approach to nature must go together with the implementation of a principle of non-regression. This principle stems from the idea that the acquired level of environmental protection should not be reduced by the adoption of a subsequent act and that the highest level of environmental protection shall always be pursued.[52] At the international level, the principle of non-regression is at the heart of two leading international projects—the Global Pact for the Environment[53] and the Pact for the Protection of Human Rights and the Environment.[54] At the national level, several states are already applying the principle of non-regression. For instance, in Belgium, the Constitutional Court stated that Article 23 of the Constitution—which recognizes the right to a healthy environment—implies a stand-still obligation which prevents the competent legislator from significantly reducing the level of protection afforded by the applicable legislation in the absence of general interest.[55] In France, the principle of non-regression was introduced in 2016. According to Article 2 of the legislation on biodiversity, the environmental code is completed with a principle of non-regression according to which the protection of the environment, as ensured by laws and regulations, can only be subject to constant improvement, taking into account current scientific and technical knowledge.[56]

Under EU law, the principle of non-regression has not yet received formal consecration. However, the EU Parliament in its resolution of

51 On the rights to nature, *see* C.M. Kaufmann, *Mapping Transnational Rights of Nature Networks & Laws: New Global Governance Structures for More Sustainable Development*, in International Studies Association Annual Conference, Toronto, Mar. 29, 2020; M. Carducci, Natura (diritti della) in R. Sacco (eds), *Digesto delle Discipline Pubblicistiche*, Bologna: Utet Giuridica, 2017.

52 M. Prieur, G. Sozzo (eds), *La non régression en droit de l'environnement*, Bruxelles, Bruylant, 2012.

53 United Nations, *Resolution adopted by the General Assembly on 10 May 2018, Towards a Global Pact for the Environment*, A/RES/72/277.

54 International Centre of Comparative Environmental Law, *Projet de Pacte international relatif au droit des êtres humains à l'environnement*, 2017, https://cidce.org/wp-content/uploads/2017/01/Projet-de-Pacte-international-relatif-au-droit-des-e%CC%82tres-humains-a%CC%80-l%E2%80%99environnement_16.II_.2017_FR.pdf.

55 Cour Constitutionnelle Belge, Judgment of 27 Janvier 2011, n° 8/2011.

56 Law of Aug. 8, 2016 for the recovery of biodiversity, nature and landscapes, n° 2016-1087.

September 29, 2011 called for "the recognition of the principle of non-regression in the context of environmental protection as well as fundamental rights."[57] The adoption under EU law of the principle of non-regression would complete the "toolbox" at the disposal of the EU institutions to ensure the protection of the environment and would constitute a necessary complement to the precautionary principle and the objective of a high level of environmental and health protection set down in Articles 191 and 168 TFEU. Not only would the EU legislator be able to anticipate the risk at stake, but it could also ensure that the high level of protection pursued by applying the precautionary principle would not be jeopardized by the adoption of subsequent legislation aimed at reducing the acquired level of protection. From this perspective, the principle of non-regression would help stabilize the environmental *acquis* and leave its legacy for future generations.

Conclusion

Over the centuries, pandemics have always laid down markers between different eras of human society. We must not wait to see if this current health crisis will open the door to the building of a new society, eventually ready to achieve the objective of the UN Sustainable Development Goals: peace and prosperity for people and the planet, now and into the future. The next pandemics are highly predictable; the effects of climate change are already visible and will increase in the coming years; it is time not only to "think the unthinkable"[58] but also to take the risk to say and to do something different. It is, in other words, time—now or never—to anticipate the predictable, yet uncertain consequences of climate change and pandemics by adopting a common, coordinated, and consistent EU risk-management strategy for the benefit of the current generation and future generations. In other words, it is essential that "once COVID-19 gradually disappears, the lessons learned from this crisis become the foundations of

---

57 European Parliament, Resolution of Sep. 29, 2011 on developing a common EU position ahead of the United Nations Conference on Sustainable Development (Rio+20), P7_TA (2011)0430, paragraph 97.

58 Financial Times, *Interview: Emmanuel Macron Says It Is Time to Think the Unthinkable*, Apr. 17, 2020, https://www.ft.com/content/55ba601d-073e-4c3c-8f6b-2d5140 8466f9.

a new approach to risk governance at EU and global levels."[59] There are many ways to pursue sustainability, but not all of them are compatible with democratic values. The challenge for the EU is to find an adequate policy mix that safeguards individual rights and liberties, protects the economy, and, at the same time, strengthens the EU's preparedness for cases of climate change and pandemics.

---

59 A. Renda, R. Castro, *Towards Stronger EU Governance of Health Threats after the Covid-19 Pandemic*, in *EJRR Special Issue, Taming Covid-19 by Regulation*, April 2020, p. 10.

Domestic Content Requirements in the Renewable Energy Sector: What Policy Space Exists under WTO Rules?

Nathan Jin Bao [*]

Osgoode Hall Law School, York University, Toronto, Canada

Introduction

Entering the twenty-first century, the UN Millennium Report warned that "[w]e are failing to provide the freedom of future generations to sustain their lives on this planet."[1] If the protection of the environment loomed large as a policy priority twenty years ago, today it is truly a matter of international urgency. Governments are devoted to resolving a variety of environmental issues including preventing pollution, preserving biodiversity, recovering the ozone layer, etc. Among these issues, reducing greenhouse gas (GHG) emissions is an urgent one, considering that even a small increase in global average temperatures would result in an increase in the type, frequency and intensity of extreme weather, such as hurricanes, typhoons, floods, droughts and storms.[2] Climate change can have widespread significant impacts ranging from falling agricultural productivity to the disappearance of low-lying countries.

* This chapter draws its inspiration from the International and Transnational Law Intensive Program at Osgoode Hall Law School (Professors Craig Scott and Geraldine Sadoway as Directors). The author would like to thank Scott Sinclair (Canadian Center for Policy Alternatives) and Craig Scott (Osgoode Hall Law School, York University) for their comments on the early draft, and Stuart Trew (Canadian Center for Policy Alternatives) for his excellent edits. All errors are the author's sole responsibility.

1 United Nations (UN), *We The Peoples, The Role of the United Nations in the 21st Century* (New York: March 2000), online: https://www.un.org/en/events/pastevents/we_the_peoples.shtml.
2 Intergovernmental Panel on Climate Change, *Climate Change 1995: The Science of Climate Change* (UK: Cambridge University Press, 1995), online: https://www.ipcc.ch/site/assets/uploads/2018/02/ipcc_sar_wg_I_full_report.pdf, at 44.

The burning of fossil fuels for energy is the dominant source of GHG emissions.[3] For that reason, a rapid transition from fossil fuels to renewable energy (RE) is an essential environmental policy goal if states are to achieve the commitments undertaken in the Kyoto Protocol, and later the Paris Agreement, to limit global warming to no more 1.5°C.[4] Justified on economic, political and social grounds, many states have employed, or sought to employ, domestic content requirements (DCR) as a condition for economic incentive for such a transition. However, DCR conditionality has been challenged under World Trade Organization (WTO) rules, with all the adjudicated dispute settlement cases decided against DCR-linked policy. By restricting this policy tool, such WTO decisions may have a chilling effect on member governments' domestic environmental policy.

This chapter seeks to identify DCR in the renewable energy sector (DCR-RE) and describe how it is used by governments; to analyze the WTO decisions to date on DCR-RE; and, finally, to determine what policy space remains for DCR-RE under WTO. This chapter is divided into four parts. The first section briefly describes the content, usage and features of DCR-RE in practice, noting how "local preference" for resources becomes the trigger of trade disputes. In the second section, the chapter then summarizes the possible justifications of DCR-RE, which could become the grounds for state defense. The third section discusses all the adjudi-cated WTO decisions on DCR-RE as of the date of writing, assessing the arguments on whether the DCR-RE has violated the WTO's cornerstone nondiscrimination principles. Considering that DCR-RE emerges from the context of environmental protection, the fourth section analyzes the pos-sible approaches to preserve DCR-RE through interpreting WTO rules based on environmental protection.

---

3 "Cities: A "Cause of and Solution to" Climate Change," *UN News* (Sept. 18, 2019), online: https://news.un.org/en/story/2019/09/1046662.

4 Almost all contributions from Member States of Paris Agreement mention RE as a mitigation sector, with more than 50% of States referring to it as a priority sector. *See* Clara Brandi, *Trade Elements in Countries' Climate Contributions under the Paris Agreement* (2017) ICTSD Working Paper, online: https://ictsd.iisd.org/sites/default/files/research/trade_elements_in_countries_climate_contributions.pdf, at vii.

DCR in Renewable Energy: Usage and Features

DCR and DCR-RE

DCR are provisions, usually under a specific law or regulation, that commit foreign investors and companies to sourcing a minimum amount of goods or services locally, as a condition of their investment or of their being granted a government procurement contract.[5] In the wake of the 2008 economic recession, many countries turned to DCR as an economically efficient tool to remedy the failure of global markets. One survey estimated that 117 new DCR measures have been proposed or implemented since 2008.[6] These measures have been applied to various sectors including health care, the auto industry, oil and gas, and RE.

DCR-RE refer to DCR measures implemented in the RE sector where equipment such as wind turbines and solar cells are used to produce electricity. DCR-RE can take many different forms including *inter alia*:

(1) minimum thresholds on the amount of locally sourced materials for production of goods;

(2) minimum thresholds on the amount of locally sourced expenditure or person-hours for the use of services;

(3) explicit or implicit requirements that companies take local content development into account; and/or

(4) requirements to locally establish facilities, factories or other operations.[7]

Wide Usage of DCR-RE in Practice

To encourage investment or production in RE, governments usually implement DCR-RE through an array of economic incentives including feed-in tariffs (FIT), government tenders, market entry conditions, subsidies, tax

---

5 United Nations Conference on Trade and Development (UNCTAD), *Local Content Requirements and the Green Economy* (New York: UNCTAD, 2014), online: https://unctad.org/en/PublicationsLibrary/ditcted2013d7_en.pdf, at 3. The definition includes local service, which is excluded in the discussion here.

6 G. Hufbauer et al., *Local Content Requirements: Report on a Global Problem* (2013) Peterson Institute for International Economics, online: https://www.piie.com/bookstore/local-content-requirements-global-problem, at 3.

7 UNCTAD, *Local Content Requirements and the Green Economy* (New York: UNCTAD, 2014), online: https://unctad.org/en/PublicationsLibrary/ditcted2013d7_en.pdf, at 4.

incentives, etc. The table[8] below indicates the widespread use of typical DCR-RE.

Countries/ Districts	Industries	DCR-RE Rate (% and year)	Incentives
China	Wind	20 (1997), 70 (2009)	State tariffs, tender requirement
Ontario	Wind	25 (2009), 50 (2012)	FIT conditionality
Ontario	Solar	50 (2009), 60 (2012)	FIT conditionality
Quebec	Wind	40 (2003), 60 (2012)	Tender requirement
Spain	Wind	70 (2012)	Market entry requirement, FIT
Turkey	Wind, Solar	Variable (2011)	Additional FIT
Brazil	Wind	60 (2002), 60 (2012)	Condition for subsidized loans
South Africa	Wind	35 (2011), >35 (2012)	Tender requirement
Italy	Solar	Variable (2011)	5-10% bonus
France	Solar	60 (2012)	10% bonus
India	Solar	30 (2011), 30 (2011)	FIT conditionality

Currently, FIT programs[9] have emerged as one of the most popular instruments to propel RE development and can be found in 111 jurisdictions including Australia, China, India, South Africa, Switzerland, most European Union countries and several states and municipalities in the

---

8 Jan-Christoph Kuntze and Tom Moerenhout, *Local Content Requirements and the Renewable Energy Industry – A Good Match?* (2013) ICTSD Working Paper, online: https://pdfs.semanticscholar.org/6872/7a8d62a9722b28a250bef0470aeb847108f9.pdf, 30-31, at 25.

9 These programs usually comprise three key elements: guaranteed electricity purchase prices, guaranteed grid access and a long-term contract.

United States (U.S.).[10] Other DCR-RE measures, such as DCR on government tenders, are endorsed in ninety-eight jurisdictions,[11] while direct grant, rebate or preferential loans are utilized in fifty-five countries to support local RE industries.[12]

Key Features of DCR-RE

Generally, DCR-RE involve some form of "local preference" for resources. Usually, this means companies are required to purchase a percentage of goods and services locally in order to qualify either for direct financial support, such as a subsidy or preferential loan, or for indirect "license" to enter into the market or win government contracts. Like "import quotas," DCR-RE use "quantity signals to influence market outcomes[13] and to restrict the importation of products from abroad." The "local preference" is reflected in the market effect of DCR-RE. The demand for imported products is diminished because of the quantitative regulation while incentives in DCR-RE are intended to drive the RE producers to purchase or use domestic products, therefore increasing demand for domestic products. Currently, domestic instruments that impose DCR-RE seem not to distinguish between local and foreign products based on grounds other than their origin of production.

Justifications for DCR-RE

DCR-RE can be justified on economic, political and social (environmental) grounds, which are interrelated. From the economic perspective, DCR-RE can help build up the capacity and competitiveness of domestic RE industries to effectively compete in global RE markets, a result which is in line with trade liberalization. From the political perspective, it is

---

10 REN21, *Renewables 2019 Global Status Report* (2019), online: https://www.ren21.net/wp-content/uploads/2019/05/gsr_2019_full_report_en.pdf, at 21.

11 REN21, *Renewables 2019 Global Status Report* (2019), online: https://www.ren21.net/wp-content/uploads/2019/05/gsr_2019_full_report_en.pdf, at 19.

12 Joanna Lewis, "The Rise of Renewable Energy Protectionism: Emerging Trade Conflicts and Implications for Low Carbon Development" (2014) 14:4 *Global Environmental Politics* 10-35, at 14.

13 G. Hufbauer et al., *Local Content Requirements: Report on a Global Problem* (2013) Peterson Institute for International Economics, online: http://files.publicaffairs.geb logs.com/files/2014/08/Local-Content-Requirements-Report-on-a-Global-Problem.pdf, at 10.

necessary for states to create jobs through DCR-RE, since otherwise, the economic incentives inherent in DCR-RE are less likely to earn the electoral support to be included in government budgets, especially during periods of austerity. Finally, DCR-RE themselves have a possible environmental justification and remain a legitimate way to reduce GHG emissions, hence achieving the principle of "sustainable development" valued by the civil society.

Economic Justifications

The primary rationale for the use of DCR is the development of domestic infant industries or strengthening of the domestic industrial base.[14] Arguably, this rationale is especially strong because of the conditions of the RE market.

First, the emerging RE market is growing robustly. Generally, very few countries have RE producers that are capable of serving as an internationally competitive platform for exploration, extraction, distribution and export of RE.[15] However, it is suggested that some countries such as China have been successful in using industrial policy including DCR-RE to promote RE.[16] Other countries have learned from the success and have implemented policies to build up capacity of production and increase the competitiveness of domestic RE industries. As a result, more competition is expected to occur in the global RE market because of the entry of more mature producers.

In addition, RE is competing with its substitute—traditional fossil fuel-based electricity generation and infrastructure that remains strong and

---

14 The economic justification is not without challenges, as shown by some scholars, it is possible that DCR would generate inefficiencies that have quite the opposite effect on the economy. *See*, e.g., Bernard Munk, "The Welfare Costs of Content Production: The Automotive Industry in Latin America" (1969) LXXVII *Journal of Political Economy* 85-98. However, the literature seems to be consistent that a properly designed DCR is an efficient industry policy, *see*, e.g., J. Kuntze & T. Moerenhout, *Local Content Requirements and the Renewable Energy Industry – A Good Match?* (2013) ICTSD Working Paper, online: https://pdfs.semanticscholar.org/6872/7a8d62a9722b28a250b ef0470aeb847108f9.pdf, at 9.

15 United Nations Conference on Trade and Development (UNCTAD), *Local Content Requirements and the Green Economy* (New York: UNCTAD, 2014), online: https://unctad.org/en/PublicationsLibrary/ditcted2013d7_en.pdf, at 6.

16 J. Kuntze & T. Moerenhout, *Local Content Requirements and the Renewable Energy Industry – A Good Match?* (2013) ICTSD Working Paper, online: https://pdfs.semantic scholar.org/6872/7a8d62a9722b28a250bef0470aeb847108f9.pdf, at 13.

heavily subsidized.[17] The exploitation of RE usually requires sophisticated and cutting-edge technology, a ready-made demand for a wide network of suppliers and ongoing employment for trained staff.[18] These factors drive up initial RE production costs. Accordingly, DCR-RE can play a positive role in lowering the cost through attracting technology from abroad, offering a market of suppliers and training experienced local workers. A lower production cost will place RE in a better position to outcompete fossil fuels.

Political Justifications

While there are economic incentives associated with DCR-RE, there are also costs. Ever since the economic slowdown post-2008, it has been harder for governments to justify higher spending on RE unless other social welfare goals, mainly job creation, are promoted in an explicit way.

According to one survey, globally the RE sector continued to increase employment from 8.1 million people in 2016 to 11 million in 2018.[19] Enabling policies that help countries capture some of this employment growth remain critical to the continued expansion of renewables.[20] These policies include financing rules to encourage local content and government auctions.[21] Take Ontario, for example. In 2011, DCR-RE implemented through the province's *Green Energy and Economy Act* (2009) (the Act) attracted CAD 7 billion in wind turbine manufacturing investment from Samsung, a South Korea-based company. In addition, the Act is

17 *See* generally David Coady, Ian Parry, Nghia-Piotr Le, and Baoping Shang, *Global Fossil Fuel Subsidies Remain Large: An Update Based on Country-Level Estimates* (2019) International Monetary Fund Report, online: https://www.imf.org/en/Publications/WP/Issues/2019/05/02/Global-Fossil-Fuel-Subsidies-Remain-Large-An-Update-Based-on-Country-Level-Estimates-46509.
18 UNCTAD, *Local Content Requirements and the Green Economy* (New York: UNCTAD, 2014), online: https://unctad.org/en/PublicationsLibrary/ditcted2013d7_en.pdf, at 6-7.
19 REN21, *Renewables 2019 Global Status Report* (2019), online: https://www.ren21.net/wp-content/uploads/2019/05/GSR2013_Full-Report_English.pdf, at 46.
20 REN21, *Renewables 2019 Global Status Report* (2019), online: https://www.ren21.net/wp-content/uploads/2019/05/GSR2013_Full-Report_English.pdf, at 46.
21 REN21, *Renewables 2016 Global Status Report* (2016), online: https://www.ren21.net/wp-content/uploads/2019/05/REN21_GSR2016_FullReport_en_11.pdf, at 40; also *see* REN21 (2019), at 46.

credited with having created 20,000 jobs among which approximately 3,000 are in new manufacturing plants under the FIT program.[22]

Furthermore, a significant transition to RE would lead to the loss of employment in the fossil fuel sector. Political support for DCR-RE may therefore depend on assurances of net job growth from the transition. In Canada, institutional reports have suggested 50,000 jobs are likely to be lost in fossil fuels while over 160,000 will be created in RE for the next decade—a net increase of 110,000 new energy jobs.[23] As part of a just transition,[24] many governments have committed to assisting displaced fossil fuel workers find new jobs in sectors with comparable wages and benefits.

Social Justifications

DCR-RE emerge from the context of environmental protection. Ever since the Rio Conference, states have confirmed that the guiding paradigm for environmental and economic policy must be sustainable development.[25] While governments remain the formal actors in reaching environmental agreements, in recent decades civil society has stepped up on the world stage and played a critical role in forming norms to link environmental protection and economic development, under the rubric of sustainable development. At the 2002 Johannesburg Summit on sustainable development, 3,200 nongovernment organizations (NGOs) were accredited to participate.[26] These groups assist countries by providing information, analyzing or even drafting treaty texts and helping monitor state compliance.[27]

---

22 UNCTAD, *Local Content Requirements and the Green Economy* (New York: UNCTAD, 2014), online: https://unctad.org/en/PublicationsLibrary/ditcted2013d7_en.pdf, at 27.

23 Clean Energy Canada, "Canada's clean energy sector set to accelerate amid fossil fuel slowdown" (Oct. 3, 2019), online: https://cleanenergycanada.org/canadas-clean-energy-sector-set-to-accelerate-amid-fossil-fuel-slowdown/.

24 *See*, e.g., International Institute for Sustainable Development, "Just Transition," online: https://www.iisd.org/topic/just-transition, which concerns the low-carbon energy transition would lead to job losses and economic hardship.

25 Brown Weiss, "The Evolution of International Environmental Law" (2011) 54 *Japanese Year Book of International Law* 1-27, at 10.

26 Brown Weiss, "The Evolution of International Environmental Law" (2011) 54 *Japanese Year Book of International Law* 1-27, at 21.

27 Brown Weiss, "The Evolution of International Environmental Law" (2011) 54 *Japanese Year Book of International Law* 1-27, at 21.

The emergence of civil society in norm-making may help justify DCR-RE in two ways. First, it legitimatizes DCR-RE as a means to attain sustainable development, as defined by the UN Sustainable Development Goals (SDGs). DCR-RE drive an expansion in the RE sector that can massively reduce GHG emissions, corresponding to SDG 13, which calls for urgent action to combat climate change. This fact can lend strength to the legitimacy of DCR-RE based on their function. Second, NGO participation in rule-making adds an environmental dimension to DCR-RE per se. The local food movement provides a helpful analogy here. For example, local food advocates have calculated that replacing one 10-ton truck loaded with California-grown produce with an Ontario-grown load is the environmental equivalent of taking two cars off the road for an entire year.[28]

WTO Decisions on DCR-RE

One of the core principles of WTO agreements is that of "national treatment," which obligates states to treat all goods, services, companies or persons equally, regardless of their country of origin, except where states have taken agreement-specific exceptions. Article III of General Agreement on Tariffs and Trade (GATT)—National Treatment on Internal Taxation and Regulation—is highly pertinent to the issue of DCR-RE.[29] Under

---

28 Jessica Leeder, "Local food movement goes national" (Jul. 1, 2011) *The Globe and Mail*, online: https://www.theglobeandmail.com/news/national/local-food-movement-goes-national/article585262/.

29 Article 2 of the Trade-Related Investment Measures (TRIMs) Agreement is also relevant. As illustrated in Canada-FIT Case, there is an inherent relation between Article III:4 of GATT and Article 2 of TRIMs in the sense that pursuant to Article 2.2 of TRIMs, if the measures at issue fall into the Illustrative List in the Annex to TRIMs, they violate the national treatment under Article III:4 of GATT. Article III:8 of GATT, which is an exemption to Article III:4 of GATT, would also apply to the measures that are in the Illustrative List. The listed measure cited in the adjudicated cases is paragraph 1(a) of the Illustrative List that reads "mandatory or enforceable under domestic law or under administrative rulings, or compliance with which is necessary to obtain an advantage, and which require: (a) the purchase or use by an enterprise of products of domestic origin from any domestic source, whether specified in terms of particular products, in terms of volume or value of products, or in terms of proportion of volume or value of its local production," WTO Panel Report, *Canada—Certain Measures Affecting the Renewable Energy Generation Sector*, WTO Doc. WT/DS412/R, *Canada—Measures Relating to the Feed-in Tariff Program*, WTO Doc. WT/DS426/R (a single document constituting these two Panel Reports, 2012), online: WTO, https://www.wto.org/english/tratop_e/dispu_e/cases_e/ds426_e.htm (hereinafter as "Panel Report Canada-FIT"), at 64; WTO Panel Report, *India—Certain Measures Relating to*

this "national treatment" obligation, states agree not to treat imports of a good any differently from similar domestically produced goods. DCR-RE potentially violate the GATT obligation because of their preference for local products over imports.[30] Even if a violation is established, however, WTO rules provide for the possibility to save the measure through either a specific exemption under Article III:8(a) or a general exemption under Article XX.

This section reviews the WTO's position on the matter by analyzing how WTO Dispute Settlement Panel ("Panel") and Appellate Body ("AB") have adjudicated cases pertaining to DCR-RE. As of the time of writing, five WTO cases addressed the issue of whether DCR-RE violate national treatment under Article III of GATT. Three cases have been adjudicated, including *Canada—Measures Relating to the Feed-In Tariff Program* (hereinafter as *Canada-FIT* case), India—*Certain Measures Relating to Solar Cells and Solar Modules* (hereinafter as *India-Solar* case), and *United States—Certain Measures Relating to the Renewable Energy Sector* (hereinafter as *US-RE* case).

Overview of Facts

Canada-FIT Case

The *Canada-FIT* case was the first WTO case to assess DCR-RE measures. Both the Panel and AB found that Canada had violated its national treatment obligations, and the Ontario policies in question have since been made compliant with the WTO decision.

Despite restructuring Ontario's electricity market, the Government of Ontario continues to play a critical role in generation, transmission, distribution and retail of electricity. In 2009, the Ontario Government enacted the *Green Energy Act* and its regulations, which implemented a FIT program "through which generators of electricity, produced from certain forms of renewable energy, are paid a guaranteed price per kWh of

---

Solar Cells and Solar Modules, WTO Doc. WT/DS456/R (2016) online: https://www.wto.org/english/tratop_e/dispu_e/456r_e.pdf (hereinafter as "Panel Report India-Solar"), at 41; WTO Panel Report, *United States—Certain Measures Relating to the Renewable Energy Sector*, WTO Doc. WT/DS510/R (2019), online: https://www.wto.org/english/tratop_e/dispu_e/510r_e.pdf (hereinafter as "Panel Report *US-RE*"), at 93.

30 Potentially, GATT Article XI ("quantitative restrictions") is also at issue but, since it is not dealt with in the WTO decisions on DCR-RE, it is not discussed here.

electricity delivered into the Ontario electricity system under 20-year or 40-year contracts with government."[31] FIT contracts were offered only to those projects which satisfied all eligibility requirements, including a "Minimum Required Domestic Content Level" involving a calculation pursuant to the methodology set out in the FIT Contract.[32] As presented by Japan and the EU (the complainants) in their WTO challenge to the Ontario policy,[33] by 2012, DCR-RE had reached 50% for FIT wind projects, while DCR-RE for solar PV and microFIT solar projects were both at 60% by 2011 (*see* table below).

	Wind (FIT)		Solar PV (FIT)		Solar PV (microFIT)	
Milestone Date for Commercial Operation	2009-2011	2012-	2009-2010	2011-	2009-2010	2011-
Minimum Required Domestic Content Level	25%	50%	50%	60%	40%	60%

Source: Panel Report *Canada-FIT*, at p. 77.

India-Solar Case

Both the Panel and AB have delivered decisions in the *India-Solar* case against India brought by the U.S. Although India has informed the WTO that it has ceased its domestic measures that are inconsistent with the decisions, the U.S. as complainant is not satisfied and has requested authorization to retaliate.

Seeking to achieve the solar power capacity planned for under India's Jawaharlal Nehru National Solar Mission ("JNNSM"), the Government of India entered into long-term power purchase agreements (PPAs) with solar power developers (SPD). Each PPA provides a guaranteed rate for a twenty-five-year term at which the electricity generated by the SPD is

31 Panel Report *Canada-FIT*, paragraph 7.64.
32 Panel Report *Canada-FIT*, paragraph 7.158-7.159.
33 Panel Report *Canada-FIT*, at p. 77.

bought by India.[34] However, a mandatory DCR was imposed on the SPD to use certain solar cells or modules manufactured in India in order to bid for or perform the PPAs.[35]

US-RE Case

In January 2017, India requested the establishment of a WTO Panel to challenge certain U.S. measures in the RE sector in various states. These included additional incentives in Washington State and Connecticut; tax incentives, credits and refunds in Montana; workforce-related bonuses in California, Michigan and Delaware; and production incentives and rebates in Minnesota. In all cases these measures provide incentives on the condition that local labor or local RE generation equipment must be used.[36] The Panel issued its report in June 2019, finding all measures violate GATT Article III. The U.S. has appealed, but the AB has yet to release a report.

Violating Article III:4 of GATT

The WTO has developed a three-part test to analyze whether measures violate national treatment under Article III:4 of GATT. The test, which was used in the *US-RE* and *India-Solar* cases, asks:
   (1) do the imported and domestic products in question qualify as "like products";
   (2) do the measure at issue constitute a "law, regulation, or requirement affecting their internal sale, offering for sale, purchase, transportation, distribution, or use"; and
   (3) are the imported products accorded "less favorable" treatment than that accorded to like domestic products.[37]

The Panels in the *Canada-FIT* case did not follow this test. Rather, the case addressed the same issue by deciding that a violation of Article 2 of

---

34 Panel Report *India-Solar*, paragraph 7.2.
35 Panel Report *India-Solar*, paragraph 7.11.
36 Panel Report *US-RE*, paragraphs 2.12, 2.17, 2.22, 2.26, 2.29-30, 2.32, 2.42, 2.53, 2.55, 2.58, 2.61 and 2.67.
37 WTO Appellate Body Report, *Korea—Measures Affecting Imports of Fresh, Chilled and Frozen Beef*, WTO Doc. WT/DS161/AB/R (2000), online: WTO, https://www.wto.org/english/tratop_e/dispu_e/161-169abr_e.pdf, paragraph 133 (hereinafter as "*Korea-Beef*"); Panel Report *India-Solar*, paragraph 7.80.

the Agreement on Trade-Related Investment Measures (TRIMs) constitutes a violation of GATT Article III:4.[38]

"Like Products"

In all three cases, the local and foreign products at issue are the equipment
to generate RE. The complainants in both the *India-Solar* and *US-RE* cases
argued that the measures provide for different treatment solely based on the
origin of the products, and therefore the local and imported products
qualify as "like products."[39] The WTO Panels in these cases accepted this
argument on the grounds that previous Panels "have repeatedly found that
products at issue were like where the sole distinguishing criterion was
origin."[40]

"Law, Regulation, or Requirement Affecting Internal Sale"

When analyzing this element, WTO Panels first consider what constitutes
a "law, regulation or requirement," which past WTO decisions have defined broadly. Pertinent to DCR-RE, the conditions that an enterprise
voluntarily accepts in order to receive an advantage have been treated as a
"requirement."[41] Then the Panels turn to the definition of "affecting." They
reframe the question into an examination of whether the measure has an
impact on the conditions of competition between domestic and imported
like products, and hold that "creating an incentive" for use of domestic
goods can be considered to "affect" the internal sale, purchase or use of
those goods.[42]

"Less Favorable Treatment"

WTO practice has developed the review of "less favorable treatment" into
a question that pertains to "whether a measure modifies the conditions of
competition in the relevant market to the detriment of imported products,"
such that "the term 'treatment no less favorable' in Article III:4 requires
effective equality of opportunities for imported products to compete with
like domestic products."[43]

---

38 *See* the discussion on TRIMs, *supra* note 29.
39 Panel Report *India-Solar*, paragraph 7.81; Panel Report *US-RE*, paragraph 7.87.
40 Panel Report *India-Solar*, paragraph 7.83.
41 Panel Report *India-Solar*, paragraph 7.87; Panel Report *US-RE*, paragraph 7.151.
42 Panel Report *India-Solar*, paragraph 7.87; Panel Report *US-RE*, paragraph 7.161.
43 Panel Report *India-Solar,* paragraph 7.92; Panel Report *US-RE*, paragraph 7.243. The
    Panel in *US-RE* acknowledges that the test may overlap with the test of "affecting"
    described above, but points out that they are different in the sense that "affecting"
    concerns whether the challenged measure impacts the conditions of competition while

After rejecting respondents' defense that an "actual," "bound or likely," or "quantified" threshold of likelihood should be established for "detrimental impact" purpose, the Panels relied on past decisions for the proposition that "the provision of incentives or advantages for the use of domestic over imported products accords less favorable treatment to such imported products."[44] The proposition operates as a prima facie rule: unless rebutted by the respondents, a less favorable treatment is deemed to be established. After finding the respondent either failed to rebut or offered an unpersuasive defense, both Panels reached the conclusion that the DCR-RE at issue violate Article III:4 of GATT.

Exemptions to Article III:4 of GATT

Specific Exemption: Article III:8(a) of GATT

In both the *Canada-FIT* and *India-Solar* cases, the Governments implemented DCR-RE through government auctions. This business model becomes the basis for the respondents to seek a government procurement exemption to Article III:4 under Article III:8(a), which specifies that national treatment "shall not apply to laws, regulations or requirements governing the procurement by governmental agencies of products purchased for governmental purposes and not with a view to commercial resale or with a view to use in the production of goods for commercial sale." This exclusion was intended to preserve government procurement as a policy tool without running afoul of GATT obligations.[45] However, the WTO AB rejected the invocation of Article III:8(a) in these cases.

Canada-FIT Case—Panel Report

The *Canada-FIT* case was the first to develop the WTO test for Article III:8(a). The Panel framed the test by assessing three questions:
  (1) whether the challenged measures can be characterized as "law, regulations or requirements governing procurement";

"less favorable treatment" concerns the impacts that are detriment of imported products. Panel Report *US-RE*, paragraph 7.244.

44 Panel Report *India-Solar*, paragraph 7.95; Panel Report *US-RE*, paragraph 7.253.

45 *See*, e.g., S. Sinclair, "Saving the Green Economy: Ontario Green Energy Act and the WTO" (2013), online: https://www.policyalternatives.ca/sites/default/files/uploads/publications/National%20Office%2C%20Ontario%20Office/2013/11/Saving_the_Green_Economy.pdf, at 9.

(2) whether the challenged measures involve "procurement by govern-
     mental agencies"; and
(3) whether any "procurement" that exists is undertaken "for govern-
     mental purposes and not with a view to commercial resale or with a
     view to use in the production of goods for commercial sale."

The Panel had no problem finding that Ontario's FIT program is
governing procurement because the DCR was a necessary prerequisite for
the alleged procurement. Recognizing that the DCR-RE requirements
were imposed on electricity generation equipment while the product of
government procurement was electricity, which were two different products, the Panel nonetheless decided that the DCR governed "procurement
of electricity," because of the close relationship between the generation
equipment and the electricity.[46]

On the second question, the Panel rejected the complainant's argument
that procurement must involve "government use, consumption or benefit
of the procured product." It interpreted procurement as meaning, simply, to
"purchase."[47] For that reason, the government contract to purchase electricity was "procurement."

Finally, the Panel read "*government purpose*" and "*not with a view to
commercial resale*" as being mutually exclusive and focused their analysis
on the latter.[48] The Panel looked at the chain of transactions regarding the
sale of electricity generated through government procurement contracts
and concluded that it is for commercial resale because the electricity was
eventually sold to consumers by government's agents.[49] For this reason, the
Panel ruled that Article III:8(a) did not apply in this case.

Canada-FIT Case—AB Review

Although Canada appealed the Panel's decision on the characterization of
"commercial resale," the AB ruled that the FIT program did not even meet
the first requirement of being tied to "laws, regulations or requirements
governing procurement." It is recalled that the Panel decided that the FIT
program governed the procurement of "electricity," though the DCR-RE
conditions in FIT were imposed on the "equipment," because the two
(electricity and electricity-generating equipment) were in close relationship. The AB acknowledged the close relationship but disagreed with the

---

46 Panel Report *Canada-FIT*, paragraph 7.127.
47 Panel Report *Canada-FIT*, paragraph 7.131.
48 Panel Report *Canada-FIT*, paragraph 7.140.
49 Panel Report *Canada-FIT*, paragraph 7.147.

Panel analysis on this point. Rather, the AB reasoned, because other paragraphs of Article III required an analysis of the "competitive relationship" between products, such an analysis should apply to the interpretation of Article III:8(a) as well. Therefore, because "electricity" and "equipment" were not in "competitive relationship," the FIT program that imposed on "equipment" could not be a measure governing the procurement of "electricity."[50] In summary, the AB came to the same conclusion as the Panel on the question of procurement—that Article III:8(a) did not apply—but for different reasons.

India-Solar Case—Panel Report and Appellate Body Review

In this case, the complainant (U.S.) invoked the AB decision in *Canada-FIT* and claimed that the respondent (India) cannot be exempted under Article III:8(a) because the government power purchase agreements imposed DCR-RE on the generation equipment while the product of procurement was electricity, therefore the two products were not in a "competitive relationship."[51] In contrast, the respondent tried, without success, to expand the "competitive relationship" test in order to argue that the equipment and electricity were "integral," "intrinsic" and "indistinguishable," and therefore should be treated as the same for the purposes of Article III:8(a).[52] The Panel generally followed the reasoning of the AB in *Canada-FIT* and delivered the decision in favor of the complainant.[53] The AB in this case upheld the Panel Report.[54]

Discussion

Considering that in both *Canada-FIT* and *India-Solar* the AB rejected the government procurement exemption (because DCR-RE are imposed on "generation equipment," a product different from the "electricity" that is procured by government), some scholars suggest the government can procure local generation equipment directly in order to maintain DCR-RE under WTO rules.[55]

---

50 WTO Appellate Body Report, *Canada-FIT*, WTO Doc. WT/DS412/AB/R (2013), online: https://www.wto.org/english/tratop_e/dispu_e/412_426abr_e.pdf, paragraph 5.79.
51 Panel Report *India-Solar*, paragraph 7.102.
52 Panel Report *India-Solar*, paragraph 7.109.
53 Panel Report *India-Solar*, paragraph 7.135.
54 WTO Appellate Body Report, *India-Solar*, WTO Doc. WT/DS456/AB/R (2014), online: http://trade.ec.europa.eu/doclib/docs/2015/august/tradoc_153729.pdf, at paragraph 5.40.
55 *See*, e.g., S. Sinclair, "Saving the Green Economy: Ontario Green Energy Act and the WTO" (2013), online: https://www.policyalternatives.ca/sites/default/files/uploads/

In that case, further issues that require analysis would include whether it is *"procurement by government agencies"* and *"for government purpose,"* and "not with a view to *commercial resale."* More controversies might arise from the second issue. The AB's reasoning in *Canada-FIT*, which was followed by the DSB Panel in *India-Solar*, was that "'commercial resale' must be assessed having regard to the entire transaction,"[56] which should include the profit-making and downstream competition of entities all the way through to final retail sale.[57] In other words, it is likely that the Panel or AB will focus on the sale of "electricity" to assess "commercial resale." Then they will need to justify why they interpret DCR-RE as targeting the generation equipment rather than electricity at the first stage while they interpret "commercial resale" through the transaction of "electricity" at a later stage (presumably they follow a "strict product-based" analysis). The undecided issue of "commercial resale" may impose uncertainty on whether respondent states would be able to structure their government procurement in a way to reserve the DCR-RE.

Furthermore, a full exemption under Article III:8(a) is subject to the changes in the state's commitment under international procurement agreements. An example is that provinces of Canada used to be free to procure local products under the WTO Government Procurement Agreement. They are now restricted from doing so because of Canada's commitment to open sub-central government procurement markets to EU suppliers pursuant to the Canada-EU Comprehensive Economic and Trade Agreement (CETA).[58]

General Exemption: Article XX of GATT

Article XX of GATT lays out a number of specific instances in which WTO members may be exempted from GATT rules including Article III:4. However, WTO Panels have interpreted Article XX narrowly, have placed the burden on the defending party to justify the exemption, and do not examine it unless the article is invoked.[59] Among the adjudicated DCR-RE

---

publications/National%20Office%2C%20Ontario%20Office/2013/11/Saving_the_Green_Economy.pdf.

56 Appellate Body Report, *Canada-FIT*, paragraph 5.70; Panel Report *India-Solar*, at paragraph 7.179.
57 Panel Report *India-Solar*, paragraph 7.178.
58 Canada-EU, Comprehensive Economic and Trade Agreement (2018), Chapter 19 "Government Procurement," Annex 19-A, online: https://www.international.gc.ca/trade-commerce/trade-agreements-accords-commerciaux/agr-acc/ceta-aecg/text-texte/toc-tdm.aspx?lang=eng.
59 GATT Panel Report, *Tuna/Dolphin I* (1991), 30 International Law Materials 1594, paragraph 5.25.

cases, only India raised an Article XX defense based on paragraphs (d) and
(j), though without success.

Defense under Paragraph (d) in *India-Solar*

Article XX(d) specifies that measures "necessary to secure compliance
with laws or regulations which are not inconsistent with the provisions of
GATT"[60] are exempted from GATT obligations including Article III:4.
WTO practice has developed the test that, to qualify as an exempted
measure, the challenged measure should be: (a) "designed to 'secure
compliance' with laws or regulations that are not themselves inconsistent
with some provision of the GATT 1994"; and (b) "necessary" to secure
such compliance.[61]

In this case, the respondent (India) provided a series of international
environmental instruments, including the preamble of the WTO Agreement, the United Nations Framework Convention on Climate Change
(UNFCCC), the Rio Declaration on Environment and Development (Rio
Declaration) and the United Nations General Assembly Rio+20 Resolution, to demonstrate its obligations to environmental protection under the
principle of sustainable development. It then claimed the domestic instruments India introduced were designed to ensure compliance with these
obligations.[62]

The first issue is "whether the international and domestic instruments"
are "laws or regulations." The AB introduced the elements to consider in
deciding on the issue, including: (i) the extent to which the instrument
operates to set out a rule of conduct, (ii) the degree of specificity, (iii)
whether the rule is legally enforceable, (iv) whether the rule has been
adopted by domestic competent authority, (v) the form and title given to
the instrument by the state, and (vi) the penalties or sanctions accompany-
ing the relevant rule.[63] The AB upheld the Panel's decision that the
international instruments are not "laws or regulations" because they are not
"automatically incorporated" into Indian law but require further domestic
implementation enactment. Regarding the domestic instruments, the Panel's interpretation of "laws or regulations" as "mandatory rules applying
across-the-board" was upheld.[64] On this ground, the AB characterized
most of the domestic instruments as falling outside of "laws or regulations"

---

60 General Agreements on Tariffs and Trade (1994) Article XX(d).
61 Panel Report *India-Solar*, paragraph 7.267.
62 Panel Report *India-Solar*, paragraph 7.269-7.283.
63 Appellate Body Report *India-Solar*, paragraph 5.113.
64 Appellate Body Report *India-Solar*, paragraph 5.128.

because they are "hortatory, aspirational, declaratory, and at times solely descriptive."[65]

Defense under Paragraph (j) in *India-Solar*

Article XX(j) establishes a general exception for measures "essential to the acquisition or distribution of products in general or local short supply."[66] As a logical starting point, the Panel first identified that the products alleged to be in "general or local short supply" refer to "solar cells and modules" rather than "electricity" generated by the equipment.[67]

Then the Panel turned to interpret "products in general or local short supply." Relying on past WTO decisions and a certain dictionary, the Panel interpreted the expression as a situation in which the "quantity of available supply of a product does not meet demand in the relevant geographical area or market."[68] However, the source of supply is not clear, and the respondent tried to direct the Panel to look solely into the "domestic production capacity" in order to determine whether supply is "available." The Panel rejected this point and developed the test as the quantity of available supply of the product "from all sources."[69] Because the respondent relied on "domestic production capacity" and failed to prove a short supply from all sources, the Panel denied the application of Article XX(j). The AB upheld the Panel's decision.[70]

Discussion

Assuming that a state uses mandatory language and imposes sanctions to enable the instruments to have a direct binding effect, or provides sufficient evidence to demonstrate that available supply of the product "from all sources" is in shortage, it can get over the hurdle set up by the WTO in adjudicated cases. In that case, the issue is whether the DCR-RE in question are "necessary," a requirement inherent in Article XX(d)[71] and XX(j).[72]

---

65 Appellate Body Report *India-Solar*, paragraph 5.133.
66 General Agreements on Tariffs and Trade (1994) Article XX(f).
67 Panel Report *India-Solar*, paragraph 7.200.
68 Panel Report *India-Solar*, paragraph 7.207.
69 Panel Report *India-Solar*, paragraph 7.234.
70 Appellate Body Report *India-Solar*, paragraph 6.1-6.8.
71 "[N]ecessary to secure compliance with laws or regulations which are not inconsistent with the provisions of this Agreement … ."
72 "[E]ssential to the acquisition or distribution of products in general or local short supply." "Essential" has the same meaning as "necessary," *see* Panel Report *India-Solar*, paragraph 7.334.

The "necessity" test has long been regarded as a high threshold to meet in cases where states invoke Article XX to exempt them from their GATT obligations.[73] In the *India-Solar* case, the AB decided it was not necessary to further analyze "necessity" because India's defense had failed the threshold to apply Article XX.[74] The jurisprudence is discussed more in detail in environment-related measures under Article XX(b)[75] and XX(g).[76] The essential lesson that can be drawn from the WTO decisions is that the "necessity" may be rebuffed if reasonable and less-trade-effecting alternative measures are available to the respondent state. Logically, respondent states will have difficulty proving the exhaustion of alternatives, and therefore it is more plausible for the arbitrators to review those alternatives proposed by the complainant state. With respect to DCR-RE, it is likely that the complainant will raise the point that an open market for foreign RE generation equipment would efficiently achieve the goal of environmental protection but with less trade restrictiveness, by lowering prices or making more advanced technology available, for example.

In summary, even if a defendant can steer clear of the hurdles of adjudicated cases, further obstacles posed by the "necessity" test would render Article XX(d) and XX(j) unavailable as a defense for DCR-RE.

Reserving DCR-RE Through Interpreting WTO Rules Based on Environmental Protection

Although currently there are only three adjudicated DCR-RE cases at the WTO, such disputes are likely to increase due to the scaling-up of the RE industry and the increasing imbalances between imports and exports of RE.[77] The justifications for DCR-RE, especially the urgency of rapidly transitioning off fossil fuels in order to avert catastrophic climate change,

---

73 *See*, e.g., Filippo Fontanelli, "Necessity Killed the GATT—Art XX GATT and the Misleading Rhetoric about 'Weighing and Balancing'" (2012) 5:2 *European Journal of Legal Studies* 36-56.
74 Appellate Body Report *India-Solar*, paragraph 5.155.
75 "[N]ecessary to protect human, animal or plant life or health."
76 "[R]elating to the conservation of exhaustible natural resources if such measures are made effective in conjunction with restrictions on domestic production or consumption."
77 Joanna Lewis, "The Rise of Renewable Energy Protectionism: Emerging Trade Conflicts and Implications for Low Carbon Development" (2014) 14:4 *Global Environmental Politics* 10-35, at 21.

demonstrate that it is desirable to consider how to reserve DCR-RE under WTO rules.

DCR-RE emerge from the context of environmental protection. The historical development of environmental protection demonstrates that ever since the 1972 Stockholm Declaration, efforts from individuals, NGOs, states and international institutions have contributed to a set of international instruments (we may call them "International Environmental Law," or IEL) to regulate or incentivize behaviors affecting the environment, within and beyond borders.

IEL consists of treaty and customary international law, both of which are public international law. It is proper to investigate whether and how possibly the IEL can impact the WTO rules in a way to reserve DCR-RE.

Interpreting Approaches

WTO rules generally impose binding obligation on states that prevent them from implementing measures that are detrimental to trade liberalization. Obligations are nailed down in strong language such as "shall," "shall not," etc., in multiple agreements. In addition, a dispute resolution system has been established to monitor compliance with these obligations, equipped with the authorization of retaliation. Furthermore, the WTO is a unifying institution where Member States negotiate, review and amend existing obligations. All these features of the WTO give rise to the idea that it is a closed, self-contained regime.[78]

However, this notion closure was rejected by the AB in *United States—Standards of Reformulated and Conventional Gasoline*, where the AB decided that WTO agreements should not be read "in clinical isolation from public international law."[79] Ever since, the AB has frequently sought additional interpretative guidance from the general principles of international law, including in trade disputes that resolve around measures of

---

78 It is so either in the sense of a narrow (set of primary and secondary rules) or a broader (wholes of primary and secondary rules to cover some particular problem) definition of "self-contained regime," *see* International Law Commission, *Fragmentation of International Law: Difficulties Arising from the Diversification and Expansion of International Law* (2006), United Nations General Assembly A/CN.4/L.682 (hereinafter "ILC Fragmentation Report") at p. 65.

79 WTO Appellate Body Report, *United States—Standards for Reformulated and Conventional Gasoline* (1996), WT/DS2/AB/R at 17.

environmental protection.[80] The relationship of the WTO agreements to customary international law may be broader than an interpretative guidance. Customary international law applies generally to the economic relations between WTO members. Such international law applies to the extent that the WTO treaty agreements do not "contract out" from it.[81]

IEL and WTO rules, as two recent types of specialized law that seek to respond to new technical and functional requirements, have highly specific objectives and rely on principles that often point in different directions,[82] and give rise to normative conflicts. The International Law Commission (ILC) has looked into the issue, which it reframes as a pragmatic interpreting process, and discusses four possible interpretation approaches for solving it. These approaches are summarized here.[83]

Lex Specialis

When there is conflict between two types of special law, *lex specialis* may provide a good means for conflict resolution.[84] The rationale for *lex specialis* is that the agreement that is most specific and approaches most nearly to the subject in hand is more effective.[85] *Lex specialis* usually has greater clarity and definiteness and is thus often felt to be "harder" or more "binding" than general rules.[86]

Lex Posterior

The principle that "later law supersedes earlier law" has its roots in Roman law and has been sometimes regarded as a "general principle of law

---

80 WTO Appellate Body Report *United States—Import Prohibition of Certain Shrimp and Shrimp Products* (1998), WT/DS58/AB/R, at 2755, also *see* Panel Report *India-Solar*, paragraph 7.202.
81 WTO Panel Report, *Korea—Measures Affecting Government Procurement,* WTO Doc. WT/DS163/R (2000), online: https://docs.wto.org/dol2fe/Pages/FE_Search/FE_S_S0 06.aspx?DataSource=Cat&query=@Symbol=WT/DS163/R&Language=English&Co ntext=ScriptedSearches&languageUIChanged=true, paragraph 7.96.
82 ILC Fragmentation Report, at p. 14, paragraph 15.
83 ILC Fragmentation Report, at p. 20, paragraph 27.
84 ILC Fragmentation Report, at p. 31, paragraphs 47. An example of such conflict is that in the 1998 *Beef Hormones* case, the Appellate Body of WTO considered the status of "precautionary principle" of IEL under WTO Agreement on Sanitary and Phytosanitary Substances. It concluded that whatever the status of that principle under IEL, it had not become binding for the WTO, ILC Fragmentation Report, at 34, paragraph 55.
85 ILC Fragmentation Report, at p. 36, paragraph 59.
86 ILC Fragmentation Report, at p. 36-37, paragraph 60.

recognized by civilized nations" or "a customary law principle of interpre-tation."[87] The rationale is that it reflects more concretely present circum-stances and the present will of the relevant actors.[88] This principle has been adopted in Article 30 of the Vienna Convention on Law of Treaties (VCLT), pursuant to which there are threshold conditions to be met before applying the principle. An important one is the question of "same subject matter" under the title and paragraph 1 of Article 30 of VCLT. The test is whether the fulfillment of the obligation under one treaty prevents the fulfillment of the obligation or undermines the object and purpose of the other treaty.[89]

Lex Superior

International law, unlike domestic law, does not have a strictly hierarchical order for its sources. However, the ILC suggests that the practice of international law has always recognized the presence of some norms that are superior to other norms.[90] The rationale is that these superior norms better secure important interests or protect important values.[91] The ILC develops *lex superior* to include *jus cogens* and *erga omnes* (owed to all) obligations, examples of which are the prohibition of genocide, slavery, racial discrimination, and so on.[92]

Systematic Integration

A systematic integration approach plays down the sense of conflict and reads the relevant materials from the perspective of their contribution to some generally shared objective.[93] The rationale is that rights or obliga-tions under one treaty have no intrinsic priority over the others.[94] Techni-cally, a process of reasoning under this approach would include "refer-ences to normal meaning, party will, legitimate expectations, good faith, and subsequent practice, as well as the 'object and purpose' and the principle of effectiveness."[95] Such approach has been embedded into

---

87 ILC Fragmentation Report, at pp. 116-117, paragraph 225.
88 ILC Fragmentation Report, at pp. 117, paragraph 226.
89 ILC Fragmentation Report, at p. 130, paragraph 254.
90 ILC Fragmentation Report, at p. 167, paragraph 326.
91 ILC Fragmentation Report, at p. 167, paragraph 325.
92 ILC Fragmentation Report, at p. 188, paragraphs 374, 405.
93 ILC Fragmentation Report, at p. 207, paragraph 412.
94 ILC Fragmentation Report, at p. 207, paragraph 414.
95 ILC Fragmentation Report, at p. 207, paragraph 412.

Article 31(3)(c) of VCLT, which reads, "There shall be taken into account, together with the context: … (c) any relevant rules of international law applicable in the relations between the parties."

Opting for a Systematic Integration Approach

DCR-RE and State Obligations under IEL

State Obligations under IEL Are Relatively Soft

When attempting to regulate behaviors, rules may be divided into a passive and an active paradigm. Such a dichotomy is helpful to illustrate hard versus soft obligations. The passive paradigm governs by negating certain behaviors. Usually, such a paradigm is embedded into specific rules restricting the person from performing certain activities, using strong language such as "shall not," and referring to "obligations," "responsibility," etc. In comparison, the positive paradigm encourages the person to achieve certain goals, leaving the discretion to the person how to act. The goals appear as obligations in the rules while soft language such as "encouraged," "endeavored," "guided," etc., is adopted to incentivize behaviors. As compared to the passive paradigm, the obligation in the active paradigm is relatively soft.

A review of history suggests that IEL has developed from the passive to the active paradigm. Many examples for the passive paradigm occur before the "maturation" of IEL in 1992.[96] One is that the International Court of Justice has developed the customary international law that a state is obliged to ensure that any activities in its territory or jurisdiction do not cause significant damage to the environment of another state.[97] Further examples include the *Montreal Protocol on Substances that Deplete the Ozone Layer* (1987) in which parties shall prohibit trade in certain products with nonparties,[98] and the *Basel Convention on the Control of Transboundary Movement of Hazardous Wastes* (1989) in which parties must

---

96 Brown Weiss, "The Evolution of International Environmental Law" (2011) 54 *Japanese Year Book of International Law* 1-27, at 10.

97 *United Kingdom v. Albania* (Corfu Channel), [1949] Merits, Judgment, International Court of Justice ("ICJ") Reports 1949, at 22; *Legality of the Threat or Use of Nuclear Weapons*, [1996] Advisory Opinion, ICJ Reports 1996 (I), at 242, paragraph 29; *Argentina v. Uruguay* (Pulp Mills on the River Uruguay), [2010] Merits, Judgment, ICJ Reports 2010, at 45, paragraph 101.

98 Montreal Protocol on Substances that Deplete the Ozone Layer, Article 4(1), https://ozone.unep.org/treaties/montreal-protocol/articles/article-4-control-trade-non-parties.

prohibit the export of hazardous wastes to parties that have prohibited the import of such wastes or that did not consent in writing to the specific import.[99]

Ever since the "maturation" of IEL, marked by the United Nations Rio Conference in 1992, the international community has embraced a set of documents including the UNFCCC, Rio Declaration, Kyoto Protocol to UNFCCC, Johannesburg Declaration, 2030 Agenda for Sustainable Development and the Paris Agreement.[100] They all recognize the imminence of climate change and share the flexible framework that states are encouraged to adopt certain measures to realize their commitments or implement the principles.

Both the features of environmental issues and practical solutions may account for the change in paradigm. Environmental issues often present a classic example of the "tragedy of the commons," since governments are faced with a nearly "irresistible temptation to ignore pollution problems."[101] Furthermore, global environmental issues offer the additional opportunity to transfer burdens to foreigners.[102] In addition, the conflict of economic interests between developing countries and developed countries render the international law only "auxiliary to the political, technical and psychological aspects of a solution,"[103] changing from the form of passive, harmful prevention to active cooperation and coordination, most of which are of an encouraging nature.

The Nexus Between DCR-RE and the Soft Obligations Is Weak

DCR-RE are one of the measures adopted by the state under an active rather than passive obligation. There is no environmental agreement that obliges the state to use DCR-RE to facilitate the rapid transition from fossil fuel to RE. In addition, the features of IEL may render a weaker link between DCR-RE and obligations under IEL. One is that IEL does not have a unifying institution, since various agreements were negotiated under

---

99 Basel Convention on the Control of Transboundary Movement of Hazardous Wastes, Article 4(1)(b) and (c), https://treaties.un.org/doc/Treaties/1992/05/19920505%2012-51%20PM/Ch_XXVII_03p.pdf.
100 United Nations, "Sustainable Development Goals." online: https://sustainabledevelopment.un.org/?menu=1300.
101 Daniel Esty, "GATTing the Greens, Not Just Greening the GATT" (1993) 72:5 *Foreign Affairs* 32-6, at 33.
102 Daniel Esty, "GATTing the Greens, Not Just Greening the GATT" (1993) 72:5 *Foreign Affairs* 32-6, at 33.
103 Oscar Schachter, "The Emergence of International Environmental Law" (1991) 44:2 *Journal of International Affairs* 457-93, at 474.

different institutional umbrellas and there has been no effort to consolidate them within one institution.[104] For this reason, states may not have a stable institution for them to negotiate and account for the new development in RE. Furthermore, the IEL does not have a mandatory dispute resolution mechanism, and this de facto leaves the settlement of trade-related climate disputes to the WTO.[105] Therefore, the positive role of DCR-RE to play down GHG emissions, a feature of environmental protection, may not attain sufficient recognition in the trade system.

Systematic Integration Approach Is the Optimal Choice

Considering the soft obligations and the weak nexus between DCR-RE and such obligations, it is better to pick up a systematic integration approach to import IEL into WTO interpretation because other approaches may not fit. First, *lex specialis* requires the special law to be more definite and specific. The argument that DCR-RE is "definitely" or "specifically" required under IEL is difficult to establish. Second, although the recent Paris Agreement (2015) emerges as a "later law" than WTO rules (1994), the *lex posterior* may not apply because of the "same subject-matter" require- ment. The opening-up of markets to foreign RE generation equipment may not necessarily frustrate the state's obligation under, or the objectives and purposes of, the Paris Agreement. Third, *lex superior* may not be a solution since the customary international law of IEL is referenced to a state's obligation to avoid activities under its jurisdiction from harming another state's environment, which bears little relevance to the context of DCR-RE. Furthermore, such an obligation is not a *jus cogens* or *erga omnes.*

Under the systematic integration approach, it is important for the respondent state to play down the conflict between the IEL and WTO rules and stress the mutually recognized goal between them, which should make reference to "sustainable development" recognized by both IEL and WTO.[106] Furthermore, such an approach ensures the reference to the system of international law as a whole when interpreting WTO rules.[107]

---

104 Brown Weiss, John Jackson & Nathalie Bernasconi-Osterwalder, *Reconciling Envi- ronment and Trade* (2nd edition) (Netherlands: Martinus Nijhoff, 2008) at 12.

105 James Bacchus, "Global Rules for Mutually Supportive and Reinforcing Trade and Climate Regimes" (2016) ICTSD Policy Options Paper, at 14.

106 WTO, "The WTO and the Sustainable Development Goals" (https://www.wto.org/ english/thewto_e/coher_e/sdgs_e/sdgs_e.htm).

107 International Law Commission, *Fragmentation of International Law: Difficulties Arising from the Diversification and Expansion of International Law* (2006), United

Importing Environmental Protection into WTO Interpretation

Adding Environmental Element to "Like" Product under Article III:4

"From the environmental perspective, the process for producing a product is very often more important than the product."[108] For example, when performing an environmental review on trade agreements, the questions raised mainly concern the characteristics of "process of production," such as "might the trade agreement increase or decrease pollution, land-use, overall levels of resource use, growth into environmental protection."[109]

In comparison, the nondiscrimination principle under WTO rules revolves around "like products." When analyzing "likeness," generally the arbitrators would look into a range of factors, including the physical characteristics, the capacity to serve the same or similar end-users, substitutability perceived by consumers, similar classification for tariff purpose, and competitive relationship of the products.[110] The "process of production" used to be excluded in characterizing products until recent WTO practice introduced the environmental element into determining the "likeness" of products.[111] The concern for WTO to remain agnostic regarding the process of production is that it would "open up the potential of thousands of societal and process differences being used to undermine the logic and principles of non-discrimination."[112] With more and more environmental protection provisions included into free trade agreements, it

---

Nations General Assembly A/CN.4/L.682, at 243, paragraphs 479-480. "This articulation is quite important in a decentralized and spontaneous institutional world whose priorities and objectives are often poorly expressed. It is also important for the critical and constructive development of international institutions, especially institutions with law-applying tasks."

108 Brown Weiss, John Jackson & Nathalie Bernasconi-Osterwalder, *Reconciling Environment and Trade* (2nd edition) (Netherlands: Martinus Nijhoff, 2008), at 33.

109 Organisation for Economic Co-operation and Development (OECD), *Methodologies for Environmental and Trade Reviews* (1994), online: http://www.oecd.org/environment/envtrade/36767000.pdf, at 16.

110 WTO Appellate Body Report, *European Communities—Measures Affecting Asbestos and Asbestos-Containing Products*, WTO Doc. WT/DS135/AB/R (2001), online: https://docs.wto.org/dol2fe/Pages/FE_Search/FE_S_S006.aspx?DataSource=Cat&query=@Symbol=WT/DS135/AB/R&Language=English&Context=ScriptedSearches&languageUIChanged=true, paragraphs 101 and 103.

111 WTO, "WTO Rules and Environmental Policies: Key GATT Disciplines," online: https://www.wto.org/english/tratop_e/envir_e/envt_rules_gatt_e.htm.

112 Brown Weiss, John Jackson & Nathalie Bernasconi-Osterwalder, *Reconciling Environment and Trade* (2nd edition) (Netherlands: Martinus Nijhoff, 2008), at 33.

seems that the development of IEL would continuously strengthen the environmental element in deciding likeness.

DCR-RE are a state means of impacting the "process of production." As stated in the social justification for DCR-RE,[113] these measures may have their own environmental impacts considering that local supply of equipment could reduce the transportation-related emissions. However, further scientific research is required regarding the lifecycle environmental impact of the equipment manufactured locally and abroad in order to strengthen the perspective of environmental risk from foreign RE equipment.

Enhancing "Necessity" under the Article XX Exemption

Currently, the WTO practice to review "necessity" under Article XX is "least trade-restrictive means."[114] This practice embraces the idea that "all deviations from the trade obligations should be minimized."[115] Reviewing an alternative measure to determine the "necessity" for Article XX purposes is problematic, given the complexity of determining a yardstick for defining what is less restrictive. As asserted by Argentina, "[a]ccepting this approach would mean supplanting the sovereignty of governments by a Panel's evaluation."[116]

Relatively speaking, a weighing and balancing (WAB) approach might be less intrusive in the sense that the analysis is targeting the measure itself

---

113 *See* above section "Key Features of DCR-RE."
114 Filippo Fontanelli, "Necessity Killed the GATT—Art XX GATT and the Misleading Rhetoric about 'Weighing and Balancing'" (2012) 5:2 *European Journal of Legal Studies* 36-56, at 35.
115 Filippo Fontanelli, "Necessity Killed the GATT—Art XX GATT and the Misleading Rhetoric about 'Weighing and Balancing'" (2012) 5:2 *European Journal of Legal Studies* 36-56, at 40.
116 WTO Panel Report, *Argentina—Measures Affecting the Export of Bovine Hides and the Import of Finished Leather* WT/DS155/R (2000), online: https://docs.wto.org/dol2fe/Pages/FE_Search/FE_S_S006.aspx?DataSource=Cat&query=@Symbol=WT/DS155/R*&Language=English&Context=ScriptedSearches&languageUIChanged=true, paragraph 8.251-8.252, also *see* WTO Panel Report, *United States—Import Prohibition of Certain Shrimp and Shrimp Products*, WTO Doc. WT/DS58/R (1998), online: https://docs.wto.org/dol2fe/Pages/FE_Search/FE_S_S006.aspx?DataSource=Cat&query=@Symbol=WT/DS58/AB/R&Language=English&Context=ScriptedSearches&languageUIChanged=true, paragraph 3.226, "the basic thrust of the GATT was to prevent protectionism, not to intrude on the decision making of the contracting parties when pursuing legitimate policy objectives such as environmental protection."

rather than introducing alternatives from the outset. In addition, function-ing as a "constitutional"[117] institute, including performing a de facto judicial review, WTO should give more weight to the WAB approach, which has been widely practiced in domestic constitutional review.[118] A shift from less-trade-distorting reviews of alternatives to WAB would encourage the arbitrators to review the effectiveness of the measures in achieving values or objectives. As adjudicated in the *Korea-Beef* case, "[t]he more vital or important those common interests or values are, the easier it would be to accept as 'necessary' a measure designed as an enforcement instrument."[119]

The justifications for DCR-RE mentioned above can be framed into the argument of "sustainable development": (1) a transition from fossil fuel to RE is desirable; (2) economic incentives are an effective way to develop the RE industry because of the high costs, presence of a low-skilled work-force, or undeveloped technology in the domestic market; (3) creating jobs through DCR-RE is an effective way to earn democratic votes in order to place the economic incentives into government budgets; (4) a transition from fossil fuel to RE should be "just" because a social acceptance or license for environmental policy is effective for the long-term implemen-tation of environmental measures.

Conclusions

The international community has been disputing ways to lower GHG emissions for decades. As fossil fuels are the main contributor to GHG emissions, a rapid transition from fossil fuel to RE is desirable.

In practice, an increasing number of states are implementing DCR-RE to incentivize the development of their domestic RE sectors. These mea-sures can be justified based on economic, political and/or social grounds. However, the prominence in DCR-RE of "local preferences" for resources

---

117 *See*, e.g., Joel Trachtman, "The Constitutions of the WTO" (2006) 17:3 *European Journal of International Law* 623-46.

118 For example, EU, U.S., Canada, Germany, and so on. *See Handyside v. the United Kingdom*, [1976] App. No. 5493/72 European Court of Human Rights; *R. v. Oakes*, [1986] 1 SCR 103; Moshe Cohen-Eliya and Iddo Porat, "American Balancing and German Proportionality: The Historical Origins" (2010) 8:2 *International Journal of Constitutional Law* 263-286.

119 WTO Appellate Body Report, *Korea—Measures Affecting Imports of Fresh, Chilled and Frozen Beef*, WTO Doc. WT/DS161/AB/R (2000), online: https://www.wto.org/english/tratop_e/dispu_e/161-169abr_e.pdf, paragraph 162.

has repeatedly triggered concerns from other states about how these measures violate the national treatment principle enshrined in WTO rules.

A review of WTO decisions on adjudicated DCR-RE cases shows that respondent states lose their arguments in defending against the national treatment principle. Considering that DCR-RE emerge from the context of environmental protection, this chapter considers the possible approaches to import environmental protection into interpreting WTO rules, therefore reserving the policy space for DCR-RE.

The systematic integration approach may be most appropriate to this task. Therefore, recommendations are made to direct WTO interpretation toward "mutual supporting" of environmental considerations, including adding production processes into analyses of "like" products for the purposes of determining violations of GATT Article III:4, and taking into account the value of sustainable development for an enhanced "necessity" analysis under GATT Article XX defenses.

WTO Panel and Appellate Body Jurisprudence on Environmental Protection of Marine Living Resources: Considerations for the Maritime Silk Road Shipping Policies

Henrik Andersen

Associate Professor at CBS Law, Copenhagen Business School, Frederiksberg, Denmark and Visiting Senior Fellow at UCLan Cyprus, Larnaca, Cyprus

Introduction

China's Belt and Road Initiative (BRI) aims at facilitating trade between Asia, Eurasia, Africa, and Europe. The means are investments in trade facilities, like improvement of infrastructure on the Maritime Silk Road. That has materialized in, for example, port investments in Piraeus, Greece;[1] building major port at Kyaukpyu in western Myanmar;[2] Chinese investors' purchase of Turkey's third largest port, Kumport,[3] etc. As part of China's Belt and Road strategy, it will connect free trade areas, and set up and support negotiation of new trade agreements between various states along the Belt and Road. From an economic perspective, it is welcoming if trade becomes smoother and world's resources can be allocated to their efficient uses. That is in line with the overall objectives of the World Trade

---

1 Frans-Paul van der Putten, "Chinese Investment in the Port of Piraeus, Greece: The Relevance for the EU and the Netherlands," *Clingendael Report*, Netherlands Institute of International Relations, 2014.
2 Ambassador Chas W. Freeman, Jr., *The Maritime Dimension of "One Belt, One Road" in Strategic Perspective*, Remarks to a Center for Naval Analysis Workshop with the Rajaratnam School of International Studies, Middle East Policy Council, 2017; https://www.mepc.org/speeches/maritime-dimension-one-belt-one-road-strategic-perspective retrieved on Sept. 10, 2020.
3 The Straits Times—Asia, "The Trains and Sea Ports of One Belt, One Road, China's New Silk Road," May 14, 2017; https://www.straitstimes.com/asia/the-trains-and-sea-ports-of-one-belt-one-road-chinas-new-silk-road, retrieved on Sept. 10, 2020.

Organization (WTO) to expand production and reduce barriers to trade to improve welfare on a global scale.[4] The opening of markets can also be seen as an environmental advantage if green goods can reach foreign markets and if the competition of such goods can drive down the market prices.[5]

However, from an environmental angle, scholars criticize the expected increase in world trade and economic interconnectedness via the Belt and Road. Increased transport and environmental problems are related.[6] Carbon dioxide (CO_2) emission from shipping is increasing[7] resulting in reduced oxygen in the sea that causes problems for marine life.[8] Furthermore, increased shipping has a negative impact on marine living resources, like changed behavior, habitat fragmentation, degradation, and invasive species.[9]

International environmental law provides the tools for states to take actions against vessels that pollute within their respective territories and exclusive economic zones.[10] It imposes duties on states to protect the

---

4 This chapter does not engage in any economic or ethical discussions about the concept of welfare and the means to improve welfare.

5 *See* WTO: Sustainable Development Goals, "Mainstreaming Trade to Attain the Sustainable Development Goals," (WTO, Genève—2018) at 44; https://www.wto.org/english/res_e/publications_e/sdg_e.htm#:~:text=sustainable%20development%20goals-,Mainstreaming%20trade%20to%20attain%20the%20Sustainable%20Developme nt%20Goals,health%2C%20education%20and%20the%20environment, retrieved on Sept. 10, 2020.

6 *See,* e.g., Danielle B. van Veen-Groot and Peter Nijkamp, "Globalisation, Transport and the Environment: New Perspectives for Ecological Economics," 31, *Ecological Economics* (1999) 331-346; Martin Cames, Jakob Graichen, Anne Siemons, and Vanessa Cook, *Emission Reduction Targets for International Aviation and Shipping*, European Parliament, Directorate General for Internal Policies: Policy Department A: Economic and Scientific Policy, IP/A/ENVI/2015-11, PE 569.964, November 2015; https://www.europarl.europa.eu/RegData/etudes/STUD/2015/569964/IPOL_STU(2015)569 964_EN.pdf, retrieved on Sept. 10, 2020.

7 Zhaofeng Lv, Huan Liu, Qi Ying, Mingliang Fu, Zhihang Meng, Yue Wang, Wei Wei, Huiming Gong, and Kebin He, "Impacts of Shipping Emissions on PM2.5 Pollution in China," 18, *Atmospheric Chemistry and Physics* (2018) 15811-15824. International Maritime Organization, "IMO's Response to Current Environmental Challenges," 2011 at 7, http://www.imo.org/en/OurWork/Environment/Documents/IMO%20and%20the%20Environment%202011.pdf, retrieved on Sept. 10, 2020.

8 UN Environment, "Greenhouse Gases Are Depriving Our Oceans of Oxygen," Apr. 10, 2019, https://www.unenvironment.org/news-and-stories/story/greenhouse-gases-are-depriving-our-oceans-oxygen, retrieved on Sept. 10, 2019.

9 Vanessa Pirotta, Alana Grech, Ian D Jonsen, William F Laurance, and Robert G Harcourt, "Consequences of Global Shipping Traffic for Marine Giants," 17(1) *Frontiers in Ecology and the Environment* (2019), 39-47.

10 For example, UNCLOS provides that a State has the right to introduce measures against vessels if they violate international rules and standards for the prevention, reduction,

environment and climate as well as duties to cooperate to protect the environment, including marine living resources, and the climate. The question is the scope of WTO law in respect of protecting marine living resources against an increase in shipping. Even though the WTO has mostly economic aims, it leaves space for its members to take sovereign decisions to protect the environment and the climate. The WTO quasi-judiciaries—Panels and the Appellate Body (AB)—uphold that line in their case law.[11] However, the imposition of trade barriers on goods—that are produced in another state and where the product in itself is not causing any harm—can be at odds with the fundamental principle of state sovereignty and the permanent sovereign right over resources. Nevertheless, deriving from the principle of state sovereignty, states have the right to protect their marine living resources from harm. With particular focus on Panel and AB jurisprudence, the overall question is whether a state legitimately under WTO law can reject goods from a state due to the environmental harm caused by shipping even if the harm takes place outside the territory of the importing state. For example, when a state imposes measures that are targeted at exporting states' goods due to a high volume of goods transported by vessel. If the answer is confirmative, the stakeholders of the BRI should address the environmental aspects of shipping. Thus, this chapter has an overall policy aim targeting the design of Belt and Road requirements. It discusses two questions:

(1) whether an importing state can apply WTO law to *protect marine living resources if they are beyond the territory of the importing state.* That can be within the territory of another state or in *res communis*, like the high seas; and

(2) whether bans on *shipping* to protect marine living resources can be legitimate under WTO law.

---

and control of pollution which result in a discharge causing major damage or threat of major damage to the coastline or related interests of the coastal State, or to any resources of its territorial sea or exclusive economic zone. The measures can be detention of the vessel, cf. UNCLOS, Article 220(3) and 220(6).

11 Disputes are first sought to be resolved through negotiations between the disputing parties. If they cannot reach agreement, a panel will be established to make a recommendation of law. That recommendation can be appealed to the AB. It is ultimately the Dispute Settlement Body (DSB), which consists of all the WTO Members, which decides whether the panel and/or AB recommendation can be accepted as a legally binding instrument. However, the panel/AB recommendation can only be rejected by the WTO DSB, which consists of all the WTO Members, if there is full consensus among *all* the WTO Members.

As these questions have various complicated aspects, this chapter needs to be delimited from questions about the *chapeau* of Article XX of the General Agreement on Tariffs and Trade (GATT) 1994. Although various states and the EU raise trade concerns about China and the BRI, and that the environmental argument is subject to the requirements of the *chapeau* of Article XX of GATT 1994, it is beyond the scope of this chapter to address the complicated questions that follows from the *chapeau*.[12] In this respect, being a member of multilateral environmental agreements, which are basis for the trade restrictive measures, can be a way of avoiding the prohibition of "arbitrary and unjustifiable discrimination" even if other WTO Members are not parties to the multilateral environmental agreement as long as negotiations to enter into international agreements are offered.[13] Furthermore, this chapter needs to build on a simple model of shipping with goods being shipped directly from the country of origin to the importing state. This chapter does not discuss questions about transit.[14] The environmental dimension is related to the increase in volume of imported goods, not to the actual compliance with environmental law by the shipping companies. Thus, the situation may be that the respective shipping companies comply with the requirements under the flag state.

As the BRI is not clearly defined in institutional terms, but rather is an initiative comprising various institutions, based on Chinese policies, and with support by a number of other states, the BRI cannot be regarded as a subject under international law. As WTO law only is applicable to its Members, this chapter will be relevant for those states and the EU. As the BRI is promoted by China, and as China is setting the overall political framework for the BRI, it is of particular relevance for China. Furthermore, this chapter is relevant for institutions that administrate other bilateral or multilateral free trade agreements along the Belt and Road.

The first section provides a brief overview of the principles of the BRI of the WTO. Next, this chapter addresses the extent of protection of marine living resources in WTO law particularly drawing on WTO case law. That

---

12 The *chapeau* of GATT 1994, Article XX provides that measures must not be "applied in a manner which would constitute a means of arbitrary or unjustifiable discrimination between countries where the same conditions prevail, or a disguised restriction on international trade."
13 *See* to this effect, *US—Shrimp (Article 21.5—Malaysia)*, WT/DS58/AB/RW, adopted by the DSB on Nov. 21, 2001, paragraph 122.
14 Article V of GATT 1994 concerns freedom of transit of goods and could also be relevant to analyze in respect of environmental and climate change questions if WTO Members impose restrictions on shipping due to environmental or climate change concerns.

includes a discussion of WTO law and policies concerning the environment and the context of international environmental law.

The BRI and the WTO: A Brief Overview

Introduction to the BRI

In 2013, the President of China, Xi Jinping, initiated the Belt and Road program. It will establish a Euro-Asian land bridge and a twenty-first century Maritime Silk Road. The BRI aims at facilitating trade between Asia, Africa, and Europe by reducing trade barriers, improving infrastructure and increasing cooperation in numerous sectors between more than sixty countries along the Belt and Road. China is the main coordinator, and China's National Development and Reform Commission, Ministry of Foreign Affairs, and Ministry of Commerce of the People's Republic of China have issued the core principles of the BRI:

- be in line with the purposes and principles of the United Nations (UN) Charter and upholding the Five Principles of Peaceful Coexistence;
- openness for cooperation for countries and international and regional organizations;
- inclusiveness and harmony with tolerance among civilizations and respect of respective countries' development and supporting dialogue between different civilizations where common ground is to be sought in order to be in peace for common prosperity;
- abiding market rules and international norms where market will have a decisive role in allocation of resources with a primary role of enterprises and where governments perform their due functions; and
- seeking mutual benefits for all parties involved.[15]

---

15 Vision and Actions on Jointly Building Silk Road Economic Belt and 21st-Century Maritime Silk Road, Issued by the National Development and Reform Commission, Ministry of Foreign Affairs, and Ministry of Commerce of the People's Republic of China, with State Council authorization, Part II: Principles.

The principles are manifested through development of infrastructure, trade liberalization, financial integration, policy coordination, and people-to-people ties. The BRI is not aiming at creating a special BRI trading bloc. However, according to China's Thirteenth Five-Year Plan:

> We will speed up efforts to implement the free trade area strategy, gradually establishing a network of high-standard free trade areas. We will actively engage in negotiations with countries and regions along the routes of the Belt and Road Initiative on the building of free trade areas; negotiations on regional comprehensive economic partnership agreements, the China-Gulf Cooperation Council Free Trade Area, and the China-Japan-RoK Free Trade Area; and work to achieve progress in developing free trade relations with Israel, Canada, the Eurasian Economic Union, and the European Union as well as in building the Free Trade Area of the Asia- Pacific. We will ensure full implementation of our free trade agreements with the Republic of Korea and with Australia as well as the Protocol to Amend the Framework Agreement on Comprehensive Economic Cooperation between China and ASEAN. We will continue to pursue progress in negotiations on investment agreements between China and the United States and between China and the European Union.[16]

China will actively—as part of its Belt and Road strategy—be involved in setting-up free trade areas along the Belt and Road. In this respect, the question is the level of promotion of environmental and climate change standards to cope with the increased shipping along the Maritime Silk Road. The Belt and Road principle of compliance with the UN Charter must also imply a general compliance with general international law,[17] including compliance with customary rules of international environmental and climate change law. Furthermore, international environmental treaty law and international climate change treaty law with wide consents across the states among the Belt and Road must also be complied with. For

---

16 "The 13th Five-Year Plan for Economic and Social Development of the People's Republic of China" (2016–2020), translated by Compilation and Translation Bureau, Central Committee of the Communist Party of China, Beijing, China, Chapter 52, Section 2.

17 Henrik Andersen, "Rule of Law Gaps and the Chinese Belt and Road Initiative: Legal Certainty for International Businesses?" in Giuseppe Martinico and Xueyan W.U. (eds.), *A Legal Analysis of the Belt and Road Initiative—Towards a New Silk Road?* (Cham, Switzerland: Palgrave Macmillan, 2020) at 119-120.

example, 197 UN members have ratified the United Nations Framework Convention on Climate Change (UNFCCC), and it has a near universal coverage, and thus must be a minimum level of legal or policy standards to combat climate change for the Belt and Road states. In addition, various international environmental treaties with wide global support must be part of the Belt and Road strategy.

The Ecological and Environmental Cooperation Plan

The Chinese Government has made an ecological and environmental cooperation plan for the BRI. It connects the BRI with the 2030 Agenda for Sustainable Development of the UN:

> The 2030 Agenda for Sustainable Development of the United Nations aims to jointly improve the welfare of all mankind and clearly specifies the targets of green development and environmental protection, mapping the road to sustainable development and international development cooperation in the next decades. The cooperation on eco-environmental protection under the framework of the Belt and Road Initiative will inject an effective impetus to accomplishment of environmental targets in the Agenda in countries along the routes.

Some of the goals under the 2030 Agenda for Sustainable Development of the UN are:
- "By 2025, prevent and significantly reduce marine pollution of all kinds, in particular from land-based activities, including marine debris and nutrient pollution."[18]
- "Enhance the conservation and sustainable use of oceans and their resources by implementing international law as reflected in (United Nations Convention on the Law of the Sea) UNCLOS, which provides the legal framework for the conservation and sustainable use of oceans and their resources."[19]

Thus, by supporting the 2030 Agenda for Sustainable Development of the UN, the BRI should in the promotion of trade agreements along the Belt

---

18 Goal Target 14.1, UN Sustainable Development Goals, https://www.un.org/sustain abledevelopment/oceans/, retrieved on Sept. 10, 2020.
19 Goal Target 14.C, UN Sustainable Development Goals, https://www.un.org/sustain abledevelopment/oceans/, retrieved on Sept. 10, 2020.

and Road make it a requirement that increased shipping would require investments in research and developments of technologies that can counter the potential environmental harm to maritime life.

The underlying principles of the ecological and environmental cooperation plan are:

- *"Green-oriented philosophy.* Guided by the philosophies of ecological civilization and green development, the Belt and Road Initiative will be advanced in an environment-friendly way to improve green competitiveness, covering policy coordination, facilities connectivity, unimpeded trade, financial integration and people-to-people bonds.
- *Joint construction through consultation to create mutual benefit and win-win situation.* With full respect for the development needs of countries along the Belt and Road, we will strengthen strategic alignment and policy communication and cooperate on eco-environmental protection based on consensus, to build a community of shared interests, responsibility and future and create a win-win situation for economic development and environmental protection.
- *Government guidance and diverse participation.* We will provide better policy support and cooperation platforms and construct a network for eco-environmental protection cooperation characterized by government guidance, business commitment and social participation. The whole society will be mobilized to actively participate in environmental governance with the business sector bearing the main responsibility and the market playing the due role.
- *Coordinated advancement and demonstration.* In accordance with unified deployment with priority areas and industries, we will make steady and orderly progress and timely summarize lessons and results to form radiation effects and cooperate at higher standards."[20]

---

20 The Belt and Road Ecological and Environmental Cooperation Plan, Belt and Road Portal, May 2017, at 2; https://eng.yidaiyilu.gov.cn/zchj/qwfb/13392.htm, retrieved on Sept. 10, 2020.

The cooperation plan also promotes cooperation with multinational enterprises.[21] In addition, it will expand import and export of environmental goods and services,[22] which is in line with China's negotiations of the Environmental Goods Agreement in the WTO. Furthermore, the cooperation plan also includes compliance with environmental conventions:

> Promote cooperation for compliance with environmental conventions. We will help relevant countries along the Belt and Road to fulfill commitments under multilateral environmental agreements (MEAs), such as Convention on Biological Diversity and Stockholm Convention on Persistent Organic Pollutants, by building up cooperation mechanisms for MEA implementation and enabling technological exchange and South-South cooperation.[23]

That is in line with the overall BRI aims of complying with "purposes and principles of the UN Charter and upholding the Five Principles of Peaceful Coexistence." In the view of this author, it implies compliance with China's commitments under public international law although the content of commitments can be debated.[24] The Plan also provides that it will explore the "feasibility of including environmental considerations into free trade

---

21 The Belt and Road Ecological and Environmental Cooperation Plan, Belt and Road Portal, May 2017, at 3; https://eng.yidaiyilu.gov.cn/zchj/qwfb/13392.htm, retrieved on Sept. 10, 2020.

22 The Belt and Road Ecological and Environmental Cooperation Plan, Belt and Road Portal, May 2017, at 4; https://eng.yidaiyilu.gov.cn/zchj/qwfb/13392.htm, retrieved on Sept. 10, 2020.

23 The Belt and Road Ecological and Environmental Cooperation Plan, Belt and Road Portal, May 2017, at 5; https://eng.yidaiyilu.gov.cn/zchj/qwfb/13392.htm, retrieved on 10 September.

24 *See*, e.g., Tim Rühlig, "How China Approaches International law: Implications for Europe," European Institute for Asian Studies, *EU-Asia at a Glance* (May 2018); Pitman B. Potter, "China and the International Legal System: Challenges of Participation," *The China Quarterly*, No. 191 (September 2007) 699. There has in particular been debates about China and its compliance with the international commitments after the South China Sea Arbitration; *The Republic of the Philippines v. The People's Republic of China* (South China Sea Arbitration), PCA Case No. 2013-19, Award by the Arbitral Tribunal on Jul. 12, 2016. *See*, for a discussion, WU Shicun and ZOU Keyuan (eds.), "Arbitration Concerning the South China Sea: Philippines Versus China" (Abingdon: Routledge, 2016); Antonios Tzanakopoulos, "Resolving Disputes over the South China Sea under the Compulsory Dispute Settlement System of the UN Convention on the Law of the Sea" (Apr. 10, 2016), the South China Sea Disputes and International Law, Oxford Legal Studies Research Paper No. 31/2016, available at SSRN: http://ssrn.com/abstract=2772659, retrieved on Sept. 10, 2020.

agreements with major countries along the Belt and Road."[25] In addition, the BRI aims at establishing a green supply chain management, which supposedly "promote green development from the perspective of the whole industrial chain ranging from production, circulation to consumption. We will carry out certification of standards and performance appraisal for green supply chain and try to establish green supply chain performance evaluation systems."[26] That should include shipping.

The Trade Aspects and the WTO

Regardless of the intentions to make a green profile for the BRI and its associated projects, it needs to be materialized in the Belt and Road projects. China's leading role in the BRI imposes moral responsibilities to ensure that the increased shipping does not increase the harmful effect on the maritime life. Otherwise, states with a greener profile than China may consider unilateral actions to preserve the environment. Besides green considerations by other states, there is a trade aspect that fuels some reluctance toward the BRI. Although the BRI also aims at abiding by market rules, there is fear of China's expansion of export along the Belt and Road. With the increased speed of shipping and improved infrastructure, there is a risk that low costs or subsidized producers from China can oust competitors in the foreign markets.[27] That concern has to some extent been expressed in the new EU antidumping regime against China. EU institutions' fear that Chinese over-capacity will reach the EU markets faster than before.[28] That has moved the EU's China policies from a "non-market approach" to the new "distorted economy" approach, which still does not

---

25 The Belt and Road Ecological and Environmental Cooperation Plan, Belt and Road Portal, May 2017, at 4; https://eng.yidaiyilu.gov.cn/zchj/qwfb/13392.htm, retrieved on May 6, 2019.

26 The Belt and Road Ecological and Environmental Cooperation Plan, Belt and Road Portal, May 2017, at 4; https://eng.yidaiyilu.gov.cn/zchj/qwfb/13392.htm, retrieved on May 6, 2019.

27 Henrik Andersen, "The New Maritime Silk Road and WTO Law: Road to Harmony or Conflict?" in Keyuan Zou, Shicun Wu, and Qiang Ye (eds.) *The 21st Century Maritime Silk Road—Challenges and Opportunities for Asia and Europe* (London, New York: Routledge, 2020) 243-263.

28 *See* European Parliament Resolution of Dec. 16, 2015 on EU-China relations (2015/2003(INI)), paragraphs 8-9 and 16; Council of the European Union, Council conclusions: *EU Strategy on China*, Brussels, Jul. 18, 2016 (OR. en) 11252/16, Appendix 1, paragraph 11; European Commission, Commission Staff Working Document, Impact Assessment, "Possible Change in the Calculation Methodology of Dumping Regarding the People's Republic of China (and Other Non-market Economies)," SWD(2016) 370 final, Brussels, 9.11.2016, p. 17.

grant Chinese producers the same market economy treatment as producers from other states.[29] In the new EU antidumping approach, part of the considerations also concerns whether states comply with international environmental law.

Obstacles to trade due to environmental concerns fall under the scope of WTO law. Although there are economic aims of "raising standards of living, ensuring full employment and a large and steadily growing volume of real income and effective demand, and expanding the production of and trade in goods and services, while allowing for the optimal use of the world's resources" they must be "in accordance with the objective of sustainable development, seeking both to protect and preserve the environment."[30] Thus, the WTO aims also at protection and preservation of the environment through sustainable development. These aims are reflected in the WTO treaties, like GATT 1994. However, protection of the environment is mainly expressed as exceptions to the trade principles of GATT 1994. Furthermore, the WTO does not contain a multilateral treaty concerning the interface between trade and environment.

The WTO's core principles are:

- *Nondiscrimination*, which is reflected in two separate principles: *most favored nations (MFN)*, i.e., a WTO Member must not discriminate between its trading partners; and *national treatment (NT)*, i.e., products which have passed the custom zone must be granted equal treatment to *like products* from domestic producers. If states target shipping due to environmental concerns about an accumulated environmental effect, it might be at odds with the nondiscrimination principles. For example, if a certain type of good gets caught through the transport restrictions by the importing state it can be a violation of the NT principle as producers of the like product in the importing state do not experience that type of restriction.
- *Market access*. It has both an import and export dimension and is reflected throughout all the WTO treaties with reduction of tariffs and elimination of quantitative restrictions and non-tariff barriers. If a state introduces a maximum of a level of volume of goods that

---

29 Article 2.6a(a) of the "Basic Regulation," introduced by Regulation (EU) 2017/2321 of the European Parliament and of the Council of Dec. 12, 2017 amending Regulation (EU) 2016/1036 on protection against dumped imports from countries not members of the European Union and Regulation (EU) 2016/1037 on protection against subsidized imports from countries not members of the European Union.

30 Preamble of the WTO Agreement.

may enter the state through its ports, it can be a quantitative restriction. In *Columbia—Ports of Entry,* the Panel found that by limiting the import by sea of goods from Panama to only one port, although it was not a quota or import license, it was a quantitative restriction in violation of Article XI of GATT 1994. The Panel stated that increased transaction costs imposed on importers due to higher costs for shipping companies reduce their competitive opportunities.[31]

– *Transparency*, which are legal requirements to make the administrative and public laws and practices transparent for importers/exporters. There are severe concerns about transparency in respect of Chinese businesses, in particular concerning governmental influence on business decisions.

– *Fair trade* is generally concerning WTO Members' rights to impose antidumping duties on goods with dumped prices, and the use of countervailing duties on subsidized products. China is the biggest target of antidumping duties. Furthermore, the EU has in its antidumping policies toward "distorted market economies" environmental aspects in the dumping determination.[32]

As transport of cargo is a *service*, it is covered by the General Agreement on Trade in Services (GATS). The exceptions to the general principles and rules for trade in services are enshrined in Article XIV(b) which covers *inter alia* measures which are necessary to protect human, animal or plant life or health. Article XIV of GATS does not have a provision resembling Article XX(g) of GATT 1994 about conservation of natural exhaustible resources. This chapter, however, addresses the situation where an importing state reduces the market access of foreign goods, not services, from states along the Belt and Road due to the potential pollution of the ocean and the threat to natural exhaustible resources resulting from increased shipping.

If national measures are in violation of the WTO rules, they can be exempted if they qualify under the legitimate policy objectives of Article

---

31 *Columbia—Ports of Entry,* WT/DS366/R, adopted by the DSB on May 20, 2009, paragraphs 7.219-7.275.

32 *See,* e.g., in situations where two or more countries can be the source of the cost determination, Article 2.6a(a) of the "Basic Regulation," introduced by Regulation (EU) 2017/2321 of the European Parliament and of the Council of Dec. 12, 2017 amending Regulation (EU) 2016/1036 on protection against dumped imports from countries not members of the European Union and Regulation (EU) 2016/1037 on protection against subsidized imports from countries not members of the European Union.

XX of GATT 1994. There have been numerous cases in the WTO Dispute Settlement System concerning the balance between the rules reflecting the free trade principles, on the one side, and states' unilateral approaches to protect national interests with basis in the legitimate policy objectives of Article XX of GATT 1994, on the other side.

WTO and Protection of Marine Living Resources

The following section concerns WTO law and the protection of marine living resources. The section will first give an overview of the overall legal and political WTO framework before it provides the context of international law that may be used in support of the argument that states under WTO law may have legitimate basis for imposing trade barriers on shipping. Next, the section discusses the development in GATT and WTO case law concerning extraterritorial jurisdiction before it discusses some of the potentials and challenges in applying the WTO exceptions to justify trade barriers based on an increased transport argument.

WTO Law and Policies on the Environment

Protection of the environment and free trade can both be complementary, e.g., green products can reach wider parts of the world, and non-complementary, e.g., green barriers, like environmental taxes or prohibitions against certain types of transport, can reduce the flow of goods. Barriers on import, including barriers on shipping of goods, based on environmental laws, may violate the general trade rules of WTO law. For example, quantitative restrictions are prohibited in Article XI of GATT 1994;[33] favoring national products over foreign products due to higher environmental standards in the importing state is a violation prohibited in

---

33 *See*, e.g., *Colombia—Ports of Entry*, WT/DS366/R, adopted by the DSB on May 20, 2009. Columbian regulations provided that all goods classifiable in Chapters 50-64 of the Customs Tariff coming from the Free Zone of Colon in Panama shall be entered and imported exclusively through the jurisdictions of the Special Customs Administration of Bogota and the Barranquilla Customs Office. That was a violation of Article XI. As the Panel stated: "In light of the Panel's conclusion that restrictions on ports of entry limit competitive opportunities for subject textiles, apparel and footwear arriving from Panama, the Panel concludes that the ports of entry measure has a limiting effect on imports arriving from Panama. On this basis, the Panel finds that the restriction to two ports of entry for subject goods arriving from Panama imposed under the ports of entry measure constitutes a restriction on importation within the meaning of Article XI:1 of

Article III of GATT 1994;[34] discrimination between trading partners based on their environmental standards are prohibited in Article I of GATT 1994.[35]

National measures which are in violation of the rules in GATT 1994 can be exempted if they qualify under the conditions of Article XX. During the GATT era,[36] environmental concerns and the protection of the environment in Article XX of GATT 1947 were introduced into the GATT dispute settlement system in cases between the GATT Contracting Parties. These concerns have increased in the time after the WTO was established. They have been expressed in soft law instruments and in policy guidelines in the WTO. In addition, the Panels and the AB are shaping a case law with relevance for the protection of the environment.[37]

The Environmental Legal Basis and Policies of the WTO

WTO law does not contain a specific agreement concerning the environment. Environmental protection is confined to the exceptions in Article XX of GATT 1994, the TBT Agreement, and the SPS Agreement. At this point, seventeen WTO Members[38] are negotiating an Environmental Goods Agreement to liberalize trade in environmental goods by lowering tariffs on those goods which contribute to generating clean and renewable energy, improving energy efficiency, controlling air pollution, managing

---

the GATT 1994. Accordingly, the Panel finds that ports of entry measure is inconsistent with Article XI:1 of the GATT 1994 … ," paragraph 7.275.

34 In particular Article III.4 is relevant. It provides: "The products of the territory of any contracting party imported into the territory of any other contracting party shall be accorded treatment no less favourable than that accorded to like products of national origin in respect of all laws, regulations and requirements affecting their internal sale, offering for sale, purchase, *transportation*, distribution or use. The provisions of this paragraph shall not prevent the application of differential internal transportation charges which are based exclusively on the economic operation of the means of transport and not on the nationality of the product." (emphasis added)

35 Article I makes explicit reference to Article III.4 of GATT 1994.

36 GATT was the predecessor to the WTO.

37 *See*, e.g., the AB's acceptance of promotion of sustainable energy as a legitimate basis for subsidies in *Canada—Renewable Energy*, WT/DS412/AB/R, adopted by the DSB on adopted on May 24, 2013; and *Canada—Feed-In Tariff Program*, WT/DS426/AB/R, adopted by the DSB on adopted on May 24, 2013.

38 The WTO Members are Australia, Canada, China, Costa Rica, the EU, Hong Kong, China, Iceland, Israel, Japan, Korea, New Zealand, Norway, Singapore, Switzerland, Separate Customs Territory of Taiwan, Penghu, Kinmen and Matsu, Turkey, and the US.

waste, and treating wastewater.[39] The aim of the Environmental Goods Agreement is to protect the environment and sustainable development.[40]

Although there is no specific agreement on environmental protection or protection against climate change, the preamble to the WTO Agreement expresses the environmental aspects of the trading system. The preamble provides:

Recognizing that their relations in the field of trade and economic endeavour should be conducted with a view to raising standards of living, ensuring full employment and a large and steadily growing volume of real income and effective demand, and expanding the production of and trade in goods and services, while allowing for the optimal use of the world's resources in accordance with the objective of sustainable development, seeking both to protect and preserve the environment and to enhance the means for doing so in a manner consistent with their respective needs and concerns at different levels of economic development, ...

The express reference to "environment" serves an important function. In the GATT era, there was no such reference to the environment in the GATT 1947 preamble. In *US—Gasoline,* the AB recognized the inclusion of "environment" into the preamble of the WTO Agreement and balanced the WTO Members' obligations to comply with the trade principles and their sovereign right to impose trade obstacles to protect the environment. With reference to the preamble, the AB stated:

Indeed, in the preamble to the WTO Agreement and in the Decision on Trade and Environment, there is specific acknowledgement to be found about the importance of coordinating policies on trade and the environment. WTO Members have a large measure of autonomy to determine their own policies on the environment (including its relationship with trade), their environmental objectives and the environmental legislation they enact and implement.[41]

---

39 *See* speech by Director General Azevêdo, "DG Azevêdo Welcomes Progress in Environmental Goods Agreement," Nairobi, Kenya, Dec. 14, 2015, WTO website, https://www.wto.org/english/news_e/news15_e/envir_14dec15_e.htm, retrieved on Sept. 10, 2020.
40 *See* EGA Chair Andrew Robb's statement, Minister for Trade and Investment, Australia, Nairobi, Kenya, Dec. 14, 2015, WTO website, https://www.wto.org/english/news_e/news15_e/egastatementmc10_e.pdf, retrieved on Sept. 10, 2020.
41 *US—Gasoline*, WT/DS2/AB/R, adopted by the DSB on May 20, 1996, p. 30.

Furthermore, the preamble makes explicit reference to *sustainable development*. The principle of sustainable development is often defined with reference to the Brundtland Report:

> Sustainable development is development that meets the needs of the present without compromising the ability of future generations to meet their own needs. It contains within it two key concepts:
>
> > the concept of "needs", in particular the essential needs of the world's poor, to which overriding priority should be given; and the idea of limitations imposed by the state of technology and social organization on the environment's ability to meet present and future needs.[42]

The principle of sustainable development is the basis for various principles of relevance to the environment which will be addressed below. The preamble has also served as relevant context for the interpretation of Article XX of GATT 1994 which will be discussed in more detail below.

Article XX(b) and XX(g) of GATT 1994 is of particular interest concerning the protection of the environment. Under Article XX(b), WTO Members may take measures which are *"necessary to protect human, animal or plant life or health,"* which includes marine life. Article XX(g) refers to the measures *"relating to the conservation of exhaustible natural resources."* In *US—Shrimps*, the AB made it clear that the term "exhaustible natural resources" also covers "living exhaustible resources" which is in line with previous GATT Panel interpretations[43] and is not confined to only non-living resources.[44] Thus both Article XX(b) and (g) is relevant for the protection of marine living resources.[45]

In the Ministerial Decision on Trade and Environment, which was a result of the Uruguay Round, the preamble provides:

> Considering that there should not be, nor need be, any policy contradiction between upholding and safeguarding an open, non-discriminatory and equitable multilateral trading system on the one

---

42 Brundtland Report, "Our Common Future, World Commission on Environment and Development" (1987), at 41.

43 *United States—Prohibition of Imports of Tuna and Tuna Products from Canada*, adopted Feb. 22, 1982, BISD 29S/91, paragraph 4.9; *Canada—Measures Affecting Exports of Unprocessed Herring and Salmon*, adopted Mar. 22, 1988, BISD 35S/98, paragraph 4.4.

44 *US—Shrimps*, WT/DS58/AB/R, adopted by the DSB on Nov. 6, 1998, paragraph 131.

45 However, they differ in other aspects. *See* more below about the differences.

hand, and acting for the protection of the environment, and the promotion of sustainable development on the other,[46]

It is an important policy consideration from the ministers;[47] the right to trade must be balanced with the protection of the environment and promotion of sustainable development. However, as the AB stated in *US—Shrimps*:

> Pending any specific recommendations by the [Committee on Trade and Environment] to WTO Members on the issues raised in its terms of reference, and in the absence up to now of any agreed amendments or modifications to the substantive provisions of the GATT 1994 and the WTO Agreement generally, we must fulfill our responsibility in this specific case, which is to interpret the existing language of the chapeau of Article XX by examining its ordinary meaning, in light of its context and object and purpose[48]

So far, the decision-making institutions of the WTO—the Ministerial Conference and the General Council—have not made any decisions under Article IX of the WTO Agreement concerning the environment nor have the Committee on Trade and Environment, which was established by the Decision on Trade and Environment, made any recommendations. The AB applied the Decision on Trade and Environment as partly justification for including environmental treaties, which are referred to in the Decision, as relevant interpretative context.[49]

The Place for International Environmental Law in WTO Law

Although WTO law does not contain a specific treaty concerning the interface between trade and environment, the explicit reference to the environment in the WTO preamble makes international environmental law relevant. WTO law is not in vacuum and is part of international law. WTO

---

46 Decision on Trade and Environment, LT/UR/D-6/2, adopted by Ministers at the Meeting of the Trade Negotiations Committee at Marrakesh, Apr. 14, 1994.

47 This Decision on Trade and Environment was not made at a Ministerial Conference. Nevertheless, it is a binding decision in the WTO system and was made during the Uruguay Round.

48 *US—Shrimps*, WT/DS58/AB/R, adopted by the DSB on Nov. 6, 1998, paragraph 155.

49 In *Brazil—Retreaded Tyres*, the Panel also made reference to the Decision on Trade and Environment in support of its argumentation concerning the importance of the environment in the interpretation of WTO law; *Brazil—Retreaded Tyres*, WT/DS332//R, adopted by the DSB after modifications by the AB on Dec. 17, 2007, footnote 1193.

law does not have an explicit catalogue of sources of law, and does not rule out any international rule of law. The scope of the WTO is defined and contained in the WTO Agreement and the multilateral agreements, like GATT 1994, which are annexed to the WTO Agreement and form an integral part of it.[50] As a result, in the interrelationship between the multilateral WTO treaties that are annexed to the WTO Agreement, they serve each other as interpretative context;[51] their rules are not in conflict but must be read harmoniously;[52] and in their relationship with the WTO Agreement, the WTO Agreement prevails in case of conflict.[53] The WTO Members are under an obligation to ensure the conformity of its laws, regulations and administrative procedures with its obligations as provided in the annexed Agreements.[54]

In case of disputes, the Panels and the AB are confined by the multilateral treaties as they cannot add to or diminish the rights and obligations of the WTO Members under the covered agreements.[55] However, as the Panel in *Korea—Procurement* rightly observed:

> Customary international law applies generally to the economic relations between the WTO Members. Such international law applies to the extent that the WTO treaty agreements do not "contract out" from it. To put it another way, to the extent there is no conflict or inconsistency, or an expression in a covered WTO agreement that implies differently, we are of the view that the customary rules of international law apply to the WTO treaties and to the process of treaty formation under the WTO.[56]

As international treaties, customary international law and principles of international law bind other states, WTO law must be seen in that context and must be applied in a manner where it as far as possible does not bring a state in a position where it must violate its other international obligations in order to comply with WTO law. However, that requires a balance between the state's obligations and rights under WTO law and its

---

50 WTO Agreement, Article II.
51 *Australia—Apples*, WT/DS367/AB/R, adopted by the DSB on Dec. 17, 2010, footnote 285.
52 *Argentina—Footwear (EC)*, WT/DS121/AB/R, adopted by the DSB on Jan. 12, 2000, paragraph 81.
53 WTO Agreement, Article XVI.3.
54 WTO Agreement, Article XVI.4.
55 Dispute Settlement Understanding (DSU), Article 3.2.
56 *Korea—Procurement*, WT/DS163/R, adopted by the DSB on Jun. 19, 2000, paragraph 7.96.

obligations and rights deriving from other international law. From a WTO perspective, the only situations where WTO law must yield in case of conflict with other rules or principles of international law are in case of conflict with the UN Charter or in situations where an interpretation of a WTO provision would lead to a violation of peremptory norms (*jus cogens*) of public international law.[57]

Scholars debate whether norms protecting the environment and the climate meet the conditions to qualify under *jus cogens*.[58] In spite of the vital importance of the environment and climate, it seems that neither environmental law, nor climate change law, or specific aspects of environmental and climate change law, have met the conditions of acceptance and recognition as peremptory norms by the international community of states as a whole.[59] Thus, at this stage, the protection of the environment and climate has the strongest legal basis in customary law, treaty law and principles of international law. However, with the wide political movements and stronger state protection of the environment and the climate, it cannot be ruled out that norms protecting the environment and climate at one point will get the required acceptance and recognition as peremptory norms by the international community of states as a whole. Nevertheless, at this point WTO law may conflict with environmental and climate change law where it is necessary to establish a balance between them. In order to avoid conflict with other international rules of law and to ensure a general consistency among international law, Article 3.2 of the Dispute Settlement Understanding further provides that the WTO treaties must be interpreted

---

57 As this writer has suggested elsewhere, WTO law must be understood in constitutional terms. Thus, higher-ranking constitutional principles, including the rule of law and certain inherent human rights, are part of WTO law. *See* Henrik Andersen, "Protection of Non-Trade Values in WTO Appellate Body Jurisprudence: Exceptions, Economic Arguments, and Eluding Questions," 18(2) *Journal of International Economic Law* (2015) 383.

58 *See*, e.g., Eva M. Kornicker Uhlmann, "State Community Interests, Jus Gogens and Protection of the Global Environment: Developing Criteria for Peremptory Norms," 11(1) *Georgetown International Environmental Law Review* (1998), 101-136; and Alexander Orakhelashvili, *Peremptory Norms in International Law*, (Oxford: Oxford University Press, 2006) at 65.

59 International Law Commission, *Fourth Report on Peremptory Norms of General International Law (Jus Cogens) by Dire Tladi, Special Rapporteur,* Seventy-First session, Geneva, April 29-June 7 and July 8-Aug. 9, 2019, UN General Assembly, A/CN.4/727, 2019, at 62.

in accordance with customary rules of interpretation of public international law which are reflected in Articles 31 and 32 of the Vienna Convention on the Law of Treaties (VCLT).[60] In *EC and Certain Member States—Large Civil Aircraft*, the AB stated with reference to Article 31(3)(c) of the VCLT that it must strike a balance between the respective WTO Members' international obligations and *"a consistent and harmonious approach to the interpretation of WTO law among all WTO members."*[61] The implication is that international law can serve as relevant context for the interpretation of WTO law, and if WTO law does not contract out from it, customary rules, other treaty law, and principles of international law can fill in the holes in WTO law.[62] Furthermore, general international law informs WTO law concerning jurisdictional aspects if a WTO Member will apply unilateral environmental standards on shipping.

International Law and Protection and Conservation of Marine Living Resources

The right to import/export under WTO law and the right to unilateral actions to follow the policy objectives of Article XX of GATT 1994 crosses into the field of international environmental law. National environmental policies may be an obstacle to trade. Yet, WTO Members have obligations under international environmental law and international climate change law to protect the environment and the climate, including a duty to protect marine living resources. It is a matter of balancing principles of trade and environment within the confinements of public international law and its legitimate basis of the sovereign state. Although states have a right to exploit their resources under WTO law—and an obligation to allow import and export of such resources—the exploitation and use of natural resources have limits under public international law. As Principle 21 of the Stockholm Declaration provides:

> States have, in accordance with the Charter of the United Nations and the principles of international law, the sovereign right to exploit

---

60 A consistent position by Panels and the AB, since the AB stated it the first time in *US—Gasoline*, WT/DS2/AB/R, adopted by the DSB on May 20, 1996, p. 17. The AB found support for this position in case law of the ICJ, the European Court of Human Rights, and the Inter-American Court of Human Rights as well as in literature.

61 *EC and Certain Member States—Large Civil Aircraft*, WT/DS316/AB/R, adopted Jun. 1, 2011, paragraph 845.

62 *See*, most explicitly, *US—Shrimps*, WT/DS58/AB/R, adopted by the DSB on Nov. 6, 1998, paragraphs 130-134.

their own resources pursuant to their own environmental policies, and the responsibility to ensure that activities within their jurisdiction or control do not cause damage to the environment of other States or of areas beyond the limits of national jurisdiction.[63]

Principle 21 reflects both the principle of sovereignty over natural resources, which implies a right to both protect natural resources within a territory and to exploit them in accordance with national environmental standards, and the principle of good neighborship, including the duty not to cause damage to the environment in other states' territories. As the BRI builds on compliance with public international law and with the ecological and environmental cooperation plan, it must comply with these principles. These principles are relevant to the question of the scope of WTO law in accepting unilateral barriers to trade in order to protect the environment from harm caused by increased shipping. The following sub-parts concern first the aspect of sovereignty and extraterritoriality under public international law, and second the principles for protection of the environment.

Sovereignty and Extraterritorial Jurisdiction

It is a fundamental principle of public international law that states are sovereign.[64] That implies that states have jurisdiction within a specific territory; that they must not interfere in another state's internal affairs; and that they are only bound by obligations under international law which they have consented to or which follows from customary rules or principles of international law.[65] It follows from customary law that within its territory,

---

63 Declaration of the United Nations Conference on the Human Environment, adopted on Jun. 16, 1972.
64 *See*, for the principles in the UN Charter, Articles 1.2, 2.1, and 2.7. *See also* the Draft Declaration on Rights and Duties of States with commentaries 1949, Adopted by the International Law Commission, taken note of by the UN General Assembly in resolution 375 (IV). *See*, for critique of the Declaration, Hans Kelsen, "The Draft Declaration on Rights and Duties of States—Critical Remarks," 44(2) *American Journal of International Law* (April 1950), 259-276.
65 *See* James Crawford, *Brownlie's Principles of Public International Law*, 9th edition (Oxford: Oxford University Press, 2019) 431. However, "sovereignty" has various definitions. *See*, e.g., from one of the first cases in the history of the US Supreme Court; "Sovereignty is the right to govern; a nation or State sovereign is the person or persons in whom that resides," *Chisholm v. Georgia*, 2 U.S. 419 (1793) at 472. *See also*, from literature, Stephen D. Krasner, "Sharing Sovereignty: New Institutions for Collapsed and Failing States," 29(2) *International Security*, (Fall, 2004), 85-120, at 88 defining

the state has permanent sovereignty over its natural resources.[66] That implies exclusive right to utilize resources.[67] States also enjoy the right to their resources in the sea within their respective exclusive economic zones.[68] UNCLOS provides in Article 56(1):

> In the exclusive economic zone, the coastal State has: a) sovereign rights for the purpose of exploring and exploiting, conserving and managing the natural resources, whether living or non-living, of the waters superjacent to the sea-bed and of the sea-bed and its subsoil,
> ... .

Within its territory and exclusive economic zone, the state has a right to protect these resources from external harm, including rights to impose measures on foreign vessels if they pollute.[69] However, the rights to own resources within a territory can be constrained by other international law.[70] For example, WTO law provides that limitation of export of a state's own resources is a quantitative restriction in violation of WTO law.[71] Furthermore, international environmental law imposes such restrictions through customary rules of good neighborship in case the state's exploitation of natural resources causes harm elsewhere. Furthermore, these rules of

---

"conventional sovereignty" as: "Recognized authorities within territorial entities regulate behavior, enjoy independence from outside interference, and enter into mutually beneficial contractual relations (treaties) with other recognized entities."

66 *See* the ICJ in *Armed Activities on the Territory of the Congo (Democratic Republic of the Congo v. Uganda)*, Judgment, I.C.J. Reports 2005, p. 168, paragraph 244. *See*, for a discussion of the evolution of the principle, Stephan Hobe, "Evolution of the Principle on Permanent Sovereignty over Natural Resources—From Soft Law to a Customary Law Principle?" in Marc Bungenberg and Stephan Hobe (eds.) *Permanent Sovereignty over Natural Resources* (Heidelberg, Germany: Springer International Publishing Switzerland, 2015), 1-13.

67 *See*, e.g., UN General Assembly resolution 1803 (XVII) of Dec. 14, 1962, "Permanent Sovereignty over Natural Resources," New York, Dec. 14, 1962.

68 UNCLOS, Article 57 provides the length of the exclusive economic zone: "The exclusive economic zone shall not extend beyond 200 nautical miles from the baselines from which the breadth of the territorial sea is measured."

69 *See* UNCLOS, Article 211(4) and (5).

70 *See*, e.g., from *Armed Activities on the Territory of the Congo (Democratic Republic of the Congo v. Uganda)*, Judgment, I.C.J. Reports 2005, p. 168, where the ICJ rejected the Democratic Republic of Congo's (DRC) claim that Uganda had violated its sovereign right to resources. Soldiers of the Ugandan army had plundered and looted resources in the territory of the DRC. The ICJ stated that the soldiers acted in violation of the *jus of bello* but that the loitering and plundering fell outside the scope of the principle of the permanent sovereignty over natural resources.

71 *China—Raw Materials*, WT/DS394/R, WT/DS395/R, and WT/DS398/R, adopted by the DSB on adopted on Feb. 22, 2012, paragraph 7.405.

international environmental law may at the same time serve as legitimate basis for a state to impose restrictions on shipping. Before discussing these issues, this chapter addresses the question whether a state can extend the right to protect its sovereign resources to the actual activities taking place outside its territory. The territorial principle is a customary rule of law and is reflected in Article 2 of the Draft Declaration on Rights and Duties of States:

> Every State has the right to exercise jurisdiction over its territory and over all persons and things therein, subject to the immunities recognized by international law

Following the territorial principle, states enjoy jurisdiction within their respective territories[72] and within the confines of the exclusive economic zone. The jurisdictional aspect concerns the competence to make judicial, legislative, and administrative decisions which are binding on the subject.[73] In that respect, states can implement their international environmental obligations into national law. In respect of vessels, they are generally under the jurisdiction of the state whose flag they are registered under when sailing on the high seas.[74] What is of interest for this chapter is the situation where a state exercises extraterritorial jurisdiction by imposing requirements on the level of emissions from shipping from a specific country even when it is in the high sea.

It follows from customary law that states cannot claim sovereignty of the high sea.[75] Nevertheless, the limit on sovereign claims does not rule out extraterritorial jurisdiction. As the Permanent Court of International Justice (PCIJ) stated in *S. S. Lotus*:

> Now the first and foremost restriction imposed by international law upon a State is that failing the existence of a permissive rule to the contrary it may not exercise its power in any form in the territory of another State. In this sense jurisdiction is certainly territorial; it cannot be exercised by a State outside its territory except by virtue of a permissive rule derived from international custom or from a

---

72 James Crawford, *Brownlie's Principles of Public International Law*, 9th edition (Oxford: Oxford University Press, 2019), at 442.

73 James Crawford, *Brownlie's Principles of Public International Law*, 9th edition (Oxford: Oxford University Press, 2019), at 440.

74 UNCLOS, Article 92.

75 UNCLOS, Article 87; James Crawford, *Brownlie's Principles of Public International Law*, 9th edition (Oxford: Oxford University Press, 2019), at 285.

convention. It does not, however, follow that international law prohibits a State from exercising jurisdiction in its own territory, in respect of any case which relates to acts which have taken place abroad, and in which it cannot rely on some permissive rule of international law.[76]

Extraterritorial jurisdiction is not prohibited under international law if there is a link between the state claiming jurisdiction and the act that is subject to the legal assessment. However, extraterritorial jurisdiction can be limited by international law. Furthermore, the exercise of extraterritorial jurisdiction can conflict with a state's sovereign right to jurisdiction, and it risks causing conflict of norms if two different institutions and sets of laws apply to the same situation.[77] For example, if a state can require a vessel to comply with its own environmental standards when it is in high sea or within the territory of another state it may cause conflict.[78]

The Principles for the Protection of the Environment

Where extraterritorial jurisdiction cannot be ruled out under international law, the next question concerns the protection of the environment. Various principles and customary rules of international law impose duties on states to protect the environment both within other states' territories and *res communis*. The duty to protect the environment is related to the overall aim of sustainable development, which, as mentioned above, is written in the WTO preamble. The principle of sustainable development integrates social, economic and environmental concerns. Although the legal strength of it is debated, several treaties refer to sustainable development. It is materialized in principles of international law including a duty for states to prevent transboundary environmental harm or damage,[79] as well as a duty

---

76 *S.S. Lotus,* Case (*France v. Turkey*), PCIJ Ser. A, No. 10, (1927). pp. 18-19.
77 Compare Panel Report in *Canada—Periodicals*, WT/DS31/R, adopted by the DSB on Jul. 30, 1997 with *United Parcels Service of America Inc. v. Canada* (ICSID Case No. UNCT/02/1), Award rendered on Jun. 11, 2007, concerning the differences of the National treatment principle of WTO law and the North American Free Trade Agreement (NAFTA).
78 *See* as an example of extraterritorial jurisdiction, Regulation (EC) No. 1013/2006 of the European Parliament and of the Council of Jun. 14, 2006 on shipments of waste, OJ L 190, 12.7.2006, pp. 1-98, with amendments.
79 *See* the International Law Commission, "Draft Articles on Prevention of Transboundary Harm from Hazardous Activities with Commentaries," Yearbook of the International Law Commission, 2001, Vol. II, Part Two, at 148, paragraphs 1 and 2. *See also*

for states to take precautionary measures according to the states' capabilities.[80] All these environmental concerns should be part of the overall strategy of the BRI in order to secure compliance with international law.

General Obligation to Protect the Environment

The duty to protect the environment reflects the often transboundary effects of pollution. The common law maxim *sic utere tuo, ut alienum non laedas*[81] has gained recognition as customary international law.[82] It implies states have a duty to keep good neighborship with other states, and thereby not cause environmental damage in other states' territories.[83] However, states have a duty beyond the good neighborship with other states: they have a duty not to cause harm in *res communis*. In the *Behring Sea Fur Seals Arbitration* from 1893, which concerned a dispute between the US and Great Britain about Great Britain's overexploitation of fur seals beyond its jurisdiction, the award expressed the freedom of the high sea to fisheries as well as the need to protect and conserve marine resources from overexploitation.[84] International treaty law has developed in that direction that marine living resources must be protected from overexploitation and from pollution. Nevertheless, early GATT case law did not seem to recognize it, which this chapter discusses below. Furthermore, states have a general obligation under international law to respect the environment. To cite the ICJ in *Legality of the Threat or Use of Nuclear Weapons*:

Principle 2 of the Rio Declaration on Environment and Development, UN General Assembly, A/CONF.151/26 (Vol. I), Aug. 12, 1992.

80 Reflected in Principle 15 of the Rio Declaration. *See* more below.

81 "Use your own property in such a way that you do not injure other people's," *Oxford—A Dictionary of Law*, Jonathan Law (ed.), (Oxford: Oxford University Press, 2018). *See* about its content—and potential common law origin—in Elmer E. Smead, "Sic Utere Tuo Ut Alienum Non Laedas A Basis of the State Police Power," 21(2) *Cornell Law Review* (1936) 276.

82 *See*, e.g., R. Malavia, "State Responsibility for Environmental Damage beyond Territorial Limits: A Legal Analysis," 27 *Indian Journal of International Law* (1987) 30 at 36; Karen Dawson, "Wag the Dog: Towards a Harmonization of the International Hazardous Waste Transfer Regime," 19(1) *Canadian Journal of Law and Society* (2004) 1, at 11 and footnote 47; An Hertogen, "The Persuasiveness of Domestic Law Analogies in International Law," 29(4) *European Journal of International Law* (2018) 1127, at 1128. *See*, for opposite view, Greg Lynham, "The Sic Utere Principle as Customary International Law: A Case of Wishful Thinking?," 2 *James Cook University Law Review* (1995) 172.

83 *See* P.W. Birnie and A.E. Boyle, *International Law and the Environment*, 2nd edition (Oxford: Oxford University Press, 2002), at 104.

84 *Behring Sea Fur Seals Arbitration*, Reports of International Arbitral Awards, Award between the United States and the United Kingdom relating to the rights of jurisdiction of United States in the Bering's sea and the preservation of fur seals Aug. 15, 1893, Vol. XXVIII, pp. 263-276.

The existence of the general obligation of states to ensure that activities within their jurisdiction and control respect the environ-ment of other States *or of areas beyond national control* is now part of the corpus of international law relating to the environment.[85] (emphasis added)

Prevention, Precaution, and Cooperation

From a duty to keep good neighborship and to protect common space emanates the preventive principle. The preventive principle is recognized as a customary rule of international law,[86] and various treaties refer to the preventive principle.[87] Of particular relevance to the case with pollution from vessels is the International Convention for the Prevention of Pollution from Ships (MARPOL), which aims at preserving the human environment in general and the marine environment in particular.[88] It covers *inter alia* prevention of pollution by oil and prevention of pollution by sewage from ships. Violations of the requirements under MARPOL are sanctioned as "[a]ny violation of the requirements of the present Convention within the jurisdiction of any Party to the Convention shall be prohibited and sanc-tions shall be established therefor under the law of that Party."[89]

However, the preventive principle implies not only the prevention of environmental harm beyond the territory of a state but also an obligation to prevent pollution within the state's own territory.[90] In that respect the preventive principle is different from the general duty to avoid causing harm to the environment in neighboring states and in *res communis*. The

---

85 *Legality of the Threat or Use of Nuclear Weapons,* Advisory Opinion, I.C.J. Reports 1996, p. 226, paragraph 29.

86 *See* to that effect from ICJ jurisprudence, *Legality of the Threat or Use of Nuclear Weapons*, Advisory Opinion, I.C.J. Reports 1996, p. 226, paragraphs 27-29, and *Pulp Mills on the River Uruguay (Argentina v. Uruguay),* Judgment, I.C.J. Reports 2010, p. 14, paragraph 101.

87 *See*, e.g., the International Convention Relating to Intervention on the High Seas in Cases of Oil Pollution Casualties (with annex, official Russian and Spanish transla-tions) and Final Act of the International Legal Conference on Marine Pollution Damage, Brussels on Nov. 29, 1969, Article I(1); Basel Convention on the Control of Transboundary Movements of Hazardous Wastes and Their Disposal, Basel on Mar. 22, 1989, Article 4(2)(c).

88 International Convention for the Prevention of Pollution from Ships (MARPOL), IMO Nov. 2, 1973, modified in 1978.

89 MARPOL, Article 4.2.

90 Max Valverde Soto, "General Principles of International Environmental Law," 3 *ILSA Journal of International and Comparative Law* (1996), 193 at 199; Philippe Sands, Jacqueline Peel, Adriana Fabra and Ruth MacKenzie, *Principles of International Environmental Law*, 4th edition, (Cambridge: Cambridge University Press, 2018), 212.

objective of the preventive principle is to avoid environmental harm in general.

The preventive principle must in the first place secure that states do not cause irreversible harm to the environment. As the ICJ noted in *Gabčíkovo-Nagymaros Project*:[91]

> The Court is mindful that, in the field of environmental protection, vigilance and prevention are required on account of the often irreversible character of damage to the environment and of the limitations inherent in the very mechanism of reparation of this type of damage.[92]

In *Pulp Mills*, the ICJ further stated that it is:

> an obligation to act with due diligence in respect of all activities which take place under the jurisdiction and control of each party. It is an obligation which entails not only the adoption of appropriate rules and measures, but also a certain level of vigilance in their enforcement and the exercise of administrative control applicable to public and private operators, such as the monitoring of activities undertaken by such operators, to safeguard the rights of the other party.[93]

It imposes obligations on all states along the Belt and Road to incorporate the political and legal instruments necessary to prevent environmental harm and to exercise due diligence. Although international law builds on customary rules of law to make reparation,[94] the problem is that environmental damage may have severe consequences that are beyond repair. Furthermore, some environmental damage—in particular in respect of damage to the climate and the direct environmental consequences on a global scale—can be difficult to trace directly to the actions or non-actions from a specific state. Prevention reduces these problems and protects the

---

91 *Gabčíkovo-Nagymaros Project* (*Hungary v. Slovakia*), Judgment, I.C.J. Reports 1997, p. 7.
92 Paragraph 140.
93 *Pulp Mills on the River Uruguay (Argentina v. Uruguay),* Judgment, I.C.J. Reports 2010, p. 14, paragraph 197.
94 *Chorzów Factory (Jurisdiction)*, PCIJ, Ser. A. No. 9, 1927, at 21. *See also* International Law Commission, "Draft Articles on Responsibility of States for Internationally Wrongful Acts, with Commentaries 2001," *Yearbook of the International Law Commission*, 2001, Vol. II, Part Two, Article 34. Environmental treaties refer to the liability of states under general international law; *see also*, for example, UNCLOS, Article 235.

res communis from irreversible harm. An increase in shipping along the Maritime Silk Road by the Belt and Road states imply heavier duty to prevent the increased harm that may follow. That duty also covers importing states to prevent environmental harm in their territorial sea from vessels coming from abroad.

The obligations on states to eliminate risks of damage can be taken further with the precautionary principle. The preventive principle and the precautionary principle overlap to some degree but differ in respect of scientifically established risks, where the precautionary principle applies to situations where the risks are not scientifically established.[95] As Principle 15 of the Rio Declaration provides:

> In order to protect the environment, the precautionary approach shall be widely applied by States according to their capabilities. Where there are threats of serious or irreversible damage, lack of full scientific certainty shall not be used as a reason for postponing cost-effective measures to prevent environmental degradation.

Nevertheless, the scope of—and the legal strength of—the precautionary principle as a principle of general international law is debated. Some treaties refer to or build upon the precautionary principle.[96] UNCLOS does not explicitly contain a precautionary principle but the International Tribunal for the Law of the Sea (ITLOS) made reference to it in the *Southern Bluefin Tuna Case (Australia and New Zealand v. Japan)* when it stated:

> Considering that, in the view of the Tribunal, the parties should in the circumstances act with prudence and caution to ensure that effective conservation measures are taken to prevent serious harm to the stock of southern bluefin tuna; ...
> Considering that there is scientific uncertainty regarding measures to be taken to conserve the stock of southern bluefin tuna and that there is no agreement among the parties as to whether the conservation measures taken so far have led to the improvement in the stock of southern bluefin tuna;

---

95 Jonathan B. Wiener, "Precaution" in Daniel Bodansky, Jutta Brunnée, and Ellen Hey (eds) *The Oxford Handbook of International Environmental Law* (Oxford University Press, 2008) at 603.
96 *See*, e.g., the Cartagena Protocol on Biosafety to the Convention on Biological Diversity, Article 1, and UNFCCC, Article 3(3).

Considering that, although the Tribunal cannot conclusively assess the scientific evidence presented by the parties, it finds that measures should be taken as a matter of urgency to preserve the rights of the parties and to avert further deterioration of the southern bluefin tuna stock.[97]

In *EC—Hormones*, which concerned human health concerning a ban on import of hormone-injected beef, the AB confined the precautionary principle to international environmental law:

The status of the precautionary principle in international law continues to be the subject of debate among academics, law practitioners, regulators and judges. The precautionary principle is regarded by some as having crystallized into a general principle of customary international environmental law. Whether it has been widely accepted by Members as a principle of general or customary international law appears less than clear. We consider, however, that it is unnecessary, and probably imprudent, for the Appellate Body in this appeal to take a position on this important, but abstract, question. We note that the Panel itself did not make any definitive finding with regard to the status of the precautionary principle in international law and that the precautionary principle, at least outside the field of international environmental law, still awaits authoritative formulation.[98]

The precautionary principle still needs further clarity as to its acceptance as a principle of general international law. Nevertheless, from a WTO perspective, the AB has clearly recognized it as a principle of international environmental law. It may provide a relevant context in cases concerning environment and trade.

Furthermore, states have a duty to cooperate to protect marine living resources. UNCLOS provides in Article 192 that states have an obligation to protect and preserve the marine environment, and in respect of migrant marine living resources in the high sea, Article 117 of UNCLOS provides:

---

97 *Southern Bluefin Tuna (New Zealand v. Japan; Australia v. Japan)*, Provisional Measures, Order of Aug. 27, 1999, ITLOS Reports 1999, p. 280, paragraphs 77-80.

98 *EC—Hormones*, WT/DS26/AB/R and WT/DS48/AB/R, adopted by the DSB on Feb. 13, 1998, paragraph 123.

All States have the duty to take, or to cooperate with other States in taking, such measures for their respective nationals as may be necessary for the conservation of the living resources of the high seas.

The duty to cooperate is also reflected in Principle 12 of the Rio Declaration as, "[u]nilateral actions to deal with environmental challenges outside the jurisdiction of the importing country should be avoided. Environmental measures addressing transboundary or global environmental problems should, as far as possible, be based on an international consensus."

The parties to MARPOL "shall co-operate in the detection of violations and the enforcement of the provisions of the present Convention, using all appropriate and practicable measures of detection and environmental monitoring, adequate procedures for reporting and accumulation of evidence."[99]

Furthermore, national action must be taken to conserve living resources in the high sea. The Convention on Fishing and Conservation of the Living Resources of the High Seas provides that all states have a duty to adopt measures toward their nationals as may be necessary for the conservation of the living resources of the high sea. The Convention on the Conservation of Migratory Species of Wild Animals provides in Article II:

The Parties acknowledge the importance of migratory species being conserved and of Range States agreeing to take action to this end whenever possible and appropriate, paying special attention to migratory species the conservation status of which is unfavourable, and taking individually or in co-operation appropriate and necessary steps to conserve such species and their habitat.

Thus, states have a duty to protect and conserve species even if they migrate and are common good. The first step is cooperation between states which should be reflected in treaties or soft law instruments. This is an area where the BRI in its policies can introduce requirements and cooperation along the Belt and Road states to counter the risk of harmful effects from increased shipping. In particular, if such efforts get a hard law basis it will inform the interpretation of WTO law. Nevertheless, the current instruments of international environmental law are a mosaic of customary rules and principles of law as well as various conventions with different numbers of participatory states, and with different degrees of legal strength.

---

99 MARPOL, Article 6.1.

However, they may all serve as relevant context for the interpretation of the WTO treaties,[100] and may prove relevant for the application of Article XX of GATT 1994 which the chapter discusses in more detail below.

WTO Law on Extraterritorial Jurisdiction

The challenges in WTO law are situations where a state applies an exception to the free trade rules as a legitimate basis to reject products from a state if there in the production process have been issues which are not in conformity with the importing states' national policies. A distinction must be made between the *product, production processes, and transport.* Products that may cause harm to the environment are generally uncontroversial under WTO law. The debate is often on a state's application of Article XX of GATT 1994 to *production processes* in other states due to the extraterritorial nature of such requirements, like working condition, animal rights, and so on. In similar line, requirements on *transport of goods*, like shipping, outside the territorial scope of a state move the discussion into questions of extraterritorial jurisdiction. As mentioned above, international law does not exclude extraterritorial jurisdiction unless specific parts of international law impose limits on it. The question is whether WTO law imposes such limits.

On a general level, a textual reading of the legitimate policy objectives, which are enshrined in the exceptions in Article XX of GATT 1994, does not rule out the possibility that Article XX may apply to measures beyond the impact a product may have inside the territory of the importing state. For example, Article XX(b) concerns measures that are "necessary to protect human, animal or plant life or health." The text does not expressly concern only products causing problems in respect of human, animal or plant life or health. Article XX(g) concerns measures "relating to the conservation of exhaustible natural resources if such measures are made effective in conjunction with restrictions on domestic production or consumption" where there is express reference to domestic production—not to domestic products. In *US—Gasoline*, where clean air was protected as an

---

100 *See*, e.g., the Panel's reference to the Rio Declaration in support of its legal argument concerning the scope of sovereign rights over natural resources in *China—Rare Earths*, WT/DS431/R, WT/DS432/R, and WT/DS433/R, adopted with modifications from the AB by the DSB on Aug. 29, 2014, paragraph 7.263. *See also* the AB's reference to the Rio Declaration as relevant legal instrument through the reference to it in the Decision of Ministers at Marrakesh to establish a permanent Committee on Trade and Environment, *US—Shrimps,* WT/DS58/AB/R, adopted by the DSB on Nov. 6, 1998, paragraph 154.

exhaustible natural resource within the meaning of Article XX(g) of GATT 1994, the AB stated that the requirement that measures are made effective in conjunction with measures is a clause requiring:

> even-handedness in the imposition of restrictions, in the name of conservation, upon the production or consumption of exhaustible natural resources.[101]

However, the case concerned the pollution resulting from gasoline *consumed inside the US*. The question is whether the statement can be applied further: if the AB by referring to "production or consumption of exhaustible resources" also suggests the production or consumption abroad by foreign producers.

In *US—Gasoline*, the AB further stated:

> Indeed, in the preamble to the WTO Agreement and in the Decision on Trade and Environment, there is specific acknowledgement to be found about the importance of coordinating policies on trade and the environment. WTO Members have a large measure of autonomy to determine their own policies on the environment (including its relationship with trade), their environmental objectives and the environmental legislation they enact and implement. So far as concerns the WTO, that autonomy is circumscribed only by the need to respect the requirements of the General Agreement and the other covered agreements.[102]

However, the line between a state's unilateral measures to protect the environment and extraterritorial jurisdiction is fine. Taking the legitimate policy objectives to also cover *production processes and transport* raises the issue of extraterritoriality. WTO Panels and the AB have in a few cases handled issues which had indirect implications concerning extraterritorial jurisdiction. There has been a progress in case law from the GATT era to present jurisprudence. It was in the 1980s that the cases concerning environment started to find their way into GATT dispute settlement.[103]

---

101 *US—Gasoline*, WT/DS2/AB/R, adopted by the DSB on May 20, 1996, p. 21.
102 *US—Gasoline*, WT/DS2/AB/R, adopted by the DSB on May 20, 1996, p. 30.
103 A GATT panel report would only be binding between the disputing parties if it had been adopted by the GATT CONTRACTING PARTIES. In the GATT system, a GATT party, including any of the disputing parties, could block its adoption. With the establishment of the WTO, these rules were changed. In the WTO, a panel or AB

GATT Case Law

In *United States—Prohibition of Imports of Tuna and Tuna Products from Canada*,[104] the US imposed import ban on tuna from Canada. The case had two jurisdictional issues:

(1) The Canadian authorities had arrested several US fishermen and seized their vessels for fishing in waters which Canada considered to be within its jurisdiction whereas the US claimed the waters were outside any state's jurisdiction. It followed from US law that if a US vessel was confiscated by a foreign state, but it had been in waters beyond the foreign state's territorial sea, the US could impose import prohibitions on fish from that state. The Panel found it was in violation of Article XI.1 and could not be justified under Article XI.2(c) of GATT 1947. The Panel did not engage directly in the jurisdictional issues.

(2) The US made a defense under Article XX(g). US law provided that to conserve certain types of fish, the US could impose limitations on their catch. According to the US, tuna was subject to overexploitation and exhaustion, and that tuna was an exhaustible natural resource. Thus, it was justified to impose the import ban on Canadian tuna. Canada agreed that tuna is an exhaustible natural resource and falls within the policy objective of Article XX(g) of GATT but held that the case did not concern the conservation of an exhaustible natural resource but was about the seizure of US vessels within Canadian jurisdiction, and that the US was together with only one other state the only ones not recognizing coastal state jurisdiction over tuna. The Panel found that the US only had restrictions on domestic production for some specific types of tuna, not all types, and thus did not meet the requirements of Article XX(g) where the measures imposing the import ban are made effective in conjunction with restrictions on domestic production or consumption. Furthermore, the Panel stated that Article XX did not provide for a policy objective which covers a state's right to impose import prohibitions of a product as a response to the arrest of its citizens by the exporting state. However, it is worth noticing that in its Article XX(g) analysis

---

report can only be blocked if there is *full consensus among all the WTO Members to reject it*. That has never happened in WTO history.

104 *United States—Prohibition of Imports of Tuna and Tuna Products from Canada*, adopted Feb. 22, 1982, BISD 29S/91.

the Panel did not rule out the possibility of extraterritorial jurisdiction as the US had made its claim concerning the conservation of tuna based on its domestic standards. Rather, the Panel noted "*that both parties considered tuna stocks, including albacore tuna, to be an exhaustible natural resource in need of conservation management and that both parties were participating in international conventions aimed, inter alia, at a better conservation of such stocks.*"[105] It seems to indirectly suggest that if the parties follow same international standards, which are reflected in the importing state's domestic law, the possibility of its application and extraterritorial jurisdiction may be within the scope of Article XX(g). However, it does not clarify what the interpretation of Article XX(g) leads to if a state makes protection of exhaustible natural resources wider than that in the international treaties.

Canada—Measures affecting the exports of unprocessed herring and salmon[106] concerned Canadian export restrictions on unprocessed sockeye salmon, pink salmon and herring. The US disputed these restrictions and claimed that they violated Article XI of GATT and with no justification under Article XX of GATT as the main purpose of the Canadian measures was to ensure employment in the Canadian industry of processors and protect them from competition. Canada claimed that the restrictions were justified under Article XX(g) as the restrictions were part of a long-time fishing policy of Canada to protect these species. The Panel found that Canada's measures violated Article XI of GATT and could not be justified under Article XX(g) of GATT as the measures did not primarily aim at conserving the exhaustible natural resources. The Panel did not engage in jurisdictional issues whether fish were caught within or outside the jurisdiction of Canada.

There are also two *unadopted* GATT panel reports[107] which are relevant to mention here as the respective panels directly discussed extraterritorial jurisdiction. *United States—Restrictions on Import of Tuna I*[108] *(Tuna I)*

---

105 Paragraph 4.9.

106 *Canada—Measures Affecting Exports of Unprocessed Herring and Salmon*, adopted on Mar. 22, 1988, L/6268.

107 The legal value of unadopted GATT panel reports is limited in WTO law. However, they may provide guidance for panels and the AB if they are relevant in the legal analysis, *see Japan—Alcoholic Beverages II*, WT/DS8/AB/R, WT/DS10/AB/R, and WT/DS11/AB/R, adopted by the DSB on Nov. 1, 1996, pp. 14-15.

108 *United States—Restrictions on Imports of Tuna (I)*, Report of the Panel on Sept. 3, 1991, (DS21/R - 39S/155), unadopted.

concerned a US-Mexico dispute where the US imposed restrictions on the import of tuna from Mexico. Under the US Marine Mammal Protection Act, the harvest of tuna should follow specific harvest methods in order to protect dolphins which otherwise could be trapped in the nets. Exporters of tuna to the US had to demonstrate that they followed those specific harvesting methods; otherwise, their products would be banned from import into the US. In this case, the US made a defense under Article XX(b) and XX(g) of GATT. The jurisdictional aspects were decisive. The Panel found that Article XX(b) could not be extended to cover the protection of human, animal, or plant life or health in the exporting states as:

> each contracting party could unilaterally determine the life or health protection policies from which other contracting parties could not deviate without jeopardizing their rights under the General Agreement. The General Agreement would then no longer constitute a multilateral framework for trade among all contracting parties but would provide legal security only in respect of trade between a limited number of contracting parties with identical internal regulations.[109]

The Panel used similar arguments in respect of Article XX(g) and found that an interpretation with extraterritorial jurisdiction could not be accepted as a state unilaterally could determine the conservation policies of other states.[110]

In *United States—Restrictions on Import of Tuna II*,[111] *(Tuna II)* the Panel followed a different line of argumentation compared to *Tuna I*. The case concerned similar issues: US import restrictions on tuna harvested in violation of US law that aimed at protecting dolphins. The US claimed that Article XX(b) and XX(g) did not have territorial or jurisdictional limitations as to the location of the tuna.[112] The Panel stated that: (1) two previous panels[113] had not distinguished between fish caught inside and outside the territorial jurisdiction of the respondent; (2) a general reading of Article XX did not proscribe a jurisdictional limitation; and (3) public

---

109 Paragraph 5.27.
110 Paragraph 5.31-5.32.
111 *United States—Restrictions on Imports of Tuna (II)*, Report of the Panel on Jun. 16, 1994, (DS29/R), unadopted.
112 Paragraph 3.16.
113 *Canada—Measures affecting the exports of unprocessed herring and salmon,* adopted 22 March and *United States—Prohibition of Imports of Tuna and Tuna Products from Canada,* adopted Feb. 22, 1982, BISD 29S/91.

international law in general does not prohibit extraterritorial jurisdiction.[114] The Panel found that conservation of exhaustible natural resources is not limited to resources that are *within the territory* of a party making a claim under Article XX(g) of GATT. Consequently, it was within the scope of Article XX(g) that the US had a policy to conserve dolphins in the eastern tropical Pacific Ocean *"which the United States pursued within its jurisdiction over its nationals and vessels."*[115] Thus, the protection of dolphins can have an extraterritorial effect.

However, the US failed in the second aspect of the Article XX(g) analysis. The Panel examined whether the US measures: (1) were *related* to the conservation of the dolphins which according to the Panel meant that the measures primarily aimed at and had the effect to protect dolphins and (2) were *made in conjunction* with restrictions on domestic production or consumption which meant that the measures should primarily be aimed at rendering the restrictions effective on domestic production or consumption. The US measures forced states to change their conservation policies irrespective of whether or not the other states' harvest policies of tuna protected dolphins. The Panel stated that Article XX(g) must be interpreted narrowly.[116] If states could force other states to change their policies within their own jurisdictions, *"the balance of rights and obligations among contracting parties, in particular the right of access to markets, would be seriously impaired."*[117] Accordingly, the Panel found that the US measures *were not primarily aimed at* conservation of exhaustible natural resources, nor primarily aimed at rendering effective restrictions on domestic production or consumption.

In contrast to the Panel in *Tuna I*, this Panel acknowledges that a state's measures to conserve exhaustible natural resources can have extra-jurisdictional effect and can apply toward a state's own nationals and vessels. However, the extraterritorial jurisdiction does not cover other states' harvesting methods within their respective jurisdictions. Such measures are not primarily aimed at conservation of exhaustible natural resources in conjunction with restrictions on domestic production or consumption as they target foreign states' policies within their own jurisdictions. The Panel does not discuss the possibility of a state to protect resources which may potentially migrate into the territory of the state.

---

114 Paragraph 5.15-5.17.
115 Paragraph 5.20.
116 WTO AB jurisprudence has taken a different approach to interpretation of exceptions of Article XX of GATT 1994. *See* more below.
117 Paragraph 5.26.

The GATT Panel jurisprudence on extraterritoriality has been significantly changed in WTO Panel and AB jurisprudence.

WTO Case Law

In *US—Shrimps*, Malaysia complained about a US ban on import of shrimps unless they had been harvested following specific US requirements to protect sea turtles. The shrimps were harvested in Malaysian territory. The AB had to examine whether sea turtles could be categorized as "exhaustible natural resources" under Article XX(g) of GATT 1994. It stated:

> We do not pass upon the question of whether there is an implied jurisdictional limitation in Article XX(g), and if so, the nature or extent of that limitation. We note only that in the specific circumstances of the case before us, there is a sufficient nexus between the migratory and endangered marine populations involved and the United States for purposes of Article XX(g).[118]

Thus, the AB does not examine WTO law and its potential extra-jurisdictional issues. The AB links the conservation of exhaustible natural resources, here sea turtles—an endangered species—with their potential migration to US territory. The AB concluded that sea turtles were an "exhaustible natural resource."[119]

The statement has two implications of relevance for the question of jurisdiction:
(1) The application of Article XX(g) of GATT 1994 can extend to conservation of animals if they can potentially migrate to the state which makes a defense under Article XX(g).
(2) By referring to "migratory" the AB seems to make it a condition that the animals can migrate into the territory of the state making the defense under Article XX(g). Thus, Article XX(g) does not have universal application where a state can use the defense even to protect animals which do not migrate into the territory of the defending state. The defense cannot be used solely on the fact that it is an endangered species.

---

118 Paragraph 133.
119 The US lost the case on other grounds, as they did not meet the requirements in the *chapeau* of Article XX of GATT 1994.

It is interesting to note that the WTO Panel had considered the question about sea turtles as "shared resources." Without specifically concluding on the question whether sea turtles are a shared resource, the Panel stated that the notion of "shared" resource implies a common interest and would be better handled through international cooperation and agreement, which several of the international environmental agreements seem to suggest, instead of unilateral measures.[120] The AB does not address the question of shared or common resources. Article XX(g) can apply as defense if the "resource" can migrate into the territory. It must be assumed that all the states, which are potential homes for the turtle, could use that defense, regardless of whether the turtle can be considered as a common good.

The important difference from GATT case law is that the AB focuses on the potential migration of the "resource" into the territory of the responding state. The keyword is *nexus*—a sufficient connection between the sea turtles, which is harmed by the conduct of people of the exporting state, and the state imposing the measures. The sea turtles can migrate into US territory and thus become a resource within the jurisdiction of US conservation law. In GATT case law, the panels did not discuss such nexus. Furthermore, in *Tuna II*, where the Panel acknowledged extraterritorial jurisdiction in its discussion of "conservation of exhaustible natural resources," it made additional jurisdictional discussions in its "relating to" and "in conjunction with" analysis. That is not the case in *US—Shrimps*. The AB takes a wider approach to "relating to" which is directly concerning the primarily aims of the US conservation laws whereas the Panel in *Tuna II* seemed to reject conservation laws if they can force other states to change their laws as such laws would have extraterritorial effect. "In conjunction with" has a separate analysis in *US—Shrimps* compared to the approach taken by the Panel in *Tuna II*. The AB states:

> we need to examine whether the restrictions imposed by Section 609 with respect to imported shrimp are *also* imposed in respect of shrimp caught by United States shrimp trawl vessels[121] (emphasis added)

Thus, it is a question of whether the measures are also imposed on domestic production methods. It is not a question of whether national measures can force the complaining state to change its policies. The sea turtles, which can migrate between US and Malaysian sea, are subject to *conservation*

---

under US law, as they under international law are regarded as an endangered species.

In *EC—Seal Products*,[122] the contested EU measures banned seal products. The EU measures aimed at seal welfare and were a response to inhumane hunting methods. It addressed hunting activities inside and outside the EU territory and thus had an extraterritorial dimension. The AB referred to its statement from *US—Shrimp* that it "would not pass upon the question of whether there is an implied jurisdictional limitation in Article XX(g), and if so, the nature or extent of that limitation." The AB made the statement in relation to Article XX(a) where WTO Members may impose trade-restricting measures to protect its *public morals* and stated:

> while recognizing the systemic importance of the question of whether there is an implied jurisdictional limitation in Article XX(a), and, if so, the nature or extent of that limitation, we have decided in this case not to examine this question further.[123]

Both the EU and the complainants, Canada and Norway, agreed that there was sufficient nexus between the public morals concerns of protecting seals due to inhuman hunting methods and the EU.[124] In line with *US—Shrimps*, it is still not clarified by the AB whether there is a jurisdictional limit in Article XX(a) and Article XX(g). It can be noted that if there is a sufficient nexus between the animals, which are protected against certain hunting or harvesting methods to protect public morals or which are an endangered species and an exhaustible natural resource, and the state imposing the protective measures, then it can be accepted that the measures apply to activities which are outside the territory of the protecting state. Although *EC—Seal Products* only indirectly addresses the issue of jurisdiction and extraterritoriality, the reference to its statements from *US—Shrimps* indicates that the AB will take a wide approach to accept a nexus between the protection of animals and the state if the protected animals potentially can migrate into the territory of the state. However, what *EC—Seal Products* does not clarify, which was unnecessary to clarify due to the agreement by all the disputing parties on the point of nexus, is whether the EU measures on animals that *does not migrate* into EU territory—and thus cannot be linked even remotely to the EU

---

122 *EC—Seal Products*, WT/DS400/AB/R and WT/DS401/AB/R, adopted by the DSB on Jun. 18, 2014.
123 Paragraph 5.173.
124 Footnote 1191.

territory—still can be accepted under the defense of Article XX(a). The difference seems to be that, in *US—Shrimps*, the AB used the nexus between the migrating animals and the US, whereas in *EC—Seal Products*, the disputing parties referred to the "public moral concerns and activities addressed by the measure, on the one hand, and the European Union."[125]

US—Tuna II (Mexico) concerned labeling of tuna products in the US.[126] In order to protect dolphins, US law provided conditions for the use of a dolphin-safe label by tuna producers. Mexico claimed that these conditions violated Articles I:1 and III:4 of GATT 1994 and Article 2.1, 2.2 and 2.4 of the TBT Agreement. The US' conditions for the dolphin-safe label had potential extra-jurisdictional issues. According to Mexico, the purpose of the US measures was to impose unilateral pressure on Mexico to change their fishing methods. Such extra-jurisdictional regulation was in violation of the NT and MFN principles. Furthermore, such extra-jurisdictional regulation would derive Mexico potential comparative advantages. According to Mexico, the US regulation left no alternative fishing methods available even though other methods could be just as safe for dolphin as the one prescribed by the US measures. However, Mexico acknowledged that under the exceptions of WTO law, unilateral approaches could be justified by a sovereign state, but the US had not made a defense with reference to these exceptions.

The Panel disagreed with Mexico. It averted questions of extraterritorial jurisdiction. It found that the US measures did not condition the import of tuna on any specific fishing method but only made requirements in respect of the product, which had to comply with the labeling scheme to be accepted as dolphin-safe. Furthermore, the US measures did not have a discriminatory effect as the incentive underlying the dolphin-safe label to harvest tuna in a manner which did not have an adverse effect on tuna applied to both the US fleet and others.[127] In the appeal case, the AB reversed parts of the Panel's findings but also found that it is not a violation of Article 2.2 of the TBT Agreement to adopt measures which create a burden to trade unless it constitutes an unnecessary obstacle to international trade. The AB did not refer to the extraterritorial aspects. It indirectly rejected Mexico's claim that the *purpose* of the US measures was to force Mexico to change its fishing methods. It stated:

---

125 Footnote 1191.
126 *US—Tuna II (Mexico)*, WT/DS381/AB/R, adopted by the DSB on Jun. 13, 2012.
127 Paragraph 7.372-7.373.

[W]hat must not be applied in a manner that would constitute a means of arbitrary or unjustifiable discrimination between countries where the same conditions prevail or a disguised restriction on international trade is a measure, and not the objective pursued by the technical regulation.[128]

Thus, the AB overcame the question of extraterritorial jurisdiction by making a textual interpretation of the text of the TBT Agreement which stipulates that *measures*—and not a state's *purposes*—are subject to the rules.

In the compliance case, *US—Tuna II (Article 21.5—Mexico)*,[129] Mexico claimed that the dolphin safe fishing methods could not be audited by the US in areas outside US jurisdiction. That left the US safe dolphin labeling system unreliable. The Panel and the AB disagreed with Mexico. Under the US National Oceanic and Atmospheric Administration (NOAA), breaches of tracking and verification requirements can be imposed with sanctions, and even without jurisdiction, the US law still provided the tools necessary to induce compliance of US processors and importers of tuna.[130]

The cases demonstrate that there have been developments in the approaches to extraterritorial jurisdiction from the GATT cases to the present WTO cases. The acceptance of extraterritorial jurisdiction has widened, and it no longer seems to be the only factor if a state can impose measures which must force other states to change their domestic policies, in particular if it is backed by international law. The focus has also shifted to the *ability* of the living natural resource to migrate into the territory of a state which seeks to protect it. If an animal can migrate, it seems to provide a sufficient nexus to the state seeking to conserve it if such measures are evenhandedly applied toward both domestic and foreign producers. For the importing state, it can refer to the international duties, like UNCLOS and the Convention on the Conservation of Migratory Species of Wild Animal, to protect the environment and migratory species within its territorial or exclusive zones as well as the duties in respect of the high sea. However, the parties in *EC—Seal Products* seem to take the protection of animals even further, as they all accepted that the measures protecting the animals should be connected with the EU. It was not a question of whether the

128 Paragraph 339.
129 *US—Tuna II (Article 21.5—Mexico)*, WT/DS381/AB/RW/USA and WT/DS381/AB/RW2, adopted by the DSB on Jan. 11, 2019.
130 Paragraph 6.237.

animals potentially could migrate into EU territory before such a nexus was established. If that view can be accepted in respect of Article XX(b) and XX(g), it would be sufficient for a state to impose protective measures on marine living resources in the high sea regardless of their migratory conduct. However, that is still unsettled in WTO case law.

The next question concerns the relationship between the exceptions of WTO law in situations where pollution from shipping can cause harm to marine living resources.

WTO Law and Pollution by Means of Transport

Context

The overall problem with the application of WTO law to provide greener products is the aim of *expanding production* on a general level and the general prohibition of discrimination and prohibition of quantitative restrictions. Nevertheless, states may apply subsidies in their efforts to promote the environment, and the AB has taken a wide interpretation in order to protect states that are using subsidies to enhance reduction of, for example, carbon dioxide in their production of goods.[131]

As mentioned above, there are a number of international treaties—as well as customary rules and principles of international law—that impose duties on states to protect the environment as well as rights of states to protect their natural resources within their territories and exclusive economic zones. Furthermore, states have a duty to protect the environment of the high sea. As mentioned by the Panel in *Korea—Procurement*, other international laws are applicable sources of WTO law as long as the WTO Agreement does not contract out from it.[132] The preventive principle and the principles of not causing transboundary environmental harm are important principles of law in respect of claims made against other states' pollution caused by shipping. These rules of international law are applicable as relevant context of WTO law. To ensure that environmental law and policies are not used as a hidden means to protect national industries

---

131 *See Canada—Renewable Energy,* WT/DS412/AB/R and *Canada—Feed-In Tariff Program*, WT/DS426/AB/R, adopted on May 24, 2013. *See,* for discussion concerning the approach taken by the AB, Henrik Andersen, "Protection of Non-trade Values in WTO Appellate Body Jurisprudence: Exceptions, Economic Arguments, and Eluding Questions," 18(2) *Journal of International Economic Law* (2015) 383.

132 *Korea—Procurement*, WT/DS163/R, adopted by the DSB on Jun. 19, 2000, paragraph 7.96.

against foreign competition, Principle 12 of the Rio Declaration adopts the trade language by providing that "[t]rade policy measures for environmental purposes should not constitute a means of arbitrary or unjustifiable discrimination or a disguised restriction on international trade." Nevertheless, the question is whether the policy objectives of Article XX can apply to situations where a state imposes restrictions on shipping due to environmental concerns.

Case Law and Practice Concerning Article XX(g) and XX(b) of GATT 1994

The question is whether Article XX(g) can apply to measures limiting transportation of goods if the measures are related to conservation of exhaustible natural resources. The text of Article XX(g) reads:

> Subject to the requirement that such measures are not applied in a manner which would constitute a means of arbitrary or unjustifiable discrimination between countries where the same conditions prevail, or a disguised restriction on international trade, nothing in this Agreement shall be construed to prevent the adoption or enforcement by any contracting party of measures: ... (g) relating to the conservation of exhaustible natural resources if such measures are made effective in conjunction with restrictions on domestic production or consumption;

It can be noted that the second subclause of Article XX(g) refers to "restrictions on domestic production or consumption" only and not "transport" which implies that Article XX(g) is not applicable to "transport," unless a wide interpretation of "domestic production or consumption" can contain transport of a product. The counterargument is that the exceptions to the general rules of WTO law should also apply to transport situations, which the general rules of WTO law seem to protect. For example, the NT principle of Article III.1 of GATT 1994, which is repeated in Article III.4, has express reference to "laws, regulations and requirements affecting ... transportation." Furthermore, Article V of GATT 1994 provides that:

> [g]oods (including baggage), and also vessels and other means of transport, shall be deemed to be in transit across the territory of a contracting party *when the passage across such territory* ... is only a portion of a complete journey beginning and terminating beyond the frontier of the contracting party across whose territory the

traffic passes. ... *There shall be freedom of transit through the territory of each contracting party*, via the routes most convenient for international transit, for traffic in transit to or from the territory of other contracting parties." (emphasis added)

These are examples of situations related to shipping which WTO law protects against national measures restricting the vessels from transporting goods. Apart from the potential exceptions directly expressed in these provisions, Article XX serves as general exceptions to the entire GATT 1994. A narrow reading of "restrictions on domestic production or consumption" of Article XX(g) would render Article XX(g) inapplicable per se to any situation concerning measures restricting transport or transit of goods. Furthermore, the first part of the text of Article XX(g), "measures relating to the conservation of exhaustible resources," is not narrowed down to cover only measures related to production or consumption. Rather, any measure that relates to conserve exhaustible natural resources, including those related to transport requirements, should be applicable under Article XX(g). Furthermore, as the AB rightly stated in *US—Shrimps*, Article XX(g) must be interpreted in light of the aim of *sustainable development* of the WTO Agreement. If states cannot impose limitations on the means of transport if they risk causing damage to exhaustible natural resources—and which technically could fall under Article I, III, V or XI—WTO law would be at odds with the aim of sustainable development as well as international law where states have a duty to protect the environment. When Article XX(g) was drafted, the focus was on the production of goods that affected exhaustible natural resources or consumption of exhaustible natural resources. It did not concern the transport of goods that affects exhaustible natural resources. However, with GATT case law and *US—Shrimps* concerning the nexus between the subject and the territory of a state, it has opened up for questions about transport of goods affecting the migrating subjects although it is so far unsettled in case law. Furthermore, in *US—Gasoline*, the Panel accepted that measures on gasoline to reduce the consumption of gasoline in order to limit the emission of pollutants to conserve the clean air fell within the scope of Article XX(g).[133] The difference to the transport situation is that the measures target gasoline specifically, not the transport of goods. The Panel refers to the consumption of gasoline. However, if the aim were to protect the environment against pollution, it would be a hollow argument if it is not

---

133 Paragraph 6.36-6.37.

applicable on polluting transportation, and it would create an imbalance in WTO law between states' rights under the general trading rules and the rights to take unilateral action to protect any of the policy objectives of Article XX, including Article XX(g). It should also be pointed out that the preventive principle and the precautionary principle are applicable as relevant context for the interpretation of Article XX(g). As mentioned above, according to the ICJ, the preventive principle reflects a customary rule of international law, and the AB has recognized the precautionary principle as a principle of international environmental law. With the preventive principle in mind, due diligence must be exercised by the states to prevent environmental damage. A reading of Article XX(g) should be in that light: the prevention of environmental damage to conserve natural exhaustible resources cannot exclude transport if there is a link between shipping and harm on marine living resources, and even if that link cannot clearly be established, the precautionary principle should give states the right to impose restrictions on shipping under Article XX(g).

If Article XX(g) is applicable to situations on transport, a few points can be made about the scope of Article XX(g). As mentioned above, both GATT and WTO case law has concerned the interpretation of Article XX(g). It can be noted that the Panel in *Tuna II* suggested that the exceptions of Article XX(g) should be interpreted narrowly. WTO AB jurisprudence has taken a different approach to interpretation of exceptions of Article XX of GATT 1994. They are not to be interpreted narrowly. The interpretation of the general rules and exceptions are subject to the same exercise in accordance with Articles 31 and 32 of the VCLT.[134] It was also discussed above that the AB has taken a wider approach to the concept "relating to" compared with GATT panel jurisprudence. It is clearly settled from both GATT and WTO jurisprudence, as mentioned above, that migrating species that may enter into the importing states territory can be protected by that state even in the high sea. Furthermore, migrating species can qualify as exhaustible natural resources within the scope of Article XX(g).

However, as there is doubt about the application of Article XX(g) on measures regulating transport of goods, the question is whether Article XX(b) provides another option to protect marine living resources. Article XX(b) does not contain a qualification about evenhandedness in respect of domestic production and consumption. Article XX(b) concerns measures which are "necessary to protect human, animal or plant life or health."

---

134 *See EC—Hormones*, WT/DS26/AB/R and WT/DS48/AB/R, adopted by the DSB on Feb. 13, 1998, paragraph 104.

There is a "necessity" requirement which is different compared to the "relating to" requirement under the conservation of exhaustible natural resources rules. The advantage for states imposing measures to protect marine living resources and its "relating to" requirement under Article XX(g) is that it does not include tests of less trade restrictive alternatives and seems to be less rigid compared to the necessity test.[135] Nevertheless, the AB has stated that in the "necessity test," the *importance* of the common interests or values must be taken into account.[136] The AB approach was refined in *Brazil—Retreaded Tyres*, where it agreed with the Panel's analysis, and with reference to its interpretation of Article XIV of GATS in *US—Gambling,*[137] stated:

> [In US—Gambling] the Appellate Body stated that the weighing and balancing process inherent in the necessity analysis "begins with an assessment of the 'relative importance' of the interests or values furthered by the challenged measure", and also involves an assessment of other factors, which will usually include "the contribution of the measure to the realization of the ends pursued by it" and "the restrictive impact of the measure on international commerce."[138]

Thus, the importance of the value is decisive for the level of standard of necessity which will be applied.[139] As the environment is considered as a "vital and important value,"[140] it must be assumed that the necessity test will not be applied rigidly in cases concerning protection of the environment, including marine living resources.

There have been several cases in both the WTO and GATT concerning Article XX(b) and protection of the environment. In *US—Gasoline*, the US referred to Article XX(b) as basis for its defense of its measures targeting

---

135 *See*, e.g., *Brazil—Retreaded Tyres*, WT/DS332/AB/R, adopted by the DSB on Dec. 17, 2007, paragraph 156.

136 *Korea—Various Measures on Beef*, WT/DS161 and 169/AB/R, adopted by the DSB on Jan. 10, 2001, paragraph 164.

137 *US—Gambling*, WT/DS285/AB/R, adopted by the DSB on Apr. 20, 2005, paragraph 306.

138 *Brazil—Retreaded Tyres*, WT/DS332/AB/R, adopted by the DSB on Dec. 17, 2007, paragraph 143.

139 Henrik Andersen, "Protection of Non-trade Values in WTO Appellate Body Jurisprudence: Exceptions, Economic Arguments, and Eluding Questions," 18(2) *Journal of International Economic Law* (2015) 383 at 396-397.

140 *Brazil—Retreaded Tyres*, WT/DS332/AB/R, adopted by the DSB on Dec. 17, 2007, paragraph 144, with reference to the Panel's Report, paragraph 7.108.

the import of gasoline. In line with the acceptance of the argument of protecting clean air as an exhaustible natural resource under Article XX(g), the Panel accepted the argument that the emission of carbon dioxide, that would pollute the air, could endanger human, animal and plant life and health under Article XX(b). In *Brazil—Taxation*,[141] the Panel found that reduction of CO_2 emission from *vehicles* is at high level of importance, and that it can be considered as an objective under Article XX(b) to protect the environment.[142] Thus, "protection of human, animal and plant life or health" covers environmental measures. Such a reading of Article XX(b) is also justified by including the context of the preamble of the WTO Agreement and its explicit reference to the environment. Furthermore, in *EC—Seal Products*, the AB held that a WTO Member has a right to determine its own level of "protection" and that they may differ between states, even if the states have similar interest of moral concern.[143] The statement was made in respect of Article XX(a) but is equally relevant in respect of Article XX(b).[144] There is wide scope for states to apply measures protecting animal and plant life health, including marine living resources, as long as the other conditions of the *chapeau* are met.[145]

However, *Brazil—Taxation* concerned EU's complaints against Brazil's taxes and charges in the automotive sector. It did not concern measures against CO_2 emission from *transport of goods* into Brazil, but it concerned the imported vehicles' CO_2 emission, which were subject to Brazil's discriminatory measures. *US—Gasoline* concerned measures targeting gasoline. That is an important difference to this scenario; WTO law promotes the trade in goods, and the cases are related to measures which are directly linked to specific *products*, which cause harm to the environment. However, as mentioned above, in respect of Article XX(g), the general trade rules of WTO law are applicable on measures related to

---

141 *Brazil—Taxation*, WT/DS472/R and AB/R, adopted by the DSB on Jan. 11, 2019.
142 Paragraph 7.914-7.916. However, Brazil failed to demonstrate that the specific measures were necessary to achieve the aim of reducing CO_2, paragraph 7.961. The Panel's analyses and findings in respect of Article XX(b) of GATT 1994 were not appealed in the appeal case.
143 *EC—Seal Products*, WT/DS400/AB/R and WT/DS401/AB/R, adopted by the DSB on Jun. 18, 2014, paragraph 5.200.
144 The AB referred to the Panel in *EC—Asbestos*, WT/DS135/AB/R, adopted with modifications from the AB by the DSB on Apr. 5, 2001: "We note that the panel in EC—Asbestos took a similar position in the context of Article XX(b) when it stated that, although it must examine the particular health risk posed by chrysotile asbestos fibres, it was not required to assess France's choice to protect its population against that risk." (Panel Report, *EC—Asbestos*, paragraph 8.170 and 8.171, footnote 1253)
145 As mentioned in the introduction, this chapter does not address the specific issues of the *chapeau* of Article XX of GATT 1994.

transport. Such measures should equally be possible to exempt generally under Article XX if the state meets the conditions of Article XX. Otherwise, WTO law would be imbalanced between the free trade rules and the rules allowing states to exercise their sovereign rights to protect those values enshrined in the policy objectives of Article XX. Furthermore—as mentioned above—the context of international environmental law, including the principles of prevention and precaution should lead to a reading of Article XX(b) that include protection of animal life and health against increased shipping of goods.

Even though there is no direct *legal* precedent from WTO or GATT case law concerning the use of Article XX(b) as a defense for measures limiting the transport of goods due to environmental concerns, the GATT trading system had a case concerning the issue. The GATT CONTRACTING PARTIES were notified about the case, which never reached panel stage, and thus did not provide us with any case law. In 1990, Austria filed a complaint against Germany for its measures to ban the circulation of 212,000 lorries from Austria at night. The German measures were a retaliation to Austria's introduction of measures to limit traffic of certain trucks, regardless of nationality, at night which in certain transit roads caused intolerable noise and pollution. Austria defended its measures under Article XX(b) of GATT 1947.[146] Austria was not challenged by any of the GATT Contracting Parties apart from the retaliatory measures from Germany. The Austrian measures did not target a specific *good*. From an Austrian position, the measures could be justified under Article XX(b) even though they imposed restrictions on *unspecified types of goods* as the transport of these goods caused intolerable pollution. The main target was the transport and its pollution, not the goods.

It should also be pointed out that the AB has made general statements concerning Article XX which are relevant in this context. In *US—Gasoline*, the AB stated generally about Article XX that:

> It is not necessary to assume that requiring from exporting countries compliance with, or adoption of, certain policies (although covered in principle by one or another of the exceptions) prescribed by the importing country, renders a measure a priori incapable of justification under Article XX.[147]

---

146 *Federal Republic of Germany—Restriction of Circulation of Austrian Lorries*, DS14/1, Feb. 28, 1990.
147 *US—Shrimps*, WT/DS58/AB/R, adopted by the DSB on Nov. 6, 1998, paragraph 121.

Thus, it cannot beforehand be excluded that limitations on shipping, even if it is related to an accumulated polluting effect, cannot be justified under Article XX(b) nor under Article XX(g).

In *US—Gasoline*, the AB also emphasized the importance of environmental protection and the autonomy of the states in that regard:

> WTO Members have a large measure of autonomy to determine their own policies on the environment (including its relationship with trade), their environmental objectives and the environmental legislation they enact and implement. So far as concerns the WTO, that autonomy is circumscribed only by the need to respect the requirements of the General Agreement and the other covered agreements.[148]

In *Brazil—Retreaded Tyres*, the AB addressed the tension between trade and protection of the environment:

> At this stage, it may be useful to recapitulate our views on the issue of whether the Import Ban is necessary within the meaning of Article XX(b) of the GATT 1994. This issue illustrates the tensions that may exist between, on the one hand, international trade and, on the other hand, public health and environmental concerns … . In this respect, the fundamental principle is the right that WTO Members have to determine the level of protection that they consider appropriate in a given context.[149]

States should be allowed to introduce and apply measures to protect the environment by making requirement in respect of potential increased shipping from specific states if there is likelihood of increased pollution resulting from the accumulated traffic in the high sea. That will be in line with international law where states are required to protect migrating living resources, are bound by customary rules of keeping good neighborship, are bound by treaty law concerning transboundary pollution, including rules to protect the high sea, are bound by varies of treaties concerning climate change, and have the right to protect their resources, which includes the migrating resources as confirmed in WTO AB jurisprudence. Article XX(b) can serve as relevant legal basis in that respect, and also Article

---

148 *US—Gasoline*, WT/DS2/AB/R, adopted by the DSB on May 20, 1996, p. 30.
149 *Brazil—Retreaded Tyres*, WT/DS332/AB/R, adopted by the DSB on Dec. 17, 2007, paragraph 210.

XX(g) should be applicable although there are some uncertain aspects in respect of measures targeting transport.

Conclusion

The potential increase in pollution caused by the expected increase in the number of vessels on the Maritime Silk Road needs to be addressed by stakeholders of the BRI, in particular by China as the anchor of the BRI. The BRI has a core principle that international law must be complied with. That includes for all the states with stakes in the BRI that they comply with their obligations under international environmental law. One of them is to conserve and protect marine living resources. That duty is not limited to a territorial protection. States must also protect marine living resources in the high sea. China has issued some ecological and environmental policies concerning the BRI. These need to address the potential increase in world trade resulting from the BRI and the risk of increased harm to marine living resources. Cooperation is a requirement under international law as well as under China's BRI policies. However, if states fail to establish tools to ensure that an increase in shipping does not increase environmental harm along the Maritime Silk Road, the question is whether states under WTO law can have legitimate basis in environmental concerns to introduce limits on import of goods through the Maritime Silk Road.

The general rules of WTO law protect trade against measures imposing restrictions on goods. That includes measures related to the transport of goods, including shipping. Although Article XX does not clearly provide whether it is applicable for states' measures against transport, including shipping, a narrow reading of Article XX, in particular Article XX(g), would lead to an imbalance between the general rules and the exceptions by excluding transport measures from being acceptable under Article XX(g). Furthermore, the context of international law, including the principles developed from international environmental law, should lead to an acceptance of such measures under Article XX(b) and XX(g) of GATT 1994. Thus, this chapter argues that states under WTO law may impose such barriers on shipping due to their accumulated environmental effect.

Nevertheless, the aim of conserving marine living resources along the Maritime Silk Road as a legitimate basis for restricting vessels from entering into a state's exclusive zone or territorial sea can cause questions about extraterritorial jurisdiction if the protection also concerns marine living resources in the high sea. General international law does not prohibit extraterritorial jurisdiction if it can be related to subjects or objects that have a connection with the territory of the state unless other international law (*lex specialis*) explicitly prohibits extraterritorial jurisdiction. WTO law does not provide a prohibition on extraterritorial jurisdiction in trade situations. Rather, WTO case law indicates an acceptance of extraterritorial jurisdiction if there is a nexus between the specific concern of the state, like conservation of marine living resources, and the state. In situations with marine living resources, such nexus can be established under Article XX(b) and XX(c) if the marine animals can migrate into the territory of the state. However, the question is whether that argument can be taken even further to include marine living resources that do not migrate into the territory of the state and if it is sufficient to establish a connection between the aim of protecting marine living resources from harm in the high sea, which also is a duty under international environmental law, and the state's national measures on conservation of marine living resources.

The stronger environmental protection of marine living resources that the Belt and Road stakeholders, in particular China, take into their Belt and Road policies, the less likely it is that states apply trade restrictions to protect the environment. However, full cooperation between the Belt and Road states to establish an agreed level of protection may be hard to achieve. Nevertheless, if China really wants to promote the BRI, China must take the lead as part of the investment policies of the BRI. For example, by promoting specific environmental requirements in the potential trade agreements between Belt and Road states, that are part of the overall BRI strategy, and by imposing strict environmental requirements in the Belt and Road contracts with suppliers of materials to improved infrastructure.

States' Environmental Obligations in Disputed Maritime Areas and the Limits of International Law

Constantinos Yiallourides [*]
British Institute of International and Comparative Law (BIICL),
University of Aberdeen, United Kingdom
Natalia Ermolina [**]
University of Tromsø – The Arctic University of Norway, Norway

Abstract

There are many cases worldwide where two or more States' maritime claims over ocean space and marine resources overlap, leading to disputed maritime areas. Many of these disputed maritime areas include rare or fragile marine ecosystems and constitute the habitat of vulnerable species. General environmental provisions under international law are binding upon States in disputed maritime areas. Yet, environmental degradation of disputed maritime areas is a live, ongoing, and potentially increasing problem. This chapter explores the specific contours of these environmental obligations and how these may be applied in dispute settlement under UNCLOS. It addresses three important environmental legal issues in international jurisprudence and State practice and which are relevant to the obligations of States acting in disputed maritime areas: (1) the duty to cooperate over environmental matters; (2) the duty to apply a precautionary approach; and (3) the duty to conduct an environmental impact assessment and monitor environmental impacts.

---

[*] Parts of this chapter are drawn from the author's earlier published work: Constantinos Yiallourides, 'Protecting and Preserving the Marine Environment in Disputed Areas: Seismic Noise and Provisional Measures of Protection' (2017) 36(2) Journal of Energy & Natural Resources Law 141-161 and a subsequent presentation at the 'Global Ocean Regime Conference: Promoting Cooperation in Overlapping Maritime Areas' organized by the Korea Maritime Institute (Jeju-do, 16-18 May 2018).

[**] Parts of this chapter are drawn from a thesis by Natalia Ermolina, 'The Law of Shared Hydrocarbon Resources and the Question of Shared State Responsibility for Environmental Harm Arising from Their Cooperative Management' (UiT, May 2019).

The Issue: Fragile Ecosystems Caught in Overlapping Maritime Claims

Crawford writes that 'there is no coastal state in the world that does not have an overlapping potential entitlement with at least one other state'.[1] Maritime boundary delimitation is crucial in determining which State is entitled to exercise sovereign rights and jurisdiction over economic activities in disputed maritime areas.[2] To date, less than half of the world's maritime boundaries have been agreed upon, whether by agreement or recourse to judicial means.[3] As a result, a large number of maritime areas are disputed by two or more coastal States.[4] Public international law has become more precise on the issue of maritime delimitation over time. Yet, resolving maritime delimitation disputes typically takes several years.[5]

---

1 James Crawford, *Brownlie's Principles of Public International Law* (Oxford University Press 2019) Chapter 12.
2 Douglas M. Johnston and Philip M. Saunders, *Ocean Boundary Making: Regional Issues and Developments* (Croom Helm 1988) 17; Yoshifumi Tanaka, *Predictability and Flexibility in the Law of Maritime Delimitation* (Hart Publishing 2006) 125, 129-130.
3 Anna Khalfaoui and Constantinos Yiallourides, 'Maritime Disputes and Disputed Seabed Resources in the African Continent' in Tina S. Hunter et al. (eds) *Routledge Handbook of Energy Law* (Routledge 2020) Chapter 31. For information regarding disputes over international land and maritime boundaries, *see* CIA World Factbook, http://teacherlink.ed.usu.edu/tlresources/reference/factbook/fields/2070.html?country Name=Haiti&countryCode=ha&regionCode=ca&#ha.
4 The BIICL Report 2016 considered the obligations of States in respect of maritime areas subject to 'overlapping entitlements'. The report drew a distinction between 'undelimited areas' (i.e., areas of overlapping maritime entitlements where no final delimitation agreement is in place) and 'disputed areas' (i.e., maritime areas that are disputed by the coastal States concerned), BIICL, 'Report on the Obligations of States under Articles 74(3) and 83(3) of UNCLOS in respect of Undelimited Maritime Areas' (30 June 2016) (hereafter, BIICL Report 2016). For present purposes, the term 'disputed area' is preferred rather than 'undelimited area' which may, depending on the context, refer to a much wider area and is not always subject to an active dispute (e.g., States may simply decide not to pursue maritime delimitation).
5 For a discussion, Constantinos Yiallourides, *Maritime Disputes and International Law: Disputed Waters and Seabed Resources in Asia and Europe* (Routledge 2019) 29-42, 144-148. *See also* Constantinos Yiallourides, 'Some Observations on the Agreement between Greece and Egypt on the Delimitation of the Exclusive Economic Zone' EJIL-Talk Blog of the European Journal of International Law (25 August 2020): 'UNCLOS, to which the vast majority of States are parties, does not provide a single delimitation method. Yet, multiple maritime boundary litigations and arbitrations have taken place since UNCLOS' adoption. Courts, tribunals and State practice have come to articulate specific delimitation methods and approaches. Going back to square one in every delimitation situation is thus no longer necessary ... The three-stage delimitation approach, which involves a provisional equidistance line drawn from the nearest

While the exact location of the maritime boundary remains uncertain, the coastal States may need to conduct economic activities in the disputed areas.[6]

The legal regime governing State activities in maritime areas subject to boundary delimitation disputes has long been a source of discussion and extensive research. International law experts, such as Lagoni, Miyoshi, Fox, Churchill and Beckman, among others, have sought to clarify the existence and content of the rights and obligations of States pending the final settlement of their boundaries and explored possible interim arrangements like joint development agreements (JDAs).[7] The literature has often focused on Article 74(3), Article 83(3) and related provisions of the 1982

---

base points of two adjacent or opposite States, adjusted for equity in light of the relevant circumstances and proportionality requirements, has now become the standard approach.'

6 Clive Schofield et al., 'From Disputed Waters to Seas of Opportunity: Overcoming Barriers to Maritime Cooperation in East and Southeast Asia' (National Bureau of Asian Research Special Report No. 30, July 2011).

7 Rainer Lagoni, 'Interim Measures Pending Maritime Delimitation Agreements' (1984) 78(2) American Journal of International Law 345; Masahiro Miyoshi, 'The Basic Concept of Joint Development of Hydrocarbon Resources on the Continental Shelf' (1988) 3(1) International Journal of Estuarine and Coastal Law 1, 10–11; Hazel Fox et al. (eds) *Joint Development of Offshore Oil and Gas* (1st edn, BIICL 1989) 35; Robin R Churchill and Geir Ulfstein, *Marine Management in Disputed Areas: The Case of the Barents Sea* (Routledge 1992); Enrico Milano and Irini Papanicolopulu, 'State Responsibility in Disputed Areas on Land and at Sea' (2011) 71(3) Zeitschrift für Ausländisches Öffentliches Recht und Völkerrecht 611, 613, 615–16; Tara Davenport, 'The Exploration and Exploitation of Hydrocarbon Resources in Areas of Overlapping Claims' in Robert Beckman et al. (eds) *Beyond Territorial Disputes in the South China Sea: Legal Frameworks for the Joint Development of Hydrocarbon Resources* (Edward Elgar 2013) 102-110; David Anderson and Youri van Logchem, 'Rights and Obligations in Areas of Overlapping Maritime Claims' in Shunmugam Jayakumar, Tommy Koh and Robert Beckman (eds) *The South China Sea Disputes and the Law of the Sea* (Edward Elgar 2014) 192-228; Youri van Logchem, 'The Scope for Unilateralism in Disputed Maritime Areas' in Clive H Schofield, Seokwoo Lee and Moon-Sang Kwon (eds) *The Limits of Maritime Jurisdiction* (Martinus Nijhoff 2014) 175-197; BIICL Report 2016 paragraphs 100-107; Constantinos Yiallourides, *Maritime Disputes and International Law: Disputed Waters and Seabed Resources in Asia and Europe* (Routledge 2019) pp. 144-169; Constantinos Yiallourides, 'Oil and Gas Development in Disputed Waters' (2016) 5(1) UCL Journal of Law and Jurisprudence 59-86; Natalia Ermolina, 'Unilateral Hydrocarbon Activities in Undelimited Maritime Areas' (2018) 15(2) Indonesian Journal of International Law 156-189; Nicholas A Ioannides, 'The Legal Framework Governing Hydrocarbon Activities in Undelimited Maritime Areas' (2019) 68 International and Comparative Law Quarterly 345-368; Sean D. Murphy, 'Obligations of States in Disputed Areas of the Continental Shelf' in Tomas Heidar (ed.) *New Knowledge and Changing Circumstances in the Law of the Sea* (BRILL 2020).

United Nations Convention on the Law of the Sea (UNCLOS), and on activities prohibited and permitted within disputed maritime areas.[8]

Significantly less attention has been paid to the environmental legal obligations of States acting in disputed maritime areas.[9] Scientific evidence indicates that many large disputed maritime areas include particularly vulnerable marine ecosystems and constitute the habitat of endangered species.[10] Examples of such areas include the East China Sea, the South China Sea, and the Gulf of Thailand in the Asia-Pacific region,[11] the Mediterranean Sea,[12] and the Indian Ocean.[13]

---

8 For a comprehensive analysis, *see* BIICL Report 2016.
9 The BIICL Report 2016 (p. 38) notes, for instance, that States should exercise caution when conducting activities in a disputed area, 'on the basis that such activities may cause harm to the environment in the maritime zones of a neighbouring State, which may prove to extend further than anticipated'. It adds that activities that cause permanent damage to the marine environment in the disputed areas would be in breach of the obligation not to 'jeopardize or hamper' in Articles 74(3) and 83(3) of UNCLOS; Becker-Weinberg notes that 'States authorizing seabed activities in maritime areas before the delimitation of maritime areas must also comply with their obligations regarding the protection and preservation of the marine environment and must ensure that these activities are developed consistently with international environmental laws and regulations', Vasco Becker-Weinberg, 'Seabed Activities and the Protection and Preservation of the Marine Environment in Disputed Maritime Areas of the Asia-Pacific Region' (Proceedings from the 2012 LOSI-KIOST Conference on Securing the Ocean for the Next Generation) 12; Vasco Becker-Weinberg, *Joint Development of Hydrocarbon Deposits in the Law of the Sea* (Springer 2014) pp. 111-120.
10 Yoshifumi Tanaka, 'The South China Sea Arbitration: Environmental Obligations under the Law of the Sea Convention' (2018) 27(1) Review of European, Comparative and International Environmental Law 90-96.
11 According to Schofield et al., 'The South and East China Seas host marine environments startlingly rich in biodiversity. In particular, the South China Sea has been recognized as an area of globally significant biodiversity, while the East China Sea and Gulf of Thailand are similarly productive. These environments also support fisheries of significance in global, and certainly regional, terms'; Weinberg, likewise: 'the Asia-Pacific region includes valuable and interrelated marine ecosystems that together have some of the richest marine biological diversity in the world and are also an important source of ecological and economic support of a large part of the world's population'; for an analysis on the conservation of endangered species and the conservation of fragile ecosystems in the South China Sea, *see* Alfredo Robles, *Endangered Species and Fragile Ecosystems in the South China Sea: The Philippines v. China Arbitration* (Springer 2020) pp. 39-86; Yoshifumi Tanaka, 'The South China Sea Arbitration: Environmental Obligations under the Law of the Sea Convention' Review of European, Comparative and International Environmental Law 27 (2018): 90–96.
12 Scovazzi writes: 'The protection of the Mediterranean environment is vital because of the very slow exchange of its waters through the strait of Gibraltar. Pollution from any source might have serious and lasting consequences', Tullio Scovazzi, 'International Law of the Sea as Applied to the Mediterranean' (1994) 24 Ocean & Coastal Management 71.

Article 194(5) of UNCLOS establishes an affirmative legal obligation for the protection of 'rare or fragile' ecosystems. However, it does not provide a definition or criteria to qualify a marine environment as a 'rare or fragile' ecosystem.[14] According to the International Union for Conservation of Nature (IUCN), 'fragile' marine ecosystems are marine areas that are highly susceptible to degradation due to natural or human-induced events.[15]

The 'rare or fragile' nature of marine ecosystems has not prevented some coastal States from exploiting their natural resources. States have designated such disputed maritime areas for seabed exploration and/or exploitation through seismic exploration surveys, petroleum drilling,

---

13 Including the Arafura and Timor Seas, *see* Vasco Becker-Weinberg, 'Maritime Boundary-Making and Improving Ocean Governance in Timor-Leste' (2020) Ocean Yearbook Online 113-135.

14 For a discussion, *see* Alfredo Robles, *Endangered Species and Fragile Ecosystems in the South China Sea: The Philippines v. China Arbitration* (Springer 2020) 97-99; If there is scientific evidence before a court or tribunal that the maritime environment of a disputed area falls under the scope of Article 194(5) of UNCLOS, it triggers enhanced environmental protection measures in the said area, according to the *South China Sea* Arbitration Tribunal, at paragraph 945. In the *Chagos Marine Protected Area Arbitration*, the Annex VII Tribunal found that Article 194(5) is 'not limited to measures aimed strictly at controlling pollution and extends to measures focused primarily on conservation and the preservation of ecosystems.' The Tribunal concluded that 'in establishing the MPA [marine protected area], the United Kingdom was under an obligation to "endeavour to harmonize" its policies with Mauritius', *Chagos Marine Protected Area Arbitration (Mauritius v. United Kingdom)* (Final Award) (PCA 2015).

15 Note that ascertaining ecosystem 'fragility' is a complex scientific exercise, strongly dependent on a number of criteria and variables, including, but not limited to, the: (a) presence of threatened, endangered or declining species and/or habitats of such species; (b) presence of nursery or juvenile areas; (c) presence of feeding, breeding or rest areas; (d) presence of species with increased sensitivity to oil spills and related disturbances; and (e) criteria relating to the social, economic and scientific value of the area in question; *see*, for instance, Hein Rune Skjoldal and Caitlyn Toropova 'Criteria for identifying ecologically important and vulnerable marine areas in the Arctic' (IUCN 2007), https://www.iucn.org/sites/dev/files/import/downloads/criteria_arctic_final.pdf. According to Nilsson and Grelsson, 'ecosystem fragility' in environmental conservation and management 'has never been satisfactorily defined … it prerequires knowledge about the effects of all impacts and activities on any ecosystem, which is virtually impossible to obtain. Radical simplifications are therefore inevitable', *see* Christer Nilsson and Gunnell Grelsson, 'The Fragility of Ecosystems: A Review' (1997) 32(4) Journal of Applied Ecology 677-692; Carolyn J. Lundquist et al., 'Ecological Criteria to Identify Areas for Biodiversity Conservation' (2017) 213 Biological Conservation 309-316.

laying of submarine pipelines and other activities; for fishing; and construction of artificial installations.[16] In a comprehensive study on East and South Asia maritime disputes, Schofield and others observed:

> Over 80% of reefs in the South China Sea and Gulf of Thailand are at risk and will collapse within 20 years unless sustainable practices are adopted; 70% of mangrove cover has been lost in the last 70 years, and at current rates of habitat loss the remainder will be lost by 2030; and 20%–60% of seagrass beds have disappeared over the last 50 years, while those still in existence are also threatened with destruction. The East China Sea is also host to fragile ecosystems, and the marine living resources that it supports are likewise extremely vulnerable to, among other threats, land-based pollution that has compromised or destroyed the spawning, breeding, feeding, and wintering grounds of important fish stocks, thus undermining the sustainability of fisheries. Competitive exploitation of shared fish stocks on the part of the rival fishing fleets of the littoral states has likewise led to significant overfishing of shared stocks. This situation is likely to further deteriorate as ocean-going traffic and oil and gas activities rise.[17]

According to Churchill and Ulfstein, the implementation of good environmental practices in disputed maritime areas largely depends on the degree of cooperation and political goodwill of the States concerned. Some States pursue activities on a unilateral basis; others collaborate. Norway and Russia have established a moratorium on hydrocarbon exploration and exploitation activities in the formerly disputed area of the Barents Sea and a regime for cooperation with respect to fishing activities to 'achieve

---

16 '[T]he potential economic and human costs of the continued deterioration of the marine environment [in the East and South China Sea] are extremely high', *see* Clive Schofield et al., 'From Disputed Waters to Seas of Opportunity: Overcoming Barriers to Maritime Cooperation in East and Southeast Asia' (National Bureau of Asian Research Special Report No. 30, July 2011); Constantinos Yiallourides, *Maritime Disputes and International Law: Disputed Waters and Seabed Resources in Asia and Europe* (Routledge 2019) pp. 144-169.

17 Clive Schofield et al., 'From Disputed Waters to Seas of Opportunity: Overcoming Barriers to Maritime Cooperation in East and Southeast Asia' (National Bureau of Asian Research Special Report No. 30, July 2011) pp. 9-10; *see also* GEF Secretariat, 'From Ridge to Reef; Water, Environment and Community Security' (Global Environment Facility 2019), https://www.thegef.org/sites/default/files/publications/GEF_Ri dgetoReef2015_r2_Final.pdf.

environmental protection to a better extent than those that authorize these activities unilaterally'.[18]

Environmental degradation of disputed maritime areas remains a live, ongoing, and potentially increasing problem. The general environmental provisions of the law of the sea together with international environmental law are binding upon States acting in disputed maritime areas. Yet, the specific contours of these obligations and how they may be used in maritime boundary adjudication under UNCLOS merit further examination. Therefore, this chapter focuses on the protection and preservation of marine environment in the specific context of disputed maritime areas. It addresses three important environmental legal obligations in international jurisprudence and State practice which are relevant to the conduct of States in disputed maritime areas: (1) the duty to cooperate over environmental matters; (2) the duty to apply a precautionary approach; and (3) the duty to conduct an environmental impact assessment and monitor environmental impacts. The analysis follows a case-study design and examines the existing body of environmental jurisprudence together with selected examples from State practice to clarify the substance of the environmental legal obligations of States in disputed maritime areas. This chapter does not claim to provide a comprehensive list of all potentially relevant jurisprudence and State practice.

Environmental Obligations under UNCLOS

UNCLOS establishes the overarching international legal framework for the protection of the marine environment.[19] When pursuing marine natural resource potentials, States must comply with their obligations on the protection and preservation of the marine environment and must ensure that their activities are conducted in conformity with international environmental laws and regulations.[20] Article 192 of UNCLOS places States

---

18 Treaty Concerning Maritime Delimitation and Cooperation in the Barents Sea and the Arctic Ocean (Russian Federation/Kingdom of Norway) (15 September 2010) 2791 United Nations Treaty Series 36; for a discussion, *see* Robin R. Churchill and Geir Ulfstein, *Marine Management in Disputed Areas: The Case of the Barents Sea* (Routledge 1992) pp. 63-65.

19 Part XII, UNCLOS; Robin Warner, *The Oceans Beyond National Jurisdiction Strengthening the International Law Framework* (Martinus Nijhoff 2009) 67.

20 Rüdiger Wolfrum, 'Means of ensuring compliance with and enforcement of international environmental law' in 272 Recueil de cours (1998) 9-154; Catherine Redgwell, 'International Environmental Law' in Malcolm D Evans, *International Law* (5th edn,

under a general legal obligation 'to protect and preserve the marine environment'.[21] Article 193 of UNCLOS adds that States have the 'sovereign right to exploit their natural resources pursuant to their environmental policies and in accordance with their duty to protect and preserve the marine environment'.[22] Giving substance to the general obligation in Article 192, UNCLOS requires States to take all measures necessary to: (a) 'prevent, reduce and control pollution of the marine environment from any source' and (b) 'ensure that activities under their jurisdiction or control' are carried out so as not to 'cause damage by pollution to other States and their environment, and that pollution ... does not spread beyond the areas where they exercise sovereign rights'.[23]

Other UNCLOS provisions stress the importance of preventive measures and proactive control of sources of pollution, rather than focus on the consequences and responsibility for recovering damages or remediating harm to the marine environment.[24] For example, Article 208(1) concerns pollution from seabed activities in areas under national jurisdiction. It provides that coastal States 'shall adopt laws and regulations to prevent, reduce and control pollution of the marine environment arising from or in connection with seabed activities subject to their jurisdiction and from

---

Oxford University Press 2018) 675; Malgosia Fitzmaurice, 'International Protection of the Environment' in 293 Recueil de cours (2001) 22-47; Yoshifumi Tanaka, 'Protection of Community Interests in International Law: The Case of the Law of the Sea' in Armin von Bogdandy and Rüdiger Wolfrum (eds), *Max Planck Yearbook of United Nations Law* Volume 15 (BRILL 2011) pp. 329-375; Thomas A Mensah, 'The International Tribunal for the Law of the Sea and the Protection and Preservation of the Marine Environment' (1999) 8(1) Review of European Community and International Environmental Law 1; Alexander Proelss, 'The Contribution of the ITLOS to Strengthening the Regime for the Protection of the Marine Environment' in Angela Del Vecchio and Roberto Virzo (eds) *Interpretations of the United Nations Convention on the Law of the Sea by International Courts and Tribunals* (Springer 2019) 93-105; Tim Stephens, *International Courts and Environmental Protection* (Cambridge University Press 2009) 45.

21   Article 192, UNCLOS.
22   Article 193, UNCLOS.
23   Articles 194(1)-(3), 207-212, UNCLOS; *see also* Article 1, UNCLOS which defines 'pollution of the marine environment': as 'the introduction ... of substances or energy into the marine environment, including estuaries, which results or is likely to result in such deleterious effects as harm to living resources and marine life, hazards to human health, hindrance to marine activities, including fishing and other legitimate uses of the sea, impairment of quality for use of sea water and reduction of amenities'.
24   For a comprehensive analysis, *see* Yoshifumi Tanaka, 'Protection of Community Interests in International Law: The Case of the Law of the Sea' in Armin von Bogdandy and Rüdiger Wolfrum (eds), *Max Planck Yearbook of United Nations Law* Volume 15 (BRILL 2011), 275-328.

artificial islands, installations, and structures under their jurisdiction'.[25] Such laws and regulations 'shall be no less effective than international rules, standards and recommended practices and procedures'.[26]

Chapter 17 of Agenda 21, adopted at the UN Conference on Environment and Development (UNCED) held in Rio de Janeiro in 1992, sets out guidelines and recommendations concerning the protection of the marine environment from various land (such as ports) and sea-based (such as oil and gas platforms) sources of pollution. On pollution from seabed activities, Chapter 17 provides that States, when 'acting individually, bilaterally, regionally or multilaterally', should assess existing regulatory measures to address discharges, emissions, and safety and assess the need for additional measures.[27] States are called to prepare coastal profiles identifying critical areas, including user conflicts and specific priorities for management; conduct prior environmental impact assessments, systematic observation, and follow-up of major projects; devise contingency plans for human-induced and natural disasters; and draft contingency plans for degradation and pollution of anthropogenic origin, including spills of oil and other materials.[28]

Environmental legal obligations under UNCLOS are absolute. They contain no qualifications and cover the ocean as a whole without distinguishing between areas under national jurisdiction (EEZ and continental shelf) and areas beyond national jurisdiction (high seas and the 'Area'), or between disputed maritime areas and areas not subject to a dispute. Whether neighbouring States have agreed to govern a disputed area under a cooperative regime, such as a JDA, is not relevant. UNCLOS makes no exception to the obligations to protect and preserve the marine environment in relation to disputes concerning maritime boundary delimitation.[29] For example, the *South China Sea Arbitration* focused on the disputed legal status of certain territorial features and the conduct of environmentally hazardous island construction activities in the disputed areas of the South China Sea. The Arbitral Tribunal considered that China had breached Article 192 and Article 194(1) and (5) of UNCLOS on environmental protection: substantively, by undertaking coral bleaching, island building,

---

25 Article 208(1), UNCLOS.

26 Article 208(3), UNCLOS.

27 Chapter 17(30), Agenda 21, United Nations Conference on Environment and Development (Rio de Janeiro, Brazil, 3-14 June 1992).

28 Agenda 21, United Nations Conference on Environment and Development (Rio de Janeiro, Brazil, 3-14 June 1992), Chapter 17(6).

29 *South China Sea Arbitration (Philippines v. China)* (Award of 12 July 2016) (hereafter, *South China Sea Arbitration*), paragraph 940.

and numerous other harmful activities, and, procedurally, by failing to communicate an adequate environmental impact assessment to the Government of the Philippines.[30] The Arbitral Tribunal noted that the general obligation to protect the marine environment encompasses both a positive obligation to 'take active measures to protect and preserve the marine environment' and a negative obligation not to degrade the marine environment.[31] The Arbitral Tribunal added that the content of the general obligation to protect and preserve the marine environment under Article 192 of UNCLOS is informed by subsequent provisions in Part XII, which runs from Articles 192-196, including Article 194, and other applicable rules of international environmental law.[32]

The International Tribunal for the Law of the Sea (ITLOS) and other adjudicative bodies operating under the dispute settlement framework of UNCLOS have developed a large body of environmental jurisprudence in the context of interlocutory proceedings relating to provisional measures on the protection of the marine environment under Article 290 of UNCLOS.[33] Article 290(1) of UNCLOS reads:

> If a dispute has been duly submitted to a court or tribunal which considers that prima facie it has jurisdiction under this Part or Part XI, section 5, the court or tribunal may prescribe any provisional measures which it considers appropriate under the circumstances to preserve the respective rights of the parties to the dispute *or* to *prevent serious harm to the marine environment*, pending the final decision (emphasis added).

The use of 'or' in Article 290(1) suggests that provisional measures may be prescribed independent of measures protecting the respective sovereign

---

30 *South China Sea Arbitration*, paragraphs 941, 992-993.
31 The Arbitral Tribunal also stated: 'This "general obligation" extends both to "protection" of the marine environment from future damage and "preservation" in the sense of maintaining or improving its present condition', *South China Sea Arbitration*, paragraph 941.
32 *See* discussion in the above section this chapter; *South China Sea Arbitration*, paragraphs 941-942.
33 Examples of such cases are the following: *Southern Bluefin Tuna (New Zealand v. Japan; Australia v. Japan)* (Provisional Measures) (1999) ITLOS Cases Nos 3 and 4; *MOX Plant (Ireland v. United Kingdom)* (Provisional Measures) (2001) ITLOS Case No. 10; *Land Reclamation by Singapore in and around the Straits of Johor (Malaysia v. Singapore)* (Provisional Measures) (2003) ITLOS Case No. 12; *The M/V 'Louisa' Case (Saint Vincent and the Grenadines v. Kingdom of Spain)* (Provisional Measures) (2010) ITLOS Case No. 18; *Maritime Boundary Delimitation in the Atlantic Ocean (Ghana/Côte d'Ivoire)* (Provisional Measures) (2015) ITLOS Case No. 23.

rights of the parties to a dispute.[34] According to Wolfrum, the reference to environmental justifications in the prescription of provisional measures 'adds a new element to their objective one, which is not directly linked to the interests of the parties to the dispute and thus makes the tribunal or court a mechanism working not only in the interest of the parties involved but in the one of the community of States'.[35] A healthy marine environment provides the foundation for all life; the protection of the marine environment can thus be considered a community interest.[36] It is a common interest of the international community of States which goes ostensibly beyond the interests of individual States.[37] Fietta and others explain:

> [A]ny State party to UNCLOS has standing to bring an environmental complaint against any other State party with respect to the conduct of its nationals or flagged vessels in any maritime area. This might be especially important where the conduct concerned threatens severe damage to the marine environment or conservation, including with respect to endangered species or fragile ecosystems.[38]

States involved in disputes concerning the application and interpretation of UNCLOS, including maritime boundary disputes, have not argued that UNCLOS does not require them to prevent, mitigate, or control pollution; to carry out environmental impact assessments; or to cooperate in the management of environmental risks, including in respect of activities in a

---

34 *See* discussion below 'The Scope of Environmental Protection: Meaning of the Marine Environment'.
35 Rüdiger Wolfrum, 'Provisional Measures of the International Tribunal for the Law of the Sea' (1997) 37(3) Indian Journal of International Law 420, 423.
36 Yoshifumi Tanaka, 'Protection of Community Interests in International Law: The Case of the Law of the Sea' in Armin von Bogdandy and Rüdiger Wolfrum (eds), *Max Planck Yearbook of United Nations Law* Volume 15 (BRILL 2011) pp. 329-375.
37 For an analysis of Article 290(1) of UNCLOS and its application to unilateral seabed activities in disputed maritime areas, focusing on environmental legal issues, *see* Constantinos Yiallourides, 'Protecting and Preserving the Marine Environment in Disputed Areas: Seismic Noise and Provisional Measures of Protection' (2018) 36(2) Journal of Energy & Natural Resources Law 141-161.
38 Stephen Fietta, Jiries Saadeh and Laura Rees-Evans, 'The South China Sea Award: A Milestone for International Environmental Law, the Duty of Due Diligence and the Litigation of Maritime Environmental Disputes?' (2017) 27(3) Georgetown Environmental Law Review 1; *see also*, David Ong, 'A Bridge too far? Assessing the Prospects for International Environmental Law to Resolve the South China Sea Disputes' (2015) 22(4) International Journal on Minority and Group Rights 578-597.

disputed maritime area. Nor have States questioned the customary character of the environmental protection regime established by UNCLOS.[39] Rather, disputing parties have contested the adequacy of measures that States have taken, or failed to take, to prevent serious harm to the environment in relation to certain maritime activities.[40] The argument has not been on whether such measures are necessary at all. For example, in *Ghana/ Côte d'Ivoire* (Provisional Measures), Côte d'Ivoire argued before ITLOS that the oil exploration and exploitation activities conducted by Ghana in the disputed maritime area resulted in marine pollution incidents.[41] Ghana countered that Ghana's environmental protection legislation 'is among the most robust in the region' and that 'constant monitoring of environmental impacts' is required by Ghanaian law.[42] Côte d'Ivoire challenged the efficacy of Ghana's environmental protection legislation; ITLOS, however, avoided to rule on this directly as discussed further below.[43]

The Scope of Environmental Protection: Meaning of the Marine Environment

Understanding the environmental legal obligations of States acting in disputed maritime areas, first, requires clarifying the meaning of the 'marine environment', i.e., the subject of protection that is independent of the alleged sovereign rights of the disputing coastal States.[44] The totality of Part XII of UNCLOS on the 'protection and preservation of the marine

---

39 For a discussion, *see* Yoshifumi Tanaka, 'The South China Sea Arbitration: Environmental Obligations under the Law of the Sea Convention' (2018) 27(1) Review of European, Comparative and International Environmental Law 90-96.

40 For a discussion, *see* Yoshifumi Tanaka, 'The South China Sea Arbitration: Environmental Obligations under the Law of the Sea Convention' (2018) 27(1) Review of European, Comparative and International Environmental Law 90-96.

41 *Ghana/Côte d'Ivoire* (Provisional Measures) (Public sitting held on Sunday, 29 March 2015, at 10 am) 40.

42 *Maritime Boundary Delimitation in the Atlantic Ocean (Ghana/Côte d'Ivoire)* (Provisional Measures) (2015) ITLOS Case No. 23 paragraphs 66-67.

43 *Ghana/Côte d'Ivoire* (Provisional Measures) (Request Submitted by Côte d'Ivoire) paragraph 51; for a commentary, *see* Yoshifumi Tanaka, 'Unilateral Exploration and Exploitation of Natural Resources in Disputed Areas: A Note on the Ghana/Côte d'Ivoire Order of 25 April 2015 before the Special Chamber of ITLOS' 46(4) Ocean Development and International Law (2015) 315; Nicholas A Ioannides, 'A Commentary on the Dispute Concerning Delimitation of the Maritime Boundary between Ghana and Côte d'Ivoire in the Atlantic Ocean (Ghana/Côte d'Ivoire)' (2017) 3 Maritime Safety and Security Law Journal 48; Constantinos Yiallourides, 'Calming the Waters in the West African Region: The Case of Ghana and Côte d'Ivoire' (2018) 26(3) African Journal of International and Comparative Law 1-29.

44 Article 290, UNCLOS.

environment' indicates that the marine environment should be construed broadly. Environmental protection under UNCLOS covers land-based and marine-based sources of marine pollution; the protection and preservation of marine ecosystems; and the conservation of living resources.[45] Agenda 21 of the Rio Conference, the Convention on Biological Diversity,[46] and the United Nations Fish Stocks Agreement[47] all give a broad reading to the responsibilities of States with regard to the protection of the marine environment. Conservation, preservation, and sustainable use of marine living and non-living resources, including endangered or depleted species, oceanic ecosystems, and biological diversity, are important elements of this legal framework.

Environmental risks posed by State activities on the conservation and sustainable use of marine living resources and ecosystems in disputed maritime areas are also covered by the general UNCLOS obligations on the protection and preservation of the marine environment. For example, *MOX Plant*,[48] *Land Reclamation*,[49] *Ghana/Côte d'Ivoire*[50] and, to some extent, *M/V 'Louisa'*[51] concerned the interpretation and application of Part XII of UNCLOS. This included provisions on prevention, reduction, and control of pollution, and the closely intertwined provisions on prior environmental impact assessment, information, and consultation. Conversely, *Southern Bluefin Tuna* is related to Part VII of UNCLOS (particularly high seas fisheries conservation) rather than Part XII. Nonetheless, ITLOS expressly considered that 'the conservation of the living resources of the sea is an element in the protection and preservation of the marine environment'.[52]

---

45 In the *South China Sea Arbitration*, the Tribunal noted that 'the obligations in Part XII apply to all States with respect to the marine environment in all maritime areas, both inside the national jurisdiction of States and beyond it', *The South China Sea Arbitration (Philippines v. China)* (Merits) (Award of 12 July 2016) paragraph 940.

46 Convention on Biological Diversity (adopted 5 June 1992, entered into force 29 December 1993) 760 United Nations Treaty Series 79.

47 Agreement for the Implementation of the Provisions of the United Nations Convention on the Law of the Sea of 10 December 1982 relating to the Conservation and Management of Straddling Fish Stocks and Highly Migratory Fish Stocks (adopted 4 August 1995, entered into force 11 December 2001) 2167 United Nations Treaty Series 3.

48 *MOX Plant (Ireland v. United Kingdom)* (Provisional Measures) (2001) ITLOS Rep 95.

49 *Land Reclamation in and around the Straits of Johor (Malaysia v. Singapore)* (Provisional Measures) (2003) ITLOS Rep 10.

50 *Maritime Boundary Delimitation in the Atlantic Ocean (Ghana/Côte d'Ivoire)* (Provisional Measures) (2015) ITLOS Case No. 23.

51 *M/V 'Louisa' (Saint Vincent and the Grenadines v. Kingdom of Spain)* (Provisional Measures) (2010) ITLOS Rep 58 (hereafter, *M/V 'Louisa'*).

52 *Southern Bluefin Tuna (New Zealand v. Japan; Australia v. Japan)* (Provisional Measures) (1999) ITLOS Rep 280 paragraph 70.

Therefore, State activities which may adversely affect or pose risks and hazards to the marine environment in a disputed maritime area fall within the scope of UNCLOS environmental obligations.

The Duty to Cooperate on Environmental Matters

The duty to cooperate to prevent and minimize pollution of the marine environment is a fundamental principle in UNCLOS and customary international law. It is highly relevant to the protection of the marine environment from State activities in disputed maritime areas.[53] As Boyle writes, 'it is undoubtedly true that co-operation in the control of environmental risks is one of the central elements of general international law on environmental protection'.[54] Under Article 194(1) of UNCLOS, States must take action to prevent pollution of the marine environment, individually or jointly as appropriate and in accordance with their capabilities. Article 197 of UNCLOS requires States to cooperate regionally or globally to develop 'international rules, standards, recommended practices and procedures' to protect and preserve the marine environment while considering characteristic regional features.[55] Besides Part XII, other Parts of UNCLOS include provisions on environmental cooperation. Article 123, for example, provides a reinforced obligation for cooperation over environmental matters in relation to States bordering 'enclosed or semi-enclosed seas'.[56]

---

53 UNCLOS, Article 194(1) and section 2 of Part XII; *MOX Plant (Ireland v. United Kingdom)* (Provisional Measures), Order of 3 December 2001, ITLOS Reports 2001, paragraph 82; *see also Request for an Advisory Opinion submitted by the Sub-regional Fisheries Commission*, Advisory Opinion of 2 April 2015, paragraph 140; *South China Sea Arbitration,* paragraph 946; Vasco Becker-Weinberg, 'Seabed Activities and the Protection and Preservation of the Marine Environment in Disputed Maritime Areas of the Asia-Pacific Region' (Proceedings from the 2012 LOSI-KIOST Conference on Securing the Ocean for the Next Generation).

54 Alan Boyle, 'The Environmental Jurisprudence of the International Tribunal for the Law of the Sea' (2007) 22(3) International Journal of Marine and Coastal Law 369, 379.

55 *MOX Plant (Ireland v. United Kingdom)* (Provisional Measures), Order of 3 December 2001, ITLOS Reports 2001, paragraph 82; *see also Request for an Advisory Opinion submitted by the Sub-Regional Fisheries Commission*, Advisory Opinion of 2 April 2015, paragraph 140; *South China Sea Arbitration,* paragraph 946.

56 Article 123, UNCLOS. According to Article 122 UNCLOS, an 'enclosed or semi-enclosed sea means a gulf, basin or sea surrounded by two or more States and connected to another sea or the ocean by a narrow outlet or consisting entirely or primarily of the territorial seas and exclusive economic zones of two or more coastal States'; Budislav Vukas, 'Enclosed or Semi-Enclosed Seas' in Max Planck Encyclopedia of Public International Law (online version, updated 2013); the South China Sea, for example, can be classified as a semi-enclosed sea, *see South China Sea Arbitration* paragraph

In the disputed maritime areas, Articles 74(3) and 83(3) of UNCLOS establish two substantive legal obligations on States operating in such areas. Pending delimitation, coastal States are obliged to 'make every effort to enter into provisional arrangements of a practical nature'. Simultaneously, concerned States shall abstain from acts that might 'jeopardize or hamper the reaching of the final agreement'. The content of the obligations in Articles 74(3) and 83(3) of UNCLOS has been addressed in *Guyana v. Suriname*,[57] *Ghana/Côte d'Ivoire*,[58] and extensively in the literature.[59] The Articles impose a restrictive obligation: parties must exercise restraint and refrain from undertaking activities that may endanger reaching a final agreement or impede negotiations to that end.[60] They also impose a positive obligation: States must pursue provisional arrangements of a practical nature to promote cooperation between States for the economic utilization and management of the disputed maritime area.[61]

Provisional arrangements, which permit the exploration and exploitation of marine through a joint development zone pending final delimitation, are the most common type of inter-State cooperation.[62] Several JDAs

---

946 and Robert Beckman, 'The UN Convention on the Law of the Sea and the Maritime Disputes in the South China Sea' (2013) 107(1) American Journal of International Law 142, 143.

57 *Arbitration Between Guyana and Suriname* (Annex VII Arbitral Tribunal) (2007) 139 International Legal Materials 566.

58 *Dispute Concerning Delimitation of the Maritime Boundary between Ghana and Côte d'Ivoire in the Atlantic Ocean (Ghana/Côte d'Ivoire)* ITLOS Case No. 23.

59 For a comprehensive analysis of both doctrine and practice in this area, *see* BIICL Report 2016.

60 *Delimitation of the Maritime Boundary in the Atlantic Ocean (Ghana/Côte d'Ivoire)* (Judgment of 23 September 2017) (Separate Opinion of Judge Paik); *Arbitration Between Guyana and Suriname* (Annex VII Arbitral Tribunal) (2007) 139 International Legal Materials 566.

61 *Guyana v. Suriname*, (2007) 139 International Legal Materials 566 at paragraph 460.

62 For a detailed study, *see* Vasco Becker-Weinberg, *Joint Development of Hydrocarbon Deposits in the Law of the Sea* (Springer 2014); Mochtar Kusuma-Atmadja, 'Joint Development of Oil and Gas by Neighbouring Countries' in Thomas A. Mensah and Bernard H. Oxman (eds) *Sustainable Development and the Preservation of the Oceans: The Challenges of UNCLOS and Agenda 21* (Law of the Sea Institute 1997) 592; Hazel Fox et al. (eds) *Joint Development of Offshore Oil and Gas* (1st edn, BIICL 1989) 45; Constantinos Yiallourides, 'Joint Development of Seabed Resources in Areas of Overlapping Maritime Claims: An Analysis of Precedents in State Practice' (2019) 31(2) University of San Francisco Maritime Law Journal 129-174. Note here that Bernard identifies four other types of provisional arrangements pending delimitation: (1) a mutually agreed moratorium on all economic activities in overlapping areas; (2) joint development or cooperation over fishing activities; (3) environmental cooperation; and (4) allocation of criminal and civil jurisdiction, *see* Leonardo Bernard, 'Prospect for Joint Development in the South China Sea' (Centre of Strategic and International Studies, 5-6 June, 2013) 4. Anderson and van Logchem suggest that a

explicitly regulate environmental issues.[63] For example, the 1974 Japan-South Korea JDA enshrines the parties' general undertaking to prevent and remove sea pollution resulting from petroleum activities in the zone. It also stipulates special arrangements for the prevention of collisions and pollution in the joint development zone. Section 1 of the Japanese note annexed to the JDA provides that the authorizing government must ensure that necessary technical measures have been taken to prevent blowouts of wells and discharge of oil and waste from ships or marine facilities and must promptly provide the other government with all available information when a major oil spill, collision at sea, or similar emergency occurs.[64] Another example is the 'International Agency' established under the Senegal and Guinea-Bissau JDA tasked with taking 'all the necessary measures for pollution prevention and control'.[65] To that end, the agency can 'lay down regulations to protect the marine environment in the Area' and 'establish an emergency plan or management plan to combat pollution and any degradation arising from resource prospecting, exploration and exploitation activities in the Area'.[66] The Parties also commit to 'cooperate with

---

wide of variety of provisional arrangements is possible, including:(a) a joint exploration and exploitation regime; (b) total moratorium on certain types of activity such as drilling; and (c) a simple arrangement of prior notification of a proposed activity in the overlapping area followed by consultations, David Anderson and Youri van Logchem, 'Rights and Obligations in Areas of Overlapping Maritime Claims' in Shunmugam Jayakumar, Tommy Koh and Robert Beckman (eds) *The South China Sea Disputes and the Law of the Sea* (Edward Elgar 2014) 192-228.

63 For a discussion, *see* Constantinos Yiallourides, *Maritime Disputes and International Law: Disputed Waters and Seabed Resources in Asia and Europe* (Routledge 2019) 242-243; David M. Ong, 'A Bridge Too Far: Assessing the Prospects for International Environmental Law to Resolve the South China Sea Disputes' (2015) 22 International Journal on Minority & Group Rights 578; Cecilia A. Low, 'Marine Environmental Protection in Joint Development Agreements' (2012) 30(1) Journal of Energy & Natural Resources Law 45-74; Vasco Becker-Weinberg, *Joint Development of Hydrocarbon Deposits in the Law of the Sea* (Springer 2014) 111-120, 133-137; Vasco Becker-Weinberg, 'Seabed Activities and the Protection and Preservation of the Marine Environment in Disputed Maritime Areas of the Asia-Pacific Region' (Proceedings from the 2012 LOSI-KIOST Conference on Securing the Ocean for the Next Generation); David M. Ong, 'The International Legal Obligations of States in Disputed Maritime Jurisdiction Zones and Prospects for Co-operative Arrangements in the East China Sea Region' (2016) 22 Asian Yearbook of International Law 109-130.

64 Masahiro Miyoshi, 'The Japan-South Korea Agreement on Joint Development of the Continental Shelf' (1985) 10(3) Energy 545, 549.

65 Article 5, Management and Cooperation Agreement between the Government of the Republic of Senegal and the Government of the Republic of Guinea-Bissau (adopted 14 October 1993, entered into force 21 December 1995) 1903 United Nations Treaty Series (1996) 34-63.

66 Senegal/Guinea-Bissau 1993 Agreement, 1903 United Nations Treaty Series (1996), Article 23; *see also* Protocol of Agreement Relating to the Organization and Operation

the Agency to prevent or minimize pollution or any other type of degradation in the marine environment resulting from resource prospecting, exploration and exploitation activities in the Area'.[67]

Ong analysed the progressive inclusion of environmental provisions within JDAs in the period from 1950 to 2001.[68] Ong observed that 'the provision for environmental protection was conspicuous in its brevity of even total absence' in earlier JDAs, while later JDAs have 'more readily' included environmental protection obligations.[69] This would reflect the increased level of environmental consciousness in joint petroleum development practice. More recently concluded JDAs have tended to address marine environmental protection more rigorously. For example, they have defined the meaning of marine pollution and empowered joint authorities to lay down health, safety, and environmental regulations and even to carry out inspections of petroleum installations situated in the zone.[70]

For instance, the Nigeria-Sao Tome joint authority has a general duty to take all steps necessary to prevent and remedy pollution and any other harm to the environment. Specifically, it can conduct, itself or through a third party, inspections of oil installations and may order the immediate cessation of any or all petroleum operations in the zone where expedient, for instance, to protect the marine area from pollution.[71] Likewise, the

---

of the Agency for Management and Cooperation between the Republic of Guinea-Bissau and the Republic of Senegal instituted by the Agreement of 14 October 1993 reproduced in Jonathan I. Charney and Lewis M. Alexander (eds) *International Maritime Boundaries* (Martinus Nijhoff Publishers 2004) pp. 2258–2278.

67 Article 23(1), Senegal/Guinea-Bissau 1993 Agreement, 1903 United Nations Treaty Series (1996).

68 David Ong, 'The Progressive Integration of Environmental Protection within Offshore Joint Development Agreements' in Malgosia Fitzmaurice and Milena Szuniewicz (eds) *Exploitation of Natural Resources in the 21st Century* (Kluwer Law International 2003).

69 David Ong, 'The Progressive Integration of Environmental Protection within Offshore Joint Development Agreements' in Malgosia Fitzmaurice and Milena Szuniewicz (eds) *Exploitation of Natural Resources in the 21st Century* (Kluwer Law International 2003), p. 120-123.

70 *See*, for instance, Article 1(21), Treaty between the Federal Republic of Nigeria and the Democratic Republic of Sao Tome and Principe on the Joint Development of Petroleum and other Resources, in respect of Areas of the Exclusive Economic Zone of the Two States (adopted 21 February 2001, entered into force 16 January 2003), https://www.un.org/Depts/los/LEGISLATIONANDTREATIES/PDFFILES/TREATIES/STP-NGA2001.PDF.

71 Article 30, Treaty between the Federal Republic of Nigeria and the Democratic Republic of Sao Tome and Principe on the Joint Development of Petroleum and other Resources, in respect of Areas of the Exclusive Economic Zone of the Two States (adopted 21 February 2001, entered into force 16 January 2003).

designated authority in the Timor Sea Treaty is instructed to 'issue regulations to protect the marine environment in the joint development area; establish a contingency plan for combating pollution from petroleum activities in the joint development area and establish safety zones to ensure the safety of navigation and petroleum operations'.[72] The Agreement further provides that companies operating in the joint development zone will be liable for damage or expenses incurred due to pollution of the marine environment inside the zone, in accordance with their contract or licence and the law of the jurisdiction, whether Australia or East Timor, in which the claim is brought.[73]

Provisions on environmental protection have been incorporated in many recent JDAs covering disputed maritime areas, such as the 2012 Seychelles/Mauritius Agreement,[74] and in framework and cross-border unitization treaties, such as the 2013 Cyprus/Egypt Agreement,[75] the 2007 Trinidad and Tobago/Venezuela Treaty,[76] and the 2012 United States (US)/Mexico Agreement[77] and the 2018 Australia/Timor-Leste Agreement.[78] This confirms the general tendency in State practice towards embracing a cooperative approach to the protection of the marine environ-

---

72 Article 10(c); Annex C under Article 6(b)(v), Timor Sea Treaty (Australia-Timor Leste) (adopted 20 May 2002, entered into force 2 April 2003), www.austlii.edu.au/au/other/dfat/treaties/2003/13.html, 2258 United Nations Treaty Series 3.

73 Article 10(d) Timor Sea Treaty; almost identical provisions were included in Articles 8, 18 and 19 of the Timor Gap Treaty, *see* Treaty on the Zone of Cooperation in an Area Between the Indonesian Province of East Timor and Northern Australia (Australia/Indonesia) (adopted 11 December 1989, entered into force 9 February 1991) (1990) 29 International Legal Materials 469 (no longer in force).

74 Article 12, Treaty Concerning the Joint Management of the Continental Shelf in the Mascarene Plateau Region (Mauritius/Seychelles) (adopted 13 March 2012, entered into force 18 June 2012) (Mauritius/Seychelles Joint Management Treaty), http://www.mfa.gov.sc/uploads/files/filepath_45.pdf.

75 Framework Agreement Concerning the Development of Cross-Median Line Hydrocarbons Resources (Republic of Cyprus/Arab Republic of Egypt) (signed 12 December 2013, entered into force 11 September 2014), www.mof.gov.cy/mof/gpo/gpo.nsf/All/A88D02909DC27F10C2257D20002C1DB5/$file/4196%2025%207%202014%20PARARTIMA%201o%20MEROS%20III%20.pdf.

76 Framework Treaty Relating to the Unitization of Hydrocarbon Reservoirs that Extend Across the Delimitation Line Between the Republic of Trinidad and Tobago and the Bolivian Republic of Venezuela (adopted 20 March 2007, entered into force 16 August 2010), 2876 United Nations Treaty Series 3.

77 Article 19, Agreement Between the United States of America and the United Mexican States Concerning Transboundary Hydrocarbon Reservoirs in the Gulf of Mexico (adopted 20 February 2012, entered into force 16 July 2013) (US/Mexico 2012 Agreement).

78 Treaty Between Australia and the Democratic Republic of Timor-Leste establishing their Maritime Boundaries in the Timor Sea (adopted 6 March 2018), https://www.dfat.gov.au/sites/default/files/treaty-maritime-arrangements-australia-timor-leste.pdf.

ment when negotiating, adopting and implementing these instruments. Conversely, practice shows that environmental cooperation is relatively easier in delimited maritime areas compared to disputed areas since there is clarity as to which State can exercise sovereign rights and jurisdiction over activities.

The Duty to Apply a Precautionary Approach

Action to protect the environment in a disputed area is not required only when a serious environmental harm has already occurred but also to prevent the risk of such harm from occurring before the settlement of the delimitation dispute.[79] Where one State requests provisional measures to halt another State's environmentally hazardous activities in a disputed maritime area pending a decision on delimitation, the court or tribunal is often asked to make predictions: what is the likely future environmental impact of these activities? It must determine whether interim action is required in view of the factual and scientific evidence. What about cases marked by disagreement on the scientific evidence? Here, making predictions as to the nature and effect of potential environmental harm is much less certain. In several legal proceedings relating to environmental issues, parties have claimed that a precautionary approach should be adopted as a matter of customary international law, particularly in the context of sustainable use of natural resources.[80] Indeed, in *Gabčíkovo-Nagymaros*

For a discussion, *see* Nigel Bankes, 'Recent Framework Agreements for the Recognition and Development of Transboundary Hydrocarbon Resources' (2014) 29 International Journal of Marine and Coastal Law 666-689.

79 Thomas A Mensah, 'Provisional Measures in the International Tribunal for the Law of the Sea (ITLOS)' (Max Planck Institute for Comparative Public Law and International Law, 2002) 43-54; Peter Tomka and Gleider Hernandez, 'Provisional Measures in the International Tribunal for the Law of the Sea' in Holger P. Hestermeyer et al. (eds) *Coexistence, Cooperation and Solidarity: Liber Amicorum Rüdiger Wolfrum* (Brill 2011) 1763-1787; Natalie Klein, 'Provisional Measures and Provisional Arrangements' in Alex G. Elferink, Tore Henriksen and Signe Veierud Busch (eds), *Maritime Boundary Delimitation: The Case Law* (Cambridge University Press 2018) pp. 117-144.

80 'The precautionary approach entails the avoidance of activities that may threaten the environment even in the face of scientific uncertainty about the direct or indirect effects of such activities', *see Whaling in the Antarctic* (Separate Opinion of Charlesworth) p. 455; for a discussion, *see* James Cameron and Juli Abouchar, 'The Precautionary Principle: A Fundamental Principle of Law and Policy for the Protection of the Global Environment' (1991) 14(1) International and Comparative Law Review 53; the Seabed

Project, precaution was seen 'as a constituent part of the wider legal principle of sustainable development'.[81]

Moreover, in *Southern Bluefin Tuna* ITLOS considered 'scientific uncertainty' in this case in light of the precautionary approach when interpreting and applying UNCLOS.[82] Judges Laing and Treves in their separate opinions stressed that environmental legal instruments should be interpreted and applied taking account of the precautionary principle.[83] Accordingly, ITLOS' order to cease Japan's unilateral experimental fishing programme de facto prescribed precautionary measures: the lack of complete scientific certainty was not a reason for refusing to take action.

Southern Bluefin Tuna remains the only ruling to date that came close to applying a precautionary approach in provisional measures proceedings. In subsequent cases, ITLOS refrained from considering the precautionary approach when ascertaining the evidentiary standard of serious harm to the marine environment. In *MOX Plant*, for example, the potential environmental impact of a plant on the marine environment was unclear, and ITLOS declined to consider the precautionary approach when assessing the probability of a serious harm to the marine environment.[84] Judge Wolfrum considered in a separate opinion that if ITLOS accepted a lower standard of proof based on scientific uncertainty, the granting of provisional measures would become 'automatic' when arguing with some plausibility that there is a risk of serious harm to the marine environment.[85]

Disputes Chamber stated that the precautionary approach was crystallized in customary international law, *Responsibilities and obligations of States with respect to activities in the Area, Advisory Opinion,* 1 February 2011, ITLOS Reports 2011, paragraph 135; *Southern Bluefin Tuna (New Zealand v. Japan; Australia v. Japan)* (Provisional Measures) (1999) ITLOS Cases Nos 3 and 4; paragraphs 31(3), 32(2), 34(3); *MOX Plant (Ireland v. United Kingdom)* (Provisional Measures) (2001) ITLOS Case No. 10 paragraph 71; *Land Reclamation by Singapore in and around the Straits of Johor (Malaysia v. Singapore)* (Provisional Measures) (2003) ITLOS Case No. 12 paragraph 74.

81 *Gabčíkovo-Nagymaros Project (Hungary v. Slovakia)*, (Judgment of 25 September 1997) (Separate Opinion of Judge Weeramantry) repr. in (1998) 37 ILM 162 at 215.

82 *Southern Bluefin Tuna (New Zealand v. Japan; Australia v. Japan)* (Provisional Measures) (1999) ITLOS Rep 280 paragraph 74.

83 *Southern Bluefin Tuna* (Separate Opinion of Judge Laing) paragraphs 16-19 and (Separate Opinion of Judge Treves) at paragraph 9.

84 *MOX Plant (Ireland v. United Kingdom)* (Provisional Measures) (2001) ITLOS Rep 95 paragraphs 78-84.

85 *MOX Plant* (Separate Opinion of Judge Wolfrum) 3.

Another example is in *Ghana/Côte d'Ivoire* where ITLOS was not swayed by Côte d'Ivoire's reports indicating that Ghana's petroleum exploration and exploitation activities could result in environmental harm.[86] ITLOS found that '[T]he exploration and exploitation activities, as planned by Ghana, may cause irreparable prejudice to the sovereign and exclusive rights invoked by Côte d'Ivoire in the continental shelf and superjacent waters of the disputed area, before a decision on the merits is given by ITLOS, and that the risk of such prejudice is imminent'.[87] Yet, ITLOS did not order Ghana to suspend its activities (including seismic surveys, production of oil, and drilling operations that were already underway) as requested by Côte d'Ivoire. However, the Ivoirian delegation had made no serious attempt, apart from citing the above reports, to highlight in specific scientific terms the causal relationship between ongoing oil-related activities and the potential adverse effects on marine organisms including fish and marine mammals.[88] Whether due to lack of solid scientific evidence or simply by oversight, Côte d'Ivoire did not detail, for instance, the types of permanent or temporary injuries and disturbance to fish and other aquatic species known to live in or near the area in question by Ghana's operations. This could have swayed the Tribunal the other way.

Thus, a problem in the context of hazardous, or potentially hazardous, activities in disputed maritime areas may be the lack of accurate and clear scientific evidence to prove actual irreparable harm to the marine environment. Nevertheless, ITLOS constantly urges disputing parties to 'act with prudence and caution to prevent serious harm to the marine environment' (*see*, e.g., *M/V 'Louisa'*, *Ghana/Côte d'Ivoire*, *MOX Plant* and *Southern Bluefin Tuna*).[89] This highlights the influence of the precautionary approach. Preventive action to deter or mitigate an activity's adverse impact on the marine environment should be taken before it is too late – even in the

---

86 Such evidence included, among other matters, satellite images showing traces of pollution in the disputed area and reports indicating an increase in the number of whales washing up on the eastern shores of Ghana since the beginning of oil-related activities in the area, *Ghana/Côte d'Ivoire* (Provisional Measures) (Public sitting held on Sunday, 29 March 2015, at 10 am) 40.

87 *Ghana/Côte d'Ivoire* (Provisional Measures), paragraph 108(b).

88 Constantinos Yiallourides, 'Protecting and Preserving the Marine Environment in Disputed Areas: Seismic Noise and Provisional Measures of Protection' (2018) 36(2) Journal of Energy & Natural Resources Law 147, 156.

89 *M/V 'Louisa'* (2010) ITLOS Rep 58 paragraph 77; *Responsibilities and Obligations of States with respect to Activities in the Area (Advisory Opinion)* (2011) ITLOS Rep paragraphs 131-132; *Ghana/Côte d'Ivoire*, paragraph 72; *Southern Bluefin Tuna*, paragraph 77; *MOX Plant*, paragraph 84.

absence of conclusive scientific certainty as to the scope and likelihood of such adverse impact.

The Duty to Conduct an Environmental Impact Assessment and Monitor Impacts

Another environmental legal obligation applicable in disputed maritime areas relates to the requirement to undertake an environmental impact assessment (EIA). An EIA is defined by the United Nations Environmental Programme (UNEP) as 'the process of identifying, predicting, interpreting and communicating the potential impacts that a proposed project or plan may have on the environment'.[90] Per Principle 17 of the Rio Declaration, an EIA, 'as a national instrument, shall be undertaken for proposed activities that are likely to have a significant adverse impact on the environment and are subject to a decision of a competent national authority'.[91] Article 206 of UNCLOS enshrines the requirement to carry out an EIA of planned activities where States have 'reasonable grounds for believing' that significant harm to the marine environment may result.[92] The requirement to undertake an EIA has been incorporated into many international, regional, and national legal instruments and is now 'a general obligation under customary international law'.[93] In the *South China Sea Arbitration*, the Tribunal found that the obligation to communicate the results of the EIA is 'absolute', even while States maintain discretion as to the content and process of the EIA.[94]

States in disputed maritime areas have not contested the existence of a duty to undertake an EIA. However, Article 206 of UNCLOS does not stipulate what is required in an EIA. Unlike other UNCLOS environmental provisions (such as Articles 207–211), Article 206 does not refer to international rules and standards. Therefore, in practice, the adequacy of an

---

90 Goals and Principles of Environmental Impact Assessment of the United Nations Environmental Programme, December 1987, UN Doc. UNEP/WG.152/4 Annex.
91 Principle 17, Rio Declaration.
92 Article 206 in conjunction with Article 205, UNCLOS.
93 Convention on Environmental Impact Assessment in a Transboundary Context, Espoo (signed 25 February 1991, entered into force 10 September 1997) 1989 United Nations Treaty Series 309; Draft Article 7, Draft Articles on Prevention of Transboundary Harm from Hazardous Activities, Report of the ILC on the Work of its Fifty-Third Session, UNGAOR, UN Doc. A/56/10; *Responsibilities and Obligations of States Sponsoring Persons and Entities with Respect to Activities in the Area* (Request for Advisory Opinion submitted to the Seabed Disputes Chamber) [2011] ITLOS Rep 10 paragraph 145.
94 *South China Sea Arbitration,* paragraph 948.

EIA and other risk-mitigating or pollution control measures taken in the undelimited area can be disputed. *Ghana/Côte d'Ivoire* illustrates that point. Côte d'Ivoire requested provisional measures under Article 290(1) of UNCLOS for Ghana to suspend immediately all oil activities in the disputed maritime area.[95] Ghana countered that EIAs had been carried out, argued that its petroleum licensing regulations were of the highest standards, and cited scientific reports to rebut any allegations that the marine environment was at risk.[96] The dispute in *MOX Plant* did not relate to boundary delimitation but to the operation of the Sellafield nuclear facility in north-east England and its possible adverse impacts on the marine environment to the Irish Sea. There, the United Kingdom argued that 'very extensive security precautions in terms of the protection of the Sellafield site' were in place.[97] In *Land Reclamation*, Malaysia argued that Singapore's actions in and around the Straits of Johor breached Malaysia's sovereignty and damaged the marine environment, including by reducing the catch of Malaysian fishermen. Singapore stated that 'the necessary steps were taken to examine possible adverse impacts on the surrounding waters'.[98] In *Ghana/Côte d'Ivoire, MOX Plant* and *Land Reclamation*, ITLOS noted the assurances given by Ghana, the United Kingdom, and Singapore that their activities were undertaken in a transparent manner and followed best industry practice and the highest international standards.[99] ITLOS did not comment on their adequacy.

Are international courts and tribunals therefore willing to review the effectiveness of preventive and risk-mitigating mechanisms or does such assessment fall squarely within the initiating State's discretion? This question was answered partly in *Pulp Mills*, which concerned a dispute between Argentina and Uruguay on the construction of pulp mills on the Uruguay River and its potential transboundary impacts on the shared waters of the

95 *Ghana/Côte d'Ivoire* (Provisional Measures), paragraph 56.
96 *Ghana/Côte d'Ivoire* (Provisional Measures), paragraph 66.
97 *MOX Plant*, paragraph 76.
98 *Land Reclamation*, paragraph 94.
99 *Ghana/Côte d'Ivoire* (Provisional Measures), paragraphs 56 and 66; for a discussion, Yoshifumi Tanaka, 'Unilateral Exploration and Exploitation of Natural Resources in Disputed Areas: A Note on the Ghana/Côte d'Ivoire Order of 25 April 2015 before the Special Chamber of ITLOS' 46(4) Ocean Development and International Law (2015) 315, 325; Constantinos Yiallourides, 'Protecting and Preserving the Marine Environment in Disputed Areas: Seismic Noise and Provisional Measures of Protection' (2018) 36(2) Journal of Energy & Natural Resources Law 141, 158.

river.[100] The parties disagreed on the scope and content of the EIA that Uruguay ought to have carried out. The International Court of Justice (ICJ) held that an EIA must take place *prior* to any operation and that continuous monitoring of environmental impact is required for long-term operations. Nevertheless, the ICJ suggested that the scope and content of the EIA could only be determined by the State carrying out the activities and in light of the specific circumstances at hand. According to the ICJ:

> [I]t is for each State to determine in its domestic legislation or in the authorisation process for the project, the specific content of the environmental impact assessment required in each case, having regard to the nature and magnitude of the proposed development and its likely adverse impact on the environment as well as to the need to exercise due diligence in conducting such an assessment.[101]

These elements do not indicate the precise consent the EIA must contain, how it should be conducted, and by whom (independent body, State agency, private entity, etc.). As the ICJ noted 'general international law [does not] specify the scope and content of an environmental impact assessment'.[102]

In *Costa Rica v. Nicaragua*, Judge ad hoc Dugard clarified that an environmental assessment should include: (a) an assessment of the risk involved in an activity and the harm to which the risk could lead; (b) an evaluation of the activity's potential transboundary harmful impact; and (c) an assessment of the activity's effects only on persons and property and on the environment of other States.[103] The Arbitral Tribunal in the *South China Sea* reviewed China's legislative standards and ruled that the statements and reports published by the Chinese authorities were 'far less comprehensive' than EIAs reviewed by other international courts and tribunals.[104] Yet, the Tribunal did not specify the meaning of 'comprehensiveness'.

---

100 *Pulp Mills on the River Uruguay (Argentina v. Uruguay)* [2010] ICJ Rep 14; for a commentary, *see* Cymie R. Payne, 'Pulp Mills on the River Uruguay (Argentina v. Uruguay)' (2011) 105(1) American Journal of International Law 94.
101 *Pulp Mills on the River Uruguay (Argentina v. Uruguay)* (Judgment) [2010] ICJ Rep 14 paragraph 205.
102 *Pulp Mills on the River Uruguay (Argentina v. Uruguay)* (Judgment) [2010] ICJ Rep 14 paragraph 205.
103 *Certain Activities Carried out by Nicaragua in the Border Area (Costa Rica v. Nicaragua) Construction of a Road in Costa Rica along the San Juan River (Nicaragua v. Costa Rica) (Judgment)* (Separate Opinion of Judge ad hoc Dugard) [2015] ICJ Rep paragraph 18.
104 *South China Sea Arbitration*, paragraphs 989-990.

An integral part of the duty to conduct an EIA is the obligation to monitor environmental impacts. This is particularly important for long-term projects, such as extraction and site restoration.[105] The Deepwater Horizon incident in the Gulf of Mexico, which caused harm to persons and the environment, illustrates the importance of the monitoring requirement. The National Commission which investigated the incident found that the US had failed to regulate and monitor hydrocarbon activities.[106]

As with EIAs in general, the relevant UNCLOS provisions do not clarify the monitoring required. Article 204 of UNCLOS obliges States to 'endeavour as far as practicable ... to observe, measure, evaluate and analyse ... the risks or effects of pollution on the marine environment' and to 'keep under surveillance the effects of any activities which they permit or in which they engage in order to determine whether they are likely to pollute the marine environment'.[107] Judge Weeramantry stated in a separate opinion to *Gabčíkovo-Nagymaros* that there must be 'a continuing assessment and evaluation as long as the project is in operation ... whether the treaty expressly so provides or not'.[108] The ICJ in *Pulp Mills* endorsed this view, holding that 'once operations have started and, where necessary, throughout the life of the project continuous monitoring of its effects on the environment shall be undertaken'.[109] Several JDAs require monitoring and follow-up.[110]

In sum, the existence of the duty to undertake an EIA and monitor environmental impacts in disputed maritime areas is uncontested. Yet, the existence of a boundary dispute may complicate the application of this

---

105 For a discussion, Rachael Lorna Johnstone, *Offshore Oil and Gas Development in the Arctic under International Law* (2014 BRILL) pp. 179-181.

106 Report of the National Commission on the BP Deepwater Horizon Oil Spill and Offshore Drilling to the President, Deep Water: The Gulf Oil Disaster and the Future of Offshore Drilling (January 2011), https://www.nrt.org/sites/2/files/GPO-OILCOMMISSION.pdf, 82-85; A. Boyle, 'Transboundary Air Pollution: A Tale of Two Paradigms' in Shunmugam Jayakumar et al. (eds) *Transboundary Pollution: Evolving Issues of International Law and Policy* (Edward Elgar Publishing 2015) pp. 239-240.

107 Article 205 of UNCLOS obligates States to publish reports of the results from such monitoring.

108 *Case Concerning the Gabčíkovo-Nagymaros Project (Hungary v. Slovakia)* (Separate Opinion of Weeramantry) [1997] ICJ 88, 112 (citing *Trail Smelter Arbitration (United States v. Canada)* (1941) 3 RIAA 1905).

109 *Pulp Mills*, paragraphs 205-266.

110 For example, Nigeria-Sao Tome and Principe Joint Development Authority, https://resourcegovernance.org/sites/default/files/Petroleum%20Regulations%20for%20Jo int%20Development%20Authority.pdf; Malaysia/Thailand MoU (1979); Senegal/Guinea-Bissau Agreement (1993).

duty. Disputing States often carry out EIAs before conducting potentially hazardous activities in, or in respect of, the disputed area. However, they maintain a wide level of discretion as to the environmental standards and impact assessment procedures used in that regard. Let us take a hypothetical situation: State A unilaterally decides to build a heavy-lift crane structure to carry out a ship-to-ship transfer of crude oil in a maritime area also claimed by State B. State B argues that such activities pose significant risks to the marine environment. State A will be able to rebut State B's claim by showing that it has undertaken and communicated an EIA, and that this EIA is adequate to deter or mitigate any potential adverse effects on the marine environment.

Concluding Remarks

States planning economic activities in disputed maritime areas must comply with their obligations regarding the protection and preservation of the marine environment. These activities must be conducted in conformity with international environmental laws and regulations. First, States should assess the environmental effects of all planned activities. Second, States must consult with and inform neighbouring States of the risks, as well as measures taken to control or mitigate possible adverse impacts on the marine environment.

Potentially affected States may bring claims against other States for any breach of environmental law obligations. Pending consideration of the merits, they may request provisional measures to preserve and protect the marine environment in the disputed area under Article 290 of UNCLOS. Such claims and associated provisional measure requests may be brought independent of the claims relating to the preservation of the parties' sovereign rights in the disputed areas or to maritime boundary delimitation. Where the complaining party adequately presents the adverse effects of a given activity on the marine environment in the disputed area, provisional measures of protection may be granted under Article 290 of UNCLOS. Provisional measures may thus provide a remedy to the complaining party. However, certain commercial activities are particularly widespread among the industry and States, for example, seismic exploration surveys and fishing activities. Obtaining a provisional measures order in such cases requires something more specific than general considerations of environmental harm. An injunction seeking to prohibit all economic activities pending the final determination of the boundary is unlikely to succeed, even where risks to the marine environment are known or plausible. A more specific submission, pending resolution of the maritime boundary, would be to seek strict monitoring, an independent expert assessment, and exchange of information and cooperation over environmental matters. Such cooperative arrangements have been made as provisional practical arrangements in maritime boundary negotiations under Articles 74(3) and 83(3) of UNCLOS; analogous measures could be ordered under Article 290 of UNCLOS.[111]

Courts and tribunals often struggle with complex issues posed by environmental disputes with scientific and technical components. Experts may play an important role.[112] In the *South China Sea Arbitration*, the opinions of independent experts were considered in assessing the environmental impact of China's island construction activities. Indeed, technically complex cases depend on experts properly trained to evaluate these issues.[113] For example, ITLOS in *Land Reclamation* prescribed that Malaysia and Singapore promptly establish a group of independent experts with the mandate to: (i) conduct a study on the effects of Singapore's land reclamation and (ii) propose, as appropriate, measures to deal with any adverse effects of such land reclamation.[114] Therefore, using independent experts to ascertain environmental impacts or foreseeable risks and subsequently monitor such risks is an option worth considering by States to protect the environment in a disputed maritime area.

---

111 Natalie Klein, 'Provisional Measures and Provisional Arrangements in Maritime Boundary Disputes' (2006) 21(4) International Journal of Marine and Coastal Law 423-460.

112 Speech by ITLOS President Judge Jin-Hyun Paik, 'Disputes Involving Scientific and Technical Matters and ITLOS' (New Knowledge and Changing Circumstances in the Law of the Sea Conference, Reykjavik 28-30 June 2018), https://www.itlos.org/fileadmin/itlos/documents/statements_of_president/paik/Iceland_Conference_President_Keynote_Speech_Final_22August2018.pdf; Lucas Carlos Lima, 'The Use of Experts by the International Tribunal for the Law of the Sea and Annex VII Arbitral Tribunals' in Angela Del Vecchio and Roberto Virzo (eds) *Interpretations of the United Nations Convention on the Law of the Sea by International Courts and Tribunals* (Springer 2019) 407.

113 Speech by ITLOS President Judge Jin-Hyun Paik, 'Disputes Involving Scientific and Technical Matters and ITLOS' (New Knowledge and Changing Circumstances in the Law of the Sea Conference, Reykjavik 28-30 June 2018).

114 *Land Reclamation by Singapore in and Around the Straits of Johor (Malaysia v. Singapore)* (Provisional Measures) (2003) ITLOS Case No. 12 paragraph 106.

Grappling with Plastic: An Increasingly Inflexible Legal Issue

Adam R. Fox, Chassica Soo & Jonathan S. King
Squire Patton Boggs (US) LLP, Los Angeles, CA and Denver, CO,
United States

Introduction

"Could the answer to our age-old, philosophical question, 'Why are we here?' be 'Plastic.'"[1]

The production of man-made plastics—a wide range of malleable, synthetic or semi-synthetic organic compounds—began in the early nineteenth century, and the last several decades have witnessed virtually exponential growth in its production, approaching 16 trillion pounds of the material in the aggregate. Today, the plastics industry produces about 1 million tons daily, and some industry observers predict the quadrupling of that figure by 2050.[2] Based on these estimates, some surmise, plastic production may by that time account for about one-fifth of the world's oil consumption, and contribute so much debris to Earth's oceans that it could literally outweigh the fish in the sea.[1]

Given the sheer volume of plastic that has been and will be produced, it is unsurprising that many people worldwide are increasingly asking tough questions about plastic production and waste management practices, with the industry stakeholders, scientists, politicians, regulators, and environmental activists all bringing to bear different perspectives and potential answers. Recently, much of their attention has focused in particular on microplastics—minute fragments of plastics found in nearly every ecosystem, ranging from polar ice to the bottom of the Mariana Trench to the guts of living beings.[3] Although evidence of the toxicity and impact of microplastics on the environment or on human health is still nascent and

---

1 *See* George Carlin https://www.youtube.com/watch?v=NBRquiS1pis; *see also* https://www.youtube.com/watch?v=eMtLdE5Zq-8.
2 Industry Agenda, *The New Plastics Economy—Rethinking the Future of Plastics. World Economic Forum* (January 2016). *See* http://www3.weforum.org/docs/WEF_The_New_Plastics_Economy.pdf.
3 Kanhai, LDK, Gardfeldt, K, Krumpen, T, Thompson, RC and O'Connor, I (2020) "Microplastics in Sea Ice and Seawater beneath Ice Floes from the Arctic Ocean" (10) *Scientific Reports* 5004.

inconclusive,[4] it has also started to give rise to litigation and regulatory efforts.

Responding to these trends, this chapter examines recent scientific and regulatory developments concerning microplastics as well as the growing but limited controversies addressing its role in the law.

State of the Science: Microplastics Are Everywhere – Are They Harmful to Environmental and Human Health?

Microplastics are generally defined as plastic particles fewer than 5 mm in diameter. In other words, any piece of plastic smaller than a lentil. They come in a myriad of shapes, sizes, and chemical structures, but are classified into two general categories. Primary microplastics are those deliberately manufactured for a specific purpose, such as cosmetic micro-beads, industrial abrasives, or precursor plastic pellets used in the manufacture of high-grade plastic materials. Secondary microplastics result from the breakdown of larger plastic products by physical, chemical, or biological degradation resulting in fragments of microplastics (<5 μm) and nanoplastics (<100 nm). Examples of secondary microplastics include fibers released from common abrasion of synthetic textiles and the wear and tear on the tires and brake pads of automobiles and even bicycles. Secondary microplastics can form on land and from weathering of marine plastic debris in the ocean. Thus far, microplastics have been found in both marine and freshwater environments,[5] as well as in soil, air, and underground aquifers. Microplastics have also been found in tap and bottled water, beer, and table salt.

Despite the widespread distribution of microplastics in the environment, limited information exists on their global distribution patterns. There is also a lack of universal measurement standards and reporting methods that might enable different parties to accurately assess the abundance and type of microplastics in the environment and thereby come to an agreement

---

4 In its Microplastics Expert Workshop Report, EPA concluded "Microplastics pollution is complex and ubiquitous, and microplastics research is in its infancy." (https://www.epa.gov/sites/production/files/2018-03/documents/microplastics_expert_work shop_report_final_12-4-17.pdf at 21)

5 It has been estimated that "approximately 90% of the plastics in the pelagic marine environment are microplastics." (Eriksen et al., 2013; Browne et al., 2010; Thompson et al., 2004)

about facts before advancing policy choices to best address them.[6] Numerous observers at least agree about these shortcomings, and thus joined a chorus calling for uniform testing and analysis and encouraging efforts in the scientific community to develop methods and tools to collect, analyze, and report micro and nanoplastics in a standardized manner.[7]

And yet there also remains a lack of peer-reviewed literature addressing these subjects and on the critical question concerning the prospect for adverse impacts of microplastics on the environment or on human health. Although many have speculated—some in very confident and conclusive terms—that microplastics have detrimental impacts on ecosystems and the health of plants and animals, the evidence remains inconclusive.[8] With respect to nanoplastics specifically, members of the scientific community readily observe that there remains a need for more information to assess possible effects that may be significantly different from any impacts that may be caused by larger microplastics.[9]

In the face of this uncertainty, the undisputed ubiquity of microplastics contamination stands out and calls out for further understanding about the impact of microplastics exposure to virtually every biota. Potential hazards to living organisms from microplastics are theorized to come in three forms: damage caused by physical particles, chemical toxicity, and exposure to microbial pathogens.[10]

To date, most of the research on the effects of microplastics exposure has focused on marine organisms, particularly invertebrates. Results of these studies vary based on study design and model organism. Nonetheless, some publications associate exposure to microplastics in marine organisms with behavioral, metabolic, and developmental changes, altered immune responses, localized inflammation, and disruption of microbiome

---

6 Koelmans, AA; Mohamed Nor, NH; Hermsen, E; Kooi, M; Mintenig, SM and De France, J (2019) "Microplastics in Freshwaters and Drinking Water: Critical Review and Assessment of Data Quality" (155) *Water Research* 410. *See* https://www.ncbi.nlm.nih.gov/pmc/articles/PMC6449537/.

7 Gomiero, A; Strafella, P and Fabi, G (2018) "From Macroplastic to Microplastic Litter: Occurrence, Composition, Source Identification and Interaction with Aquatic Organisms. Experiences from the Adriatic Sea," *Plastics in the Environment*, available at: https://www.intechopen.com/books/plastics-in-the-environment/from-macroplastic-to-microplastic-litter-occurrence-composition-source-identification-and-interactio.

8 State Water Resources Control Board Resolution No. 2020-0021, at paragraph 5.

9 "Nanoplastic Should Be Better Understood" (2019) 14 *Nature Nanotechnology* 299. *See* https://www.nature.com/articles/s41565-019-0437-7.

10 WHO Information Sheet (2019), *Microplastics in Drinking-Water*, https://www.who.int/water_sanitation_health/water-quality/guidelines/microplastics-in-dw-information-sheet/en/.

compositions.[11] Other publications have documented many of these per-
turbations as well in larger marine vertebrates such as fish, turtles, seals,
dolphins, and whales.[12] Scientists are engaged in an ongoing effort to study
the potential health risks to marine animals and humans by understanding
which types of microplastics are more likely to present real world risks of
toxic exposure based upon how much of those types marine life actually
ingests.[13] The toxicity of many microplastics may be caused by the leaching of endogenous chemicals commonly used as additives in the manufacturing process of the plastics, or their having absorbed regulated chemicals
like polychlorinated biphenyls (PCBs), but parsing out these potential
contributors to any toxic effects presents challenges.[14]

These studies fail to evaluate meaningfully any risk of various microplastics to human health for a number of reasons, including differences in
experimental design, particularly the type of microplastics exposure used
in selected studies. Indeed, scientists have legitimate questions surrounding whether many of these laboratory studies recapitulate real life exposures, as environmental microplastics are likely more complex in chemical
composition, more unique in shape, etched to a greater degree and perhaps

---

11 Limonta, G; Mancia, A; Benkhalqui, A; Bertolucci, C; Abelli, L; Fossi, MC and Panti,
    C (2019) "Microplastics Induce Transcriptional Changes, Immune Response and
    Behavioral Alterations in Adult Zebrafish" (9) *Scientific Reports*, available at: https://
    www.ncbi.nlm.nih.gov/pmc/articles/PMC6823372/. Yong, CQY; Valiyaveetill, S and
    Tang, BL (2020) "Toxicity of Microplastics and Nanoplastics in Mammalian Systems"
    (17) *International Journal of Environmental Research and Public Health*, available at:
    https://www.ncbi.nlm.nih.gov/pmc/articles/PMC7084551/. Wang, W; Gao, H; Jin, S;
    Li, R and Na, G (2019) "The Ecotoxicological Effects of Microplastics on Aquatic
    Food Web, from Primary Producer to Human: A Review" (173) *Ecotoxicology and
    Environmental Safety* 110, available at: https://pubmed.ncbi.nlm.nih.gov/30771654/.
12 Ajith, N; Arumugam, S; Parthasarathy, S; Manupoori, S and Janakiraman, S (2020)
    "Global Distribution of Microplastics and Its Impact on Marine Environment—A
    Review" (27) *Environmental Science and Pollution Research* 25970, available at:
    https://link.springer.com/article/10.1007/s11356-020-09015-5#Abs1. Hale, RC; See-
    ley, ME; Guardia, MJL; Mai, L and Zeng, EY (2020) "A Global Perspective on
    Microplastics" (125) *Journal of Geophysical Research: Oceans* e2018JC014719
    (https://agupubs.onlinelibrary.wiley.com/doi/full/10.1029/2018JC014719). Yong   et
    al., *supra* note 11.
13 Woods Hole Oceanographic Institution, Marine Microplastics (last visited Nov. 2,
    2020)   https://www.whoi.edu/know-your-ocean/ocean-topics/pollution/marine-micro
    plastics/.
14 Campanale, C; Massarelli, C; Savino, I; Locaputo, V and Uricchio, VF (2020) "A
    Detailed Review Study on Potential Effects of Microplastics and Additives of Concern
    on Human Health" (17) *International Journal of Environmental Research and Public
    Health*, available at: https://www.ncbi.nlm.nih.gov/pmc/articles/PMC7068600/.

smaller than those commonly employed in lab studies.[15] Physical differences may also prove highly relevant, as the chemical composition of microplastics as well as the physical shape and size can result in profoundly different effects on organisms, and existing experiments do not adequately address the added effects of sorbed chemicals and biofilm formation—both significant issues with environmental microplastics.

Studies on the presence of microplastics in non-marine organisms, including humans, are far fewer, and studies of actual impacts of microplastics to non-marine organisms are even more limited. Ample evidence demonstrates that humans face consistent exposure to microplastics, through inhalation, ingestion (drinking water and consuming many foods shown to contain microplastics), and even via skin contact.[16] Indeed, microplastics have been found in human fecal samples, human tissue samples, and plastics monomers have been identified in blood, urine, and crossing the placenta.[17]

Despite a growing concern about human and animal exposure to micro and nanoplastics,[18] there remains a paucity of research on the health impacts of microplastics, particularly in mammals. A number of recent studies on mouse show disruption of the gut microbiota as well as effects on cellular and metabolic processes by micro and nanoplastics.[19] Due to the obvious challenges of performing experiments on human subjects, a controlled analysis of microplastics effects is virtually impossible, and even limited *in-vitro* work using human cells has offered only inconclusive results.[20] Although some groups have reported cytotoxic effects, their

---

15 Paul-Pont, I; Tallec, K; Gonzalez-Fernandez, C; Lambert, C; Vincent, D; Mazurais, D; Zambonino-Infante, J-L; Brotons, G; Lagarde, F; Fabioux, C; Soudant, P and Huvet, A (2018) "Constraints and Priorities for Conducting Experimental Exposures of Marine Organisms to Microplastics" (5) *Frontiers in Marine Science*, available at: https://www.frontiersin.org/articles/10.3389/fmars.2018.00252/full.
16 Campanale et al., *supra* note 14.
17 Müller, JE; Meyer, N; Santamaria, CG; Schumacher, A; Luque, EH; Zenclussen, ML; Rodriguez, HA and Zenclussen, AC (2018) "Bisphenol A Exposure during Early Pregnancy Impairs Uterine Spiral Artery Remodeling and Provokes Intrauterine Growth Restriction in Mice" (8) *Scientific Reports* 9196, available at: https://www.nature.com/articles/s41598-018-27575-y. Cox, KD; Covernton, GA; Davies, HL; Dower, JF; Juanes, F and Dudas, SE (2019) "Human Consumption of Microplastics" (53) *Environmental Science & Technology* 7068, available at: https://pubs.acs.org/doi/abs/10.1021/acs.est.9b01517. Wright, SL and Kelly, FJ (2017) "Plastic and Human Health: A Micro Issue?" (51) *Environmental Science & Technology* 6634, available at: https://pubs.acs.org/doi/10.1021/acs.est.7b00423.
18 Jiang et al. "Health Impacts of Environmental Contamination of Micro- and Nanoplastics," https://pubmed.ncbi.nlm.nih.gov/32664857/.
19 Yong et al., *supra* note 11.
20 Campanale et al., *supra* note 14.

studies evaluated exposure to extremely high amounts of microplastics unlikely to be encountered in a real world setting; lower dose exposure resulted in immunologic responses but not in significant toxicity.[21] *Such studies* suggest that exposure to microplastics may not represent a significant health risk.[22] Large long-term epidemiological studies are underway as well as to address exposure to known toxins including plastic components.[23] Findings from this work suggest that a person's unique exposures influence the compounds that might make their way into our bodies, as this study found that mother-child pairs had shared chemical compounds in their urine resulting from shared home environments, diets, and consumer products suggesting that specific products will have different impacts on health and epidemiological studies may be able to hone in on the origin of certain exposures.[24] Inconclusive results and inadequate information have major global research entities calling for proposals on comprehensive and stringent microplastics studies.[25]

After conducting a meta-analysis of studies of microplastics in drinking water, the World Health Organization (WHO) stated that the limited data currently available suggests chemicals and biofilms associated with microplastics in drinking water "pose a low concern for human health."[26] Moreover, the WHO found, "there is insufficient information to draw firm conclusions on the toxicity related to the physical hazard of plastic particles," and "no reliable information suggests it is a concern."[27] Nevertheless, the WHO proclaimed it "urgently need[s] to know more about the

---

21 WHO (2019), *Microplastics in Drinking-Water*, available at: https://www.who.int/water_sanitation_health/publications/microplastics-in-drinking-water/en/.
22 Yong et al., *supra* note 11.
23 Schwedler, G. et al. (2017) "Human Biomonitoring Pilot Study DEMOCOPHES in Germany: Contribution to a Harmonized European Approach" (220) *International Journal of Hygiene and Environmental Health* 686.
24 Koppen, G. et al. (2019) "Mothers and Children Are Related, Even in Exposure to Chemicals Present in Common Consumer Products" (175) *Environmental Research* 297.
25 Hwang, J; Choi, D; Han, S; Jung, SY; Choi, J and Hong, J (2020) "Potential Toxicity of Polystyrene Microplastic Particles" (10) *Scientific Reports* 7391.
26 WHO (2019), *Information Sheet: Microplastics in Drinking-Water*, available at: http://www.who.int/water_sanitation_health/water-quality/guidelines/microplastics-in-dw-information-sheet/en/.
27 WHO (2019), *Information Sheet: Microplastics in Drinking-Water*, available at: http://www.who.int/water_sanitation_health/water-quality/guidelines/microplastics-in-dw-information-sheet/en/.

health impact of microplastics because they are everywhere"[28] and micro-plastics exposure impacts remain relatively unstudied. A 2019 report from the European Commission's Science Advice for Policy similarly stated that "the absence of evidence of microplastics risks currently does not allow on to conclude that risk is either present or absent with sufficient certainty."[29] It further stated "[t]he best available evidence suggests that microplastics and nanoplastics do not pose widespread risk to humans and the environment."[30]

Challenges to Studying Potential Human Health Effects of Microplastics

The confounding and inconclusive results coming out of microplastics studies should not be surprising as there are a multitude of challenges to studying the impacts of microplastics. As previously discussed, the term "microplastics" lacks precision and is a catch-all for an incredibly diverse scope of materials that vary in shape, size, and chemical composition. Furthermore, the actual impact of any given microplastics may vary based on environmental conditions, what organic and inorganic substances it may be carrying along with it, the concentration of contamination, and the circumstances of exposure.

It should not be overlooked that "microplastics" are more often than not degraded microplastics on the path to becoming nanoplastics, and as this progression, occurs they may leach additives or sorb environmental toxins, form sharp edges or be dulled into innocuous sizes and shapes, all the while they will be moving through changing ecosystems and varying conditions. Determining the specific effects of something so varied and dynamic, either in the field or in the laboratory, presents tremendous challenges to those who study them. It will take a massive effort to parse out these complexities, which will be necessary for producers and consumers to be informed on the true impacts of micro and nanoplastics.

28 WHO (2019), *Calls for More Research into Microplastics and a Crackdown on Plastic Pollution*, available at: https://www.who.int/news/item/22-08-2019-who-calls-for-more-research-into-microplastics-and-a-crackdown-on-plastic-pollution.

29 SAPEA (2019), *Evidence on Microplastics Does Not yet Point to Widespread Risk, Say Europe's Top Scientists*, available at: https://www.sapea.info/microplastics-launch/.

30 SAPEA (2019), *A Scientific Perspective on Microplastics in Nature and Society*, available at: https://doi.org/10.26356/microplastics.

Microplastics Do Not Exist in a Void: Contaminating the Contaminants

Further complicating the issue is the fact that many of the lab studies on microplastics have used pure compounds composed of a single chemical. Microplastics found in the environment frequently have additives, which may have their own independent health consequences. Many commonly used additives are known to be toxic, causing scientists to wonder whether microplastics could serve as an exposure pathway for toxic compounds. Common additives include regulated compounds such as PCBs, heavy metals, flame retardants, and phthalates, all of which have documented adverse health effects in humans.[31] The risk of such additives leaching out of micro or nanoplastics is itself a highly variable process, likely influenced by many factors including but not limited to the age of the plastic, the wear on the structure, the pH of the environment, etc. It is important to keep in mind, "[d]ifferent plastic types have different toxicities."[32]

There is also scientific interest in whether microplastics can sorb environmental constituents known to be toxic to humans and animals. Physical properties of microplastics enhance their ability to sorb ambient persistent organic pollutants (POPs)—with some studies showing concentrations of certain chemicals sorbed to plastic microparticles being up to six orders of magnitude greater than the concentration of that chemical in the surrounding solution.[33] In addition to POPs, plastics have been found to sorb antimicrobials and other pharmaceutical compounds.

Finally, there is concern that microplastics may act as vectors for pathogens as they have a unique capacity to form biofilms. Coral reefs exposed to microplastics with biofilms appear to ingest the microplastics and expire due to microbial infection.[34] The impacts of these interactions are again complicated—the rate of sorption may be influenced by a given

---

31 Campanale et al., *supra* note 14.

32 *Microplastics: A Big Problem for the Environment*, available at: https://www.horiba. com/en_en/science-in-action/microplastics-a-big-problem-for-the-environment/.

33 Menéndez-Pedriza, A and Jaumot, J (2020) "Interaction of Environmental Pollutants with Microplastics: A Critical Review of Sorption Factors, Bioaccumulation and Ecotoxicological Effects" (8) *Toxics*, available at: https://www.ncbi.nlm.nih.gov/pmc/ articles/PMC7355763/.

34 Rotjan, RD; Sharp, KH; Gauthier, AE; Yelton, R; Lopez, EMB; Carilli, J; Kagan, JC and Urban-Rich, J (2019) "Patterns, Dynamics and Consequences of Microplastic Ingestion by the Temperate Coral, Astrangia Poculata" (286) *Proceedings of the Royal Society B: Biological Sciences* 20190726, available at: https://royalsocietypublishing. org/doi/10.1098/rspb.2019.0726.

microplastics' physical properties (size, age, weathering, plastic type, etc.) as well as by the chemical properties of the pollutants and the environment in which the two interact.

The complexity of understanding the science of microplastics these questions is highlighted by the inconsistent findings of studies to date. Indeed, some studies have proposed synergistic detrimental effects of plastics and sorbed chemicals, while others have reported no increased damage caused by these interactions,[35] and still others surmise that depending on the conditions, some microplastics in the environment may even reduce the bioaccumulation of toxic contaminants in animals.[36] These mixed results have resulted in the general conclusion that the scientific community must, as a threshold matter, develop standardized testing methodologies to better understand the presence and effects of various microplastics in different scenarios. Meanwhile, the regulatory community, informed by the evolving science, faces an equally daunting task to define and regulate, where appropriate, microplastics that are found to pose a threat, if any.

Regulatory Framework

Even though they are understood to be a great source of pollution in virtually all media, microplastics are to date largely unregulated. Regulating secondary microplastics is especially difficult because they lack any sort of uniformity and emanate from virtually anything plastic. Perhaps in large part because the release of secondary microplastics is practically unmanageable as long as larger plastics are used and circulating through the economy, environmentalists and activists are focused on limiting the production of plastic.[37] Moreover current definitions of microplastics lack the nuance to address the fact that they exist in virtually limitless shapes,

---

35 *Microplastics as Vectors for Bioaccumulation of Hydrophobic Organic Chemicals in the Marine Environment: A State-of-the-Science Review—PubMed*, available at: https://pubmed.ncbi.nlm.nih.gov/27093569/.

36 Wang, J; Coffin, S; Schlenk, D and Gan, J (2020) "Accumulation of HOCs via Precontaminated Microplastics by Earthworm Eisenia Fetida in Soil" (54) *Environmental Science & Technology* 11220, available at: https://pubs.acs.org/doi/10.1021/acs.est.0c02922.

37 *See* Nov. 19, 2019 Opposition Letter to Save Our Seas 2.0, Senate Bill 1982 available at acoel.org/Site/DrawMembers.as.

sizes, and chemical compositions. To date, the only definition of micro-plastics by any regulatory body of which the authors are aware is the definition California in the United States (U.S.) recently promulgated under its Safe Drinking Water Act. Thus, regulating microplastics may also prove difficult because the term represents such a broad category of pollutants.

Despite scant regulation of microplastics, an urgent global push to better understand and then to reduce their release into the environment is mounting.[38] Painstaking discussions and scientific and policy disagree-ments over the most effective and appropriate manner to address micro-plastics issues are likely. Environmentalists are gravitating heavily toward halting plastic production and consumption to the greatest possible ex-tent,[39] and some in the scientific community opine that "extraordinary efforts to transform the global plastics economy are needed."[40] Other environmental groups call for less drastic measures but still stringent regulations on plastic production and concerted cleanup efforts.[41] Industry, meanwhile, is focused on better waste management practices, while regu-lators and scientists undertake exhaustive efforts to bolster their knowledge and understanding of issues that will inform the best policy solutions.

International Trade and Treaty Issues

From a global waste management perspective, changes worldwide and to international treaties affecting plastic waste disposal are occurring at an

---

38 In the fall of 2019, the WHO called for more research into microplastics contamination and the potential impacts on human health (https://www.who.int/news-room/detail/22-08-2019-who-calls-for-more-research-into-microplastics-and-a-crackdown-on-plastic-pollution#:~:text=The%20World%20Health%20Organization%20(WHO,to%20micro plastics%20in%20drinking%2Dwater). In addition, the National Science Foundation ("NSF") released a letter in March of 2020 encouraging proposals to address looming questions regarding micro and nanoplastics pollution and its impacts (https://www. nsf.gov/pubs/2020/nsf20050/nsf20050.pdf). California, ever at the vanguard of envi-ronmental lawmaking, is similarly seeking a broad spectrum of information from all corners of the globe to assess the microplastics problem and to develop a comprehensive strategy to address it.

39 Winnie W.Y. Lau, Evaluating scenarios toward zero plastic pollution (September 2020), *see* https://science.sciencemag.org/content/369/6510/1455; https://theconversation. com/recycling-isnt-enough-the-worlds-plastic-pollution-crisis-is-only-getting-worse-144175.

40 Stephanie B. Borrelle, *Predicted Growth in Plastic Waste Exceeds Efforts to Mitigate Plastic Pollution* (September 2020), *see* https://science.sciencemag.org/content/369/ 6510/1515.

41 One Percent for the Planet, *Nonprofits Fighting Plastic Pollution* (July 2020), *see* https://www.onepercentfortheplanet.org/stories/nonprofits-fighting-plastic.

almost frenetic pace. With the U.S. having never fully developed a market for recycling to match its waste output, China has historically been the world's largest importer of recycled materials,[42] but its efforts to scale back the amount of waste flowing into it from abroad threaten to disrupt waste management, including plastic disposal practices, in developed countries like the U.S. In another disruption to the international movement of plastic waste, the parties to the Basel Convention in 2019 adopted plastic scrap and waste amendments to expand the Convention's controls on trans-boundary shipment of plastic waste for disposal or recycling. The Basel Convention amendments, which took effect from January 1, 2021, bring plastic wastes within the control of the Basel Convention and mandate specific requirements for various categories of plastic waste. The below section explores the impact international efforts to curb the transboundary movement of plastic waste, as well as how domestic efforts in large economies like the European Union (EU) and the U.S. to implement policies regarding plastic production, use, and disposal are shaping the microplastics issue.

China's Waste Ban

In 2013, China enacted Operation Green Fence, whereby it increased inspections of foreign recycling bales and returned bales that failed to meet standards at the exporter's expense.[43] In 2017, China, overwhelmed with its intake of the world's trash, including 56% of the world's recyclable plastic by weight,[44] steeply curbed the import of foreign waste with the announce-ment of Operation National Sword. China's National Sword heavily re-stricts the country's importation of recyclables including plastics. It has resulted in a market disruption in the international trade of plastic waste that has affected developed countries accustomed to shipping their waste to China.[45] Some people speculate China's new domestic waste policy could be the event that serves as the catalyst for a circular plastics economy that

---

42 California Senate Resolution 47 (June 2019), *see* https://trackbill.com/bill/california-senate-resolution-47-relative-to-the-basel-convention/1756209/#/details=true.

43 California Senate Resolution 47 (June 2019), *see* https://trackbill.com/bill/california-senate-resolution-47-relative-to-the-basel-convention/1756209/#/details=true.

44 California Senate Resolution 47 (June 2019), *see* https://trackbill.com/bill/california-senate-resolution-47-relative-to-the-basel-convention/1756209/#/details=true.

45 Alan Crawford and Haley Warren, *China Upended the Politics of Plastic and the World is Still Reeling* (January 2020), *see* https://www.bloomberg.com/graphics/2020-world-plastic-waste/.

encourages and emphasizes reuse and regeneration of plastic products.[46] China followed National Sword with a 25% tariff on U.S. recycling in 2018.[47]

In January 2019, China announced it would be banning additional types of scraps for recycling and reuse, including post-consumer plastics like shampoo and soda bottles.[48] The U.S. briefly pivoted in 2019 to sending its waste to other developing countries with lenient regulations, like India, but by March 2019, India too had announced a ban on imported plastic waste scrap.[49] Since then, China announced its plastics ban on imported waste would not only be expanded to include additional plastic products, but it would also be permanent.[50] These domestic policy changes of foreign countries that have historically accepted for ultimate disposal plastic produced, used, and thrown away in the U.S. are almost certain to require U.S. decision-makers from all levels of government and in the private sector to reconsider alternatives for managing plastic waste. For example, California has experienced a negative 19% change in all recyclables exported to China since 2017.[51] California reported that China's "stringent import inspection restrictions" greatly contributed to the reduced exports of recyclables to China from 2017 to 2018.[52]

Basel Convention

The Basel Convention is a multilateral agreement governing the international movement of transboundary hazardous waste. Only two countries in the world are not parties to the Basel Convention—Haiti and the U.S. The

---

46 Joe Meyers, *China Has Announced Ambitious Plans to Cut Single-Use Plastic* (January 2020), *see* https://www.weforum.org/agenda/2020/01/china-has-an-announced-ambitious-plans-to-cut-single-use-plastic/.
47 *Editorial: A Trade War with China Is Harming the Recycling Market* (August 2018), *see* https://www.sfchronicle.com/opinion/editorials/article/Editorial-A-trade-war-with-China-is-harming-the-13156372.php.
48 California Senate Resolution 47 at 3 (June 2019), *see* https://trackbill.com/bill/california-senate-resolution-47-relative-to-the-basel-convention/1756209/#/details=true.
49 California Senate Resolution 47 at 3 (June 2019), *see* https://trackbill.com/bill/california-senate-resolution-47-relative-to-the-basel-convention/1756209/#/details=true.
50 *China Indicates Foreign Recyclables Shutdown Will Be Permanent* (May 2020), https://www.waste360.com/recycling/china-indicates-foreign-recyclables-shutdown-will-be-permanent?utm_source=Bibblio&utm_campaign=Related.
51 CalRecycle, *Calendar Year 2018 California Exports of Recycled Materials* at 5 (September 2019), https://www2.calrecycle.ca.gov/Publications/Download/1427.
52 CalRecycle, *Calendar Year 2018 California Exports of Recycled Materials* at 5 (September 2019), https://www2.calrecycle.ca.gov/Publications/Download/1427.

2019 Basel Convention amendments aim to regulate the transboundary movement and disposal of plastic waste by distinguishing clean and sorted plastic waste suitable for immediate recycling from unsorted and contaminated plastics that will be labeled in some cases as "other" or "hazardous" plastic waste.[53] These amendments will require prior informed consent of the importing country before "other" and "hazardous" plastic wastes may be received.[54] Moreover, of extreme importance to the U.S., Basel Convention parties seeking to import regulated plastic waste from nonparties must enter into a bilateral Chapter 11 Agreement[55] to permit the nonparty to export plastic recyclables other than those that are pre-sorted, cleaned, and destined for "recycling in an environmentally sound manner."[56] Chapter 11 Agreements "shall stipulate provisions which are not less environmentally sound than" the Convention's, "in particular taking into account the interests of developing countries."[57] Chapter 11 Agreements may not circumvent the environmental management of hazardous waste set forth in the Convention.[58] With every potential trade partner other than Haiti a party to the Basel Convention, the U.S. now needs individual Chapter 11 Agreements to export waste internationally.[59]

---

53 Basel Convention Plastic Waste Amendments, BC-14/12: Amendments to Annexes II, VIII and IX to the Basel Convention (April 29-May 10, 2019), *see* http://www.basel.int/ Portals/4/download.aspx?d=UNEP-CHW-COP.14-BC-14-12.English.pdf.

54 DeAnne Toto, *New Rules Place Restrictions on Global Plastic Scrap Trade* (May 2019), *see* https://www.recyclingtoday.com/article/basel-convention-restrictions-on-plastic-scrap-trade/.

55 The U.S. has bilateral Chapter 11 Agreements with Canada, Mexico, Costa Rica, Malaysia, and the Philippines. The Agreements with Costa Rica, Malaysia, and the Philippines only permit a one-way flow of hazardous waste, with the United States able to import hazardous wastes from those countries, but not permitted to export such waste. The United States also has a multilateral agreement with OECD member countries, although EPA is unsure "whether OECD countries will allow trade in Basel-controlled non-hazardous plastic scrap, [mixed and uncle ned scrap], … with the United States." If such international trade is allowed, it is unclear what the requirements OECD would impose. U.S. Environmental Protection Agency, *New International Requirements for the Export and Import of Plastic Recyclables and Waste, see* https://www.epa.gov/hwgenerators/new-international-requirements-expo rt-and-import-plastic-recyclables-and-waste.

56 U.S. Environmental Protection Agency, *New International Requirements for the Export and Import of Plastic Recyclables and Waste, see* https://www.epa.gov/hwgenera tors/new-international-requirements-export-and-import-plastic-recyclables-and-waste.

57 Basel Convention, Article 11, *see* http://archive.basel.int/article11/multi.html.

58 Basel Convention, Article 11, *see* http://archive.basel.int/article11/multi.html.

59 The Maritime Executive, Report: U.S. Plastic Waste Exports May Violate the Basel Convention (March 2021), *see* https://www.maritime-executive.com/article/report-u-s-plastic-waste-exports-may-violate-basel-convention.

Private industry and government in the U.S. are concerned over the limitations the Basel Convention amendments will create. At least one recycling trade group expressed concern that the Convention's amendments will inhibit worldwide plastic recycling and increase the risk of pollution by placing an administrative burden on countries like the U.S. that rely on shipping plastic waste abroad.[60] Moreover, the California Senate in 2019 urged Congress to join the treaty to avoid the limitations plastic amendments are expected to create when they take effect.[61] The Environmental Protection Agency (EPA) has also expressed concern, recognizing practically every other country in the world will be legally bound not to accept most plastic scrap and wastes from the U.S. absent a bilateral agreement that meets the Basel Convention's criteria.[62] The Basel Convention does allow nonparties to participate in the Plastic Waste Partnership, a forum to discuss and "promote the environmentally sound management (ESM) of plastic waste at the global, regional and national levels and to prevent and minimize its generation."[63] The U.S., through various EPA offices, participates in the Plastic Waste Partnership.[64]

EU Single-Use Plastic Directive

In the EU, legislators passed a Single-Use Plastics Directive aimed to prevent and reduce the impact of certain single-use plastics on the environment, with particular focus on the marine environment and human health. Member States must incorporate effective, proportionate, and dissuasive penalties for infringements of the rules adopted pursuant to the

---

60 DeAnne Toto, *New Rules Place Restrictions on Global Plastic Scrap Trade* (May 2019), *see* https://www.recyclingtoday.com/article/basel-convention-restrictions-on-plastic-scrap-trade/.
61 California Senate Resolution 47 at 2-3 (June 2019), *see* https://trackbill.com/bill/california-senate-resolution-47-relative-to-the-basel-convention/1756209/#/details=true.
62 U.S. Environmental Protection Agency, *New International Requirements for the Export and Import of Plastic Recyclables and Waste*, *see* https://www.epa.gov/hwgenerators/new-international-requirements-export-and-import-plastic-recyclables-and-waste.
63 Basel Convention, *Plastic Waste Partnership Overview, see* http://www.basel.int/Implementation/Plasticwaste/PlasticWastePartnership/tabid/8096/Default.aspx#:~:text=A%20Plastic%20Waste%20Partnership%20(PWP,national%20levels%20and%20to%20prevent.
64 Basel Convention Plastic Waste Partnership Working Group, *Current Membership* (Oct. 2, 2020), *see* http://www.basel.int/Portals/4/download.aspx?d=UNEP-CHW-PWP-LST-Members-20201002.English.pdf.

EU directive into their national laws.[65] Affecting a broad category of "producers," including retail shops responsible for first placing a single-use plastic product in the market,[66] the Directive's scope includes products "made wholly or partly from plastic."[67] Accordingly, "even the smallest share of plastic" brings a product within the Directive's definition,[68] although products returned to another producer for refill are excluded.

The EU's Directive also comprehensively bans all products made of "oxo-degradable plastics" within two years of entry into force, or early 2021. The Directive defines oxo-degradable plastics as "plastic materials that include additives which, through oxidation, lead to the fragmentation of the plastic material into micro-fragments or to chemical decomposition." The EU targeted oxo-degradable plastic because "that type of plastic does not properly biodegrade and thus contributes to microplastics pollution in the environment."[69]

Microplastics Related Legislation in the U.S.

Federal legislative efforts to address microplastics are limited. Congress banned one type of primary microplastics in 2015 when it prohibited the manufacturing, packaging, and distribution of rinse-off cosmetics containing microplastics beads due to concerns over their presence in water

---

65 Wolfgang Maschek and Ken Huestebeck, *The New EU Single-Use Plastic Directive* at 5 (January 2019), *see* https://www.squirepattonboggs.com/-/media/files/insights/publi cations/2019/01/the-new-eu-single-use-plastics-directive-eu-to-adopt-law-on-the-red uction-of-the-impact-of-certain-plastic-products-on-the-environment/new_singleuse_ plastics_directive_alert.pdf.

66 Wolfgang Maschek and Ken Huestebeck, *The New EU Single-Use Plastic Directive* at 1 (January 2019), *see* https://www.squirepattonboggs.com/-/media/files/insights/pub lications/2019/01/the-new-eu-single-use-plastics-directive-eu-to-adopt-law-on-the-re duction-of-the-impact-of-certain-plastic-products-on-the-environment/new_singleuse_ plastics_directive_alert.pdf.

67 Wolfgang Maschek and Ken Huestebeck, *The New EU Single-Use Plastic Directive* at 1 (January 2019), *see* https://www.squirepattonboggs.com/-/media/files/insights/ publications/2019/01/the-new-eu-single-use-plastics-directive-eu-to-adopt-law-on-the- reduction-of-the-impact-of-certain-plastic-products-on-the-environment/new_singleuse_ plastics_directive_alert.pdf.

68 Wolfgang Maschek and Ken Huestebeck, *The New EU Single-Use Plastic Directive* at 2 (January 2019), *see* https://www.squirepattonboggs.com/-/media/files/insights/publi cations/2019/01/the-new-eu-single-use-plastics-directive-eu-to-adopt-law-on-the-red uction-of-the-impact-of-certain-plastic-products-on-the-environment/new_singleuse_ plastics_directive_alert.pdf.

69 Directive of the European Parliament and of the Council on the Reduction of the Impact of Certain Plastic Products on the Environment (Jun. 5, 2019), *see* https://data.co nsilium.europa.eu/doc/document/PE-11-2019-REV-1/en/pdf.

supplies.[70] Notably, FDA expressly states that the microbead legislation does not address consumer safety, and it "do[es] not have evidence suggesting that plastic microbeads, as used in cosmetics, pose a human health concern."[71] The Micro Plastics Act of 2020, introduced in February 2020, is a bill that would establish a research pilot program, overseen by EPA in consultation with interagency Marine Debris Program Coordinating Committee, to test the effectiveness of tools designed to address microplastics issues, including treatment technologies to remove microplastics from the environment.[72]

Most plastics legislation in the U.S. to date has focused on marine debris. Critics argue Congress has thus far failed to legislatively aim to reduce domestic plastic production and target plastic pollution, including secondary microplastics that result from marine debris. They disapprove of a perceived federal government focus on securing international waste disposal options rather than addressing the inadequacies of domestic waste management infrastructure. They believe state and local laws to reduce plastic use have been more effective than federal efforts.[73]

In 2006, Congress enacted the Marine Debris Act,[74] which assembled a coalition of federal agencies,[75] led by the National Oceanic and Atmospheric Administration (NOAA), to administer a Marin Debris Program (MDP) and make recommendations on research priorities, monitoring, and regulation of marine debris to address adverse impacts on the economy and

70 U.S. Food and Drug Administration, *The Microbead-Free Waters Act: FAQ, see* https://www.fda.gov/cosmetics/cosmetics-laws-regulations/microbead-free-waters-act-faqs#:~:text=The%20Microbead%2DFree%20Waters%20Act%20of%202015%20prohibits%20the%20manufacturing,)%20drugs%2C%20such%20as%20toothpastes.

71 U.S. FDA, *Microbead-free Waters Act: FAQs* (last visited Nov. 2, 2020) https://www.fda.gov/cosmetics/cosmetics-laws-regulations/microbead-free-waters-act-faqs#:~:text=The%20Microbead%2DFree%20Waters%20Act%20of%202015%20prohibits%20the%20manufacturing,)%20drugs%2C%20such%20as%20toothpastes.

72 Micro Plastics Act of 2020, *see* https://www.congress.gov/bill/116th-congress/senate-bill/3306#:~:text=Introduced%20in%20Senate%20(02%2F13%2F2020)&text=This%20bill%20directs%20the%20Environmental,of%20microplastics%20into%20the%20environment.

73 *See* https://www.breakfreefromplastic.org/globalbrandauditreport2019/.

74 Marine Debris Research, Prevention, and Reduction Act (33 United States Code § 1951 et seq.).

75 The Marine Debris Act reestablished the Interagency Marine Debris Coordinating Committee ("IMDCC"), which includes Department of Interior's Bureau of Safety and Environmental Enforcement, U.S. Fish and Wildlife Service, National Park Service, Department of Justice, Department of State, Marine Mammal Commission, U.S. Army Corps of Engineers, U.S. Coast Guard, U.S. EPA, and U.S. Navy.

the environment.[76] In 2018, the Save Our Seas Act[77] allocated USD 10 million annually to the MDP through 2022. The Act allowed NOAA to declare severe marine debris events and authorize funds for cleanup and response. The Save Our Seas Act has been criticized for its focus on international waste management and for failing to recognize the role of domestic plastic production and consumption of single-use plastic as a source of plastic pollution.[78]

More recently, the Save our Seas Act 2.0 was introduced in the U.S. Senate in late 2019 and focuses: (1) on strengthening the U.S.' domestic marine debris response capabilities through incentivizing innovation; (2) on international cooperation and exploration of the potential for a new international agreement to address marine plastic debris; and (3) improving domestic infrastructure to prevent marine debris by studying waste management and mitigation strategies.[79] Environmental groups responded to this bill with great resistance, and they submitted an opposition letter stating "the legislation does not provide an effective approach."[80] Instead, they assert, Congress should "pass legislation that reduces generation of plastic, particularly single-use plastic packaging."[81] They point to four major flaws in the legislation: (1) the bill would not reduce plastic pollution because it does not curb upstream production or provide for a transition to reusable and refillable packaging; (2) climate change cannot be solved without reducing plastic pollution; (3) spending tax dollars to study false solutions is a waste of valuable time and resources; and (4) international negotiations should focus on reducing plastic pollution. It was particularly critical of the GHG contributions of plastic production facilities, the focus on studying waste disposal methods instead of reduction of plastics production, and the bill's failure to include single-use plastic bans. Moreover, the proponents of the letter assert the bill fails to recognize the U.S.'

---

76 NOAA and the Department of Commerce are required to submit biennial reports on Interagency Coordination of Efforts on Marine Debris. 33 United States Code § 1954(a).

77 Save Our Seas Act of 2018, *see* https://www.congress.gov/bill/115th-congress/senate-bill/3508/text?q=%7B%22search%22%3A%5B%22S.3508%22%5D%7D&r=1.

78 Surfrider Foundation, *Movement on Federal Plastics Legislation with Save Our Seas Act* (October 2018), *see* https://www.surfrider.org/coastal-blog/entry/movement-on-federal-plastics-legislation-with-save-our-seas-act.

79 https://www.foreign.senate.gov/press/ranking/release/save-our-seas-20-act-passes-senate-unanimously-new; https://thehill.com/opinion/energy-environment/519273-the-ocean-is-sending-out-an-sos-congress-is-responding.

80 *See* Nov. 19, 2019 Opposition Letter to Save Our Seas 2.0, Senate Bill 1982, acoel.org/Site/DrawMembers.aspx.

81 *See* Nov. 19, 2019 Opposition Letter to Save Our Seas 2.0, Senate Bill 1982, acoel.org/Site/DrawMembers.aspx.

inadequate waste management and recycling infrastructure or the ongoing exports of "unrecyclable" plastic to other countries.[82]

The "Break Free From Plastic Pollution Act" (BFFPPA) is another recent plastics bill that environmentalists favor and has been described as "a comprehensive tool-kit that tackles packaging waste issues and plastic pollution from extraction to disposal."[83] The BFFPPA targets plastic producers themselves, pushing them to support recycling programs, use more recycled feedstock in their production lines, and calls for more rigorous EPA standards for plastic production.[84] Recognizing the greater progress at the state level, the federal bill's sponsors reached out to state legislators "who have demonstrated an interest in and commitment to environmental legislation"[85] and encouraged them to package relevant portions of the BFFPPA in their own future legislation "that suits [their jurisdiction's] needs to aggressively reduce plastic pollution and waste."[86]

Among its key provisions, the BFFPPA would introduce a national "bottle bill"—a nationwide requirement for a 10-cent beverage container refund. Some of the funds would be used to supplement recycling collection and infrastructure investment. The bill would also include a national recycled plastic content requirement for beverage containers, with the requirements for the proportion of recycled content in containers increasing over the years, similar to a recycled content law California recently adopted. The bill would also put a temporary moratorium on new plastics production facilities for three years or until EPA promulgates stricter air and water pollution standards on production facilities, whichever is later. The law seeks to nationally ban certain single-use plastic products, impose a nationwide fee on carryout bags, and limit cigarette waste. It would impose new labeling requirements to inform consumers of recyclability and compostability of various plastic products. These comprehensive

---

82 *See* Nov. 19, 2019 Opposition Letter to Save Our Seas 2.0, Senate Bill 1982, acoel.org/Site/DrawMembers.aspx.

83 Letter from U.S. Senators Tom Udall and Alan Lowenthal to National Caucus of Environmental Legislators Regarding Legislative Blueprints for Reducing Plastic and Packaging Pollution (Aug. 10, 2020), *see* https://www.freshlawblog.com/wp-content/uploads/sites/15/2020/08/Udall-Lowenthall-letter.pdf.

84 Bothwell Nicole, *Supporters of US Plastic Pollution Reduction Bill Press on Despite Challenging Times* (Sep. 9, 2020), *see* https://www.natlawreview.com/article/supporters-us-plastic-pollution-reduction-bill-press-despite-challenging-times.

85 *See* https://www.ncel.net/about/#members.

86 Letter from U.S. Senators Tom Udall and Alan Lowenthal to National Caucus of Environmental Legislators Regarding Legislative Blueprints for Reducing Plastic and Packaging Pollution (Aug. 10, 2020), *see* https://www.freshlawblog.com/wp-content/uploads/sites/15/2020/08/Udall-Lowenthall-letter.pdf.

measures, although they do not expressly target microplastics, would presumably limit the release of microplastics into the environment by reducing source products.

Federal Environmental Statutes and Regulatory Efforts to Regulate Microplastics Directly and Indirectly under the CWA and CAA

While a comprehensive assessment of U.S. environmental laws is beyond the scope of this chapter, the petitions for EPA to regulate under the Clean Water Act (CWA) and the Clean Air Act (CAA) are notable efforts to impose stricter standards on plastic production facilities. Moreover, the CWA petition seeks specific regulation of microplastics discharges to surface waters where feasible.

The goal of the CWA is to "to restore and maintain the chemical, physical and biological integrity of the Nation's waters."[87] The CWA achieves this goal largely by regulating point source discharges of specific pollutants to waters of the U.S. (generally defined as navigable surface waters). Point source discharges are those from discrete conveyances such as industrial facility or wastewater treatment plant outfalls where effluent enters a water body. The CWA requires these point sources to obtain a section 402 National Pollution Discharge Elimination System (NPDES) permit which regulates the amount of pollutants they can safely discharge to protected waters. The NPDES permit is required for all point source discharges of pollutants to navigable surface waters of the U.S.[88]

Microplastics are not currently directly regulated under any major U.S. Environmental laws, although, as the BFFPPA recognizes, petitions have been filed requesting EPA regulate plastics production facilities under the CWA and CAA. In 2019, seeking to compel regulation, 280 private parties filed a CWA petition for EPA to "adopt strict new water-pollution limits for industrial plants that create plastic."[89] The petition focuses heavily on primary microplastics, which make up 30% of all microplastics,[90] as well

---

87 33 United States Code § 1251(a).
88 33 United States Code § 1342(p).
89 Center of Biological Diversity, *Legal Petition Seeks Ban on Plastic Pollution from Petrochemical Plants* (Jul. 23, 2019), *see* https://biologicaldiversity.org/w/news/press-releases/ban-plastic-pollution-from-petrochemical-plants-2019-07-23/.
90 Petition to Revise the Clean Water Act Effluent Limitations Guidelines and Standards for the Petro-Plastics Industry under the 40 C.F.R. Part 419 Petroleum Refining Industrial Category (Cracking and Petrochemicals Subparts) and Part 414 Organic Chemicals, Plastics, and Synthetic Fibers Industrial Category (Jun. 23, 2019), *see* https://www.biologicaldiversity.org/campaigns/ocean_plastics/pdfs/CWA-Petro-Plastics-Petition-to-EPA-6-23-19.pdf.

as pollutants associated with plastic production.[91] In January 2020, many of the same organizations filed a second petition,[92] this time under the CAA, to regulate the same plastics production facilities.

The CWA petition urges EPA "to update the 26-year-old water pollution rules it uses to approve industrial facilities that create plastic and to eliminate plastic discharges from these plastic plants."[93] The petition specifically addresses microplastics pollution associated with plastic production facilities that "push massive quantities of plastic pellets and other plastic particles into waterways through stormwater discharge—affecting the recreational, aesthetic, biological, cultural, water quality, and economic values and uses of our shorelines and waterways."[94] Accordingly, the petition asserts "EPA must update its Effluent Limitations Guidelines and Standards [that apply to plastics facilities] to reflect … [n]ew and emerging pollutants of concern, including microplastics pollution."[95] Updating effluent limitations would restrict plastic facilities from discharging microplastics and other pollutants directly into surface waters or indirectly into surface waters through publicly owned treatment works that treat

---

91 Petition to Revise the Clean Water Act Effluent Limitations Guidelines and Standards for the Petro-Plastics Industry under the 40 C.F.R. Part 419 Petroleum Refining Industrial Category (Cracking and Petrochemicals Subparts) and Part 414 Organic Chemicals, Plastics, and Synthetic Fibers Industrial Category at 13-19 (Jun. 23, 2019), *see* https://www.biologicaldiversity.org/campaigns/ocean_plastics/pdfs/CWA-Petro-Plastics-Petition-to-EPA-6-23-19.pdf.

92 Petition to the U.S. Environmental Protection Agency to Revise the Clean Air Act section 111 and section 112 Standards Applicable to Petro-Plastics Production Facilities (Dec. 3, 2019), *see* https://www.biologicaldiversity.org/campaigns/plastic-production/pdfs/19-12-3-NSPS-Petition.pdf.

93 Petition to Revise the Clean Water Act Effluent Limitations Guidelines and Standards for the Petro-Plastics Industry under the 40 C.F.R. Part 419 Petroleum Refining Industrial Category (Cracking and Petrochemicals Subparts) and Part 414 Organic Chemicals, Plastics, and Synthetic Fibers Industrial Category at ES-1 (Jun. 23, 2019), *see* https://www.biologicaldiversity.org/campaigns/ocean_plastics/pdfs/CWA-Petro-Plastics-Petition-to-EPA-6-23-19.pdf.

94 Petition to Revise the Clean Water Act Effluent Limitations Guidelines and Standards for the Petro-Plastics Industry under the 40 C.F.R. Part 419 Petroleum Refining Industrial Category (Cracking and Petrochemicals Subparts) and Part 414 Organic Chemicals, Plastics, and Synthetic Fibers Industrial Category at ES-1 (Jun. 23, 2019), *see* https://www.biologicaldiversity.org/campaigns/ocean_plastics/pdfs/CWA-Petro-Plastics-Petition-to-EPA-6-23-19.pdf.

95 Petition to Revise the Clean Water Act Effluent Limitations Guidelines and Standards for the Petro-Plastics Industry under the 40 C.F.R. Part 419 Petroleum Refining Industrial Category (Cracking and Petrochemicals Subparts) and Part 414 Organic Chemicals, Plastics, and Synthetic Fibers Industrial Category at 44-45 (Jun. 23, 2019), *see* https://www.biologicaldiversity.org/campaigns/ocean_plastics/pdfs/CWA-Petro-Plastics-Petition-to-EPA-6-23-19.pdf.

wastewater.[96] EPA's Office of Inspector General responded with a Notice of Audit that it is investigating the effectiveness of the CWA to protect the nation's waters from Plastic Pollution.[97] The CWA petition does not seek regulation of secondary microplastics.[98]

Diffuse Sources of Water Pollution and EPA's Total Maximum Daily Load (TMDL) Program

Although plastic production facilities discharging to surface waters either directly or through their discharges to publicly owned wastewater treatment facilities are covered under CWA's NPDES permit program as point sources, many nonpoint sources release secondary microplastics that are widely dispersed into the environment. Regulating sources of secondary microplastics may not be feasible under the existing framework of U.S. environmental laws. Some secondary microplastics, such as fibers from synthetic clothing that flake off in household washing machine or fragments from car tires that runoff into storm drains feeding municipal wastewater collection systems, may be captured by wastewater treatment plants, which are point sources whose discharges are subject to a NPDES permit. However, for most other secondary microplastics preventing their introduction to a navigable river, lake, or coastal waterbody is likely to prove a difficult, if not insurmountable, regulatory challenge because EPA has no enforceable mechanisms to regulate pollution from nonpoint sources.[99]

---

96 Petition to Revise the Clean Water Act Effluent Limitations Guidelines and Standards for the Petro-Plastics Industry under the 40 C.F.R. Part 419 Petroleum Refining Industrial Category (Cracking and Petrochemicals Subparts) and Part 414 Organic Chemicals, Plastics, and Synthetic Fibers Industrial Category at 31 (Jun. 23, 2019), *see* https://www.biologicaldiversity.org/campaigns/ocean_plastics/pdfs/CWA-Petro-Plastics-Petition-to-EPA-6-23-19.pdf.

97 U.S. Environmental Protection Agency, Notification of Audit: Effectiveness of Clean Water Act to Protect from Plastic Pollution, Project No. OA&E-FY19-0086 (Oct. 30, 2019), *see* https://www.epa.gov/sites/production/files/2019-10/documents/_epaoig_notificationmemo_10-30-19_plasticpollution.pdf.

98 Petition to Revise the Clean Water Act Effluent Limitations Guidelines and Standards for the Petro-Plastics Industry under the 40 C.F.R. Part 419 Petroleum Refining Industrial Category (Cracking and Petrochemicals Subparts) and Part 414 Organic Chemicals, Plastics, and Synthetic Fibers Industrial Category at 13 (Jun. 23, 2019), *see* https://www.biologicaldiversity.org/campaigns/ocean_plastics/pdfs/CWA-Petro-Plastics-Petition-to-EPA-6-23-19.pdf.

99 Mark A. Ryan, *The Clean Water Act Handbook* 193 (American Bar Association, 3rd ed. 2011).

Nonpoint source pollution of all kinds has confounded EPA and other environmental regulators. Secondary microplastics shedding from plastic products and marine debris already in the environment are likely no different from other nonpoint sources in that limiting them in surface water is a difficult regulatory task. EPA's nonpoint source pollution control program requires individual states to identify waters impaired by nonpoint source pollution and develop a plan to control nonpoint sources. In 1987, aware that nonpoint sources were limited by the CWA's ability to achieve its goal of restoring and maintaining the quality of the nation's waters, Congress added section 319 requiring states to submit assessment reports to EPA identifying waterbodies that would not meet applicable water quality standards without additional controls of nonpoint sources.[100] EPA's TMDL program began in 2003 to require each state to calculate the amount of specific pollutants that may be discharged into an impaired water body from all sources, including nonpoint sources, to meet water quality standards.[101] While the TMDL program does not offer specific enforcement mechanisms, it limits the amount of a given pollutant in a water body, and thus can restrict point source discharges where nonpoint source discharges contribute to a water body's impairment.[102] Thus, the TMDL program is one indirect way in which microplastics might be regulated under the CWA. Specifically, the CWA compels a state or EPA to develop for each pollutant causing impairment of a water body TMDLs that determine how much of the pollutant a water body may receive without exceeding water quality standards.[103] Because EPA lacks the authority to directly regulate nonpoint sources under the CWA, implementation of load allocations in TMDLs is left to the state's discretion. When a water body is included in a state's section 303(d) list, the state has the authority and duty to consider and control pollutants from all sources that are causing the impairment, not just point sources.[104] TMDLs do not offer an enforceable mechanism against nonpoint source pollution, but they can be restrictive to point sources where nonpoint source pollution causes exceedances water quality standards. In such a scenario, point source discharges will be limited under NPDES permits. This circumstance has the potential to create tension and

---

100 Mark A. Ryan, *The Clean Water Act Handbook* 193 (American Bar Association, 3rd ed. 2011).
101 *See* 40 Code of Federal Regulations § 130.2(i).
102 *Pronsolino v. Marcus*, 91 F. Supp. 2d 1337 (N.D. Cal. 2000), *aff'd sub nom. Pronsolino v. Nstri*, 291 F.3d 1123 (9th Cir. 2002); 40 Code of Federal Regulations § 130.2.
103 33 United States Code § 1313(d).
104 33 United States Code § 1313(d).

lead to litigation where public bodies responsible for treating and managing microplastics, such as wastewater treatment facilities, are required to spend more money on treatment because their discharges are limited by microplastics TMDLs established because of nonpoint sources.

California's Microplastics Regulation Efforts: Define, Investigate, and Protect

The hurdles governments face in regulating secondary microplastics pollution explains in part why waste management and plastic production, generally associated with larger plastic products, or macroplastics, have an impact on the microplastics discussion. California is clearly tuned into microplastics issues, having already started a regulatory process for microplastics in drinking water, appears generally concerned that existing plastic production, use, and disposal activities will exacerbate marine debris and plastic pollution issues of which microplastics are a subset. In late 2020, California passed a novel "recycled content" plastics bill requiring beverage containers to be made of increasing percentages of recycled plastics over time. The law expressly recognizes the impact of "China's 2018 National Sword Policy," recognizes California's "struggling … markets for recycled materials," and need to "reduce its reliance on unpredictable foreign markets for its recycled materials."[105] If California's effort is any indication, at least some states in the U.S., may seek to control plastic production in the future as an indirect means of regulating microplastics and other plastic waste issues.

California is the largest economy in the U.S.,[106] and it is a coastal region that relies heavily on exportation of recyclables. These factors, combined with the state's frequent position at the vanguard of environmental and sustainability laws and regulations, means California will almost undoubtedly influence the plastics and microplastics discussion in the foreseeable future. California argues that China's National Sword Policy and the Basel Convention amendments will both limit traditional plastic waste disposal options for the U.S. and create significant new domestic waste management and recycling challenges. California's concerns over plastic recycling and waste disposal as well as marine plastic pollution

---

105 *See* https://leginfo.legislature.ca.gov/faces/billTextClient.xhtml?bill_id=201920200 AB793#:~:text=AB%20793%2C%20Ting.,have%20a%20minimum%20refund%20 value.
106 *See* https://www.statista.com/statistics/248023/us-gross-domestic-product-gdp-by-state/.

have it at the vanguard of legislative and regulatory efforts in the U.S. where efforts to legislate and regulate plastic issues, including microplastics, have occurred most prominently at the state and local levels. Many states have passed "bottle bills" requiring a minimum refundable deposit on beverage containers to encourage recycling.[107] States and local governments have also focused on banning specific single-use products like straws, plastic bags, and styrofoam takeout containers.[108] Indeed, it was existing legislation in a handful of states that prompted the federal ban on cosmetic microbead legislation in 2015.[109] Still, outside of banning microbeads, states have largely left microplastics unaddressed, although efforts to ban single-use plastic products indirectly reduce microplastics by removing from economic circulation plastic products likely to end up in landfills or improperly disposed of abroad.

In 2018, California, acting as the microplastics bellwether, took a direct and proactive measure to address microplastics,[110] instructing its top water quality agency, the California State Water Resources Control Board ("State Water Board"), to develop a definition for microplastics in drinking water by July 2020. Accordingly, in 2020, the State Water Board became "the first regulatory agency in the world to specifically define 'Microplastics in Drinking Water.'"[111]

After responding to public comments on its proposed microplastics definition, the State Water Board adopted a final resolution with the following microplastics definition:[112]

"Microplastics in Drinking Water" are defined as solid[113] polymeric materials to which chemical additives or other substances may have

---

107 *See* http://www.bottlebill.org/index.php/current-and-proposed-laws/usa/additional-links.
108 *See* https://www.ncsl.org/research/environment-and-natural-resources/plastic-bag-legislation.aspx.
109 *See* https://www.ncel.net/microbeads/.
110 California Senate Bill 1422, signed into law in September 2018 and codified in California Health and Safety Code section 116376.
111 State Water Resources Control Board, *Proposed Definition of "Microplastics in Drinking Water"* at 3 (Jun. 3, 2020), *see* https://www.waterboards.ca.gov/drinking_water/certlic/drinkingwater/docs/stffrprt_jun3.pdf.
112 State Water Resources Control Board, *State Water Board Addresses Microplastics in Drinking Water to Encourage Public Water Systems Awareness* (Jun. 16, 2020), *see* https://www.waterboards.ca.gov/press_room/press_releases/2020/pr06162020_microplastics.pdf.
113 State Water Resources Control Board, Proposed Definition of "Microplastics in Drinking Water" at 6 (Jun. 3, 2020), *see* https://www.waterboards.ca.gov/drinking_water/certlic/drinkingwater/docs/stffrprt_jun3.pdf.

been added, which are particles which have at least three dimensions that are greater than 1 nm and less than 5,000 micrometers (μm). Polymers that are derived in nature that have not been chemically modified (other than by hydrolysis) are excluded.

The microplastics definition was promulgated under California's Safe Drinking Water Act, which requires the State Water Board to protect water supply sources of "public water systems."[114] With the vast majority of the State's population relying on public water systems, the State's efforts to define and monitor microplastics are likely to have sweeping statewide implications. In promulgating its microplastics definition, the State Water Board received numerous comments from various sectors, including comments expressing concern the proposed microplastics definition was too broad.[115] Other comments suggested State Water Board update the definition subject to new information,[116] a comment with which the agency agreed, later noting that "[p]lastic particles are a diverse contaminant suite and may be differentiated by a variety of criteria such as substance, state at a given temperature and pressure, ... dimensions, shape and structure, ... and color."[117]

Perhaps recognizing deficiencies in its own definition due to limited current information, the State Water Board broadcasted it "intends to consider revisions to the [microplastics] definition in response to new information, including but not limited to toxicity and exposure to humans, standards adopted by other nations, regulatory agencies or authoritative

---

114 Public Water Systems provide water for human consumption to 15 or more connections or regularly serves 25 or more people daily for at least 60 days out of the year. California Health and Safety Code § 116275(h).

115 State Water Resources Control Board, Draft – Initial Response to Comments for Proposed Definitions of "Microplastics in Drinking Water," Comment No. 1.01 (Jun. 15, 2020), see https://www.waterboards.ca.gov/drinking_water/certlic/drinkingwater/docs/mcrplstcs_cmmnt.pdf.

116 State Water Resources Control Board, Draft – Initial Response to Comments for Proposed Definitions of "Microplastics in Drinking Water," Comment Nos. 1.03, 3.03, 14.03 (Jun. 15, 2020), see https://www.waterboards.ca.gov/drinking_water/certlic/drinkingwater/docs/mcrplstcs_cmmnt.pdf.

117 State Water Resources Control Board, Proposed Definition of "Microplastics in Drinking Water" (Jun. 3, 2020), at 7. The State Water Board also acknowledged "[e]vidence concerning the toxicity and exposure of humans to microplastics is nascent and rapidly evolving." Indeed, it noted, "[f]ew studies are available regarding human exposure and health hazards of plastic particles, and significant data gaps remain (World Health Organization 2019)."

bodies, as well as advances in analytical techniques and/or the standardization of analytical methods," taking into account domestic and international developments."[118] Recognizing the need for an additional information, the State Water Board was perhaps reluctant to develop what it perceived to be a likely ephemeral microplastics definition. Likely struggling to precisely define microplastics, the State Water Board was careful to distinguish between larger and smaller particles, and also notably set a size floor of 1 nm for microplastics. A primary purpose of defining microplastics in drinking water is to ultimately be able to universally characterize their presence in California's public water systems. Moving forward, besides potential modification to the existing definition, the State Water Board also must develop a standard methodology for testing microplastics in drinking water, to accredit qualified California laboratories for microplastics testing, and to sampling and reporting requirements by July 1, 2021.[119]

Other 2018 California Legislation[120] required California Ocean Protection Council (OPC) to adopt and implement a comprehensive Statewide Microplastics Strategy[121] by December 31, 2021. To meet the requirements of this legislation, OPC partnered with the Ocean Science Trust in early 2020 to convene an interdisciplinary working group of the OPC Science Advisory Team. Scientific experts from this team are tasked with developing a risk assessment framework for microplastics pollution in California. They will identify information gaps impeding risk assessment and provide guidance on the research necessary to fill those gaps. Taking the entire landscape into account, California is actively seeking to bolster the science surrounding microplastics and appears poised to apply new information to implement regulations wherever it deems appropriate.

---

118 State Water Resources Control Board Resolution No. 2020-0021, at paragraph 6.
119 California Senate Bill 1422, signed into law in September 2018 and codified in Health and Safety Code section 116376.
120 Codified as Public Resources Code § 35635.
121 The State's comprehensive strategy must include development of risk assessments, development of standardized sampling methods, characterization of ambient microplastics concentrations by particle age, size, shape, type, and location; investigations of sources and importance of exposure; research on approaches to reducing microplastics in the environment; and utilization of research to develop improvements to products and to policies to reduce microplastics pollution. In addition to submitting the strategy report, OPC must provide a progress report on the implementation of the strategy by 2025.

Litigation Issues

Although the current research is limited, there has been a discernible increase in litigation aimed at addressing marine plastic debris and micro-plastics recently. In general, these cases have been brought under federal environmental statutes seeking to compel action or enforcement under the CWA. Moreover, the Earth Island Institute filed in a complaint ("Earth Island Complaint" or "Earth Island Litigation") in California state court alleging statutory and common law tort claims against major food and beverage companies using plastic containers.

The Earth Island Litigation bears a substantive and procedural resemblance to climate change lawsuits states and local governments have filed in state courts around the country seeking to hold fossil fuel companies responsible for the localized effects of climate change. Substantively, there are similarities between the Earth Island Complaint and current climate change litigation. Plastic pollution, like climate change, represents a potential ubiquitous global problem that emanates from innumerable sources. Unlike climate change, however, the possible adverse effects of microplastics are not yet discerned. Climate litigants have generally focused on rising sea levels and increased infrastructure costs as localized injuries that result from the effects of increased GHG emissions. The Earth Island Complaint mentions microplastics off hand, but its primary focus is on marine debris made up of larger pieces of plastic trash that have littered coastlines and local water bodies, allegedly causing public nuisance. Procedurally, the Earth Island Complaint arguably even more closely resembles the state-based climate suits that are ongoing throughout the country. Typically these lawsuits have been brought in state courts alleging public nuisance and other state common law and statutory claims, and defendants have responded by seeking to remove the cases to federal court on a variety of grounds, including federal preemption.

A brief discussion of the legal efforts to compel regulation and hold plastic producers responsible for plastic pollution is below. As more studies are conducted and the intake of microplastics by living marine organisms and humans is better understood, businesses that are responsible or even potentially responsible for an individual's exposure to plastics could face a range of liabilities.

Microplastics Litigation Relating to Federal Environmental Statutes

Unsurprisingly, some of the recent litigation regarding microplastics pollution were brought under environmental statutes. In 2017, private parties brought a lawsuit under the CWA's citizen suit provision[122] against an owner and operator of a Texas petrochemical facility, seeking injunctive relief and civil penalties for illegal discharges of plastic pellets and plastic dust into San Antonio Bay. That lawsuit resulted in a 2019 court-approved consent decree that included a USD 50 million payment into a settlement fund and prescribed remediation measures, including the defendant's agreement to pay steep fines for additional recorded plastics discharges.[123] Within a year of the settlement for the CWA violations in Texas, environmental groups sued for a preliminary injunction[124] in federal court under the National Environmental Policy Act (NEPA) and the CWA, seeking to halt the development of another plastics facility in Louisiana.[125]

Also in 2019, environmental plaintiffs filed a lawsuit against EPA to compel it to require the state of Hawaii to evaluate all data available to it and include two water bodies on its CWA section 303(d) impaired water bodies list for plastic pollution.[126] The Complaint alleged microplastics harm wildlife via ingestion and by exposing them to "dangerous toxins."[127] The Complaint charged EPA with overlooking Hawaii's failure to consider all available water quality data[128] in assembling its CWA section 303(d) list and sought to compel the state to develop a plan to curtail microplastics pollution in the ocean. The plaintiffs alleged toxic chemicals associated with plastics come from the "breakdown of plastic itself" (into microplastics), and from "chemicals the plastic has accumulated," including DDT and PCBs, in the surrounding environment.[129] Accordingly, the complaint

---

122 33 United States Code § 1365(a).
123 Consent Decree, *San Antonio Bay Estuarine Waterkeeper v. Formosa Plastics Corp.*, CV No. 6:17-CV-47 (Oct. 15, 2019), *see* https://www.law360.com/articles/1209830/attachments/0.
124 Complaint for Declaratory and Injunctive Relief, *Center for Biological Diversity v. U.S. Army Corps of Engineers*, CV No. 1:20-cv-00103 (Jan. 15, 2020), *see* https://www.biologicaldiversity.org/campaigns/plastic-production/pdfs/2020_01_14-Formosa-404-Complaint.pdf.
125 *See* https://www.biologicaldiversity.org/programs/climate_law_institute/pdfs/2020-07-14-Prelim-Inj-Brief-Formosa-Plastics.pdf.
126 *Center for Biological Diversity v. U.S. Environmental Protection Agency*, Complaint, at ¶ 6-8.
127 *Center for Biological Diversity v. U.S. Environmental Protection Agency*, at ¶ 1.
128 *Center for Biological Diversity v. U.S. Environmental Protection Agency*, at ¶ 6-8.
129 *Center for Biological Diversity v. U.S. Environmental Protection Agency*, at ¶ 40.

alleged, "[p]lastic particles … provide a pathway to transfer environmental pollutants dissolved in seawater to the marine food web."[130]

Shortly after the Center for Biological Diversity filed its complaint, the EPA withdrew the portion of Approval of the Hawaii's 2018 Impaired Waters List specifically with respect to consideration of plastic pollution and gave the state sixty days to evaluate whether plastic pollution was impairing any of its water bodies. Upon further review, Hawaii still decided not to list any waters as impaired due to plastics pollution. In response, the EPA Region 9 Administrator unilaterally decided to add Kamilo Beach and Tern Island and to the State's 2018 section 303(d) list for "trash impairments of marine waters and marine bottom ecosystems designated uses."[131] Such a designation requires Hawaii to develop a plan for reducing plastic pollution for these impaired water bodies, although it does not provide a mechanism for enforcement or directly threaten to hold any specific party liable for causing plastic pollution in the marine trash impairing the water bodies.

Finally, with the recent petitions to the EPA for regulation of plastic and plastic production facilities under the CWA and CAA, including regulation of microplastics under the CWA, plastic production facilities and wastewater treatment plants may face stricter regulations that increase their operating expenses and may lead to legal disputes over such cost. Moreover, more stringent regulations would also likely encourage new citizen suits by environmental groups seeking enforcement for violations. The types of claims and plaintiffs in future plastics lawsuits are developments likely to be shaped in part by EPA's response to these petitions.

State Litigation Against Retailers, Distributors, and Manufacturers

The Earth Island Complaint filed in California state court alleges localized harms caused by a deficient global recycling system and single-use plastic contributions of a handful of food and beverage companies.[132] The crux of Earth Island's plastics complaint is that the defendants allegedly created a public nuisance through their continued marketing and sale of their products in single-use plastic containers, and they misled consumers about the

---

130 *Center for Biological Diversity v. U.S. Environmental Protection Agency*, at ¶ 40.
131 https://www.biologicaldiversity.org/programs/oceans/pdfs/HI-303d-List-Suplemental-Submission-EPA-Response.pdf.
132 Complaint in Case No. 20CIV01213 (San Mateo County Superior Court) (Feb. 26, 2020), at ¶¶ 1-21.

recyclability of their products' containers. The complaint alleges state-based claims for statutory violations of the California Consumers Legal Remedies Act, Cal. Civil. Code §§ 1750 et seq. and common law claims for public nuisance, breach of warranty, failure to warn, design defect, and negligence.[133]

Imbedded in the Earth Island Complaint is the notion that defendants' actions are responsible for microplastics pollution, which Earth Island alleges are present in "greater abundance" just in Monterey Bay than in the entire pacific garbage patch.[134] Consistent with existing scientific knowledge, the complaint generally describes the ubiquity of microplastics in the environment, including in human water supplies, but does not allege any specific harm microplastics pollution or exposure causes to Earth Island.[135] Rather, the mention of microplastics in the complaint is contextual. Still, the multiple allegations of microplastics in human water supplies and human ingestion of microplastics[136] arguably broadcast that future litigation targeting drinking water pollution may crop up depending on how the science surrounding microplastics exposure evolves. Notwithstanding the Earth Island Complaint's handful of references to microplastics' ubiquity, the primary focus of the complaint is on the alleged public nuisance in California's waterways created by marine debris, or larger macro plastic trash.[137] The complaint also focuses heavily on defendants' alleged misrepresentations over the recyclability of their products and their failure to adopt sustainable practices, leading to a global trash problem.[138] Included in its prayer for relief, the Earth Island seeks compensatory damages, equitable relief for nuisance abatement to address local issues caused by marine plastic debris.[139] They also seek an order requiring defendants to

---

133 Complaint in Case No. 20CIV01213 (San Mateo County Superior Court) (Feb. 26, 2020), at ¶ 161-226.
134 Complaint in Case No. 20CIV01213 (San Mateo County Superior Court) (Feb. 26, 2020), at ¶ 154.
135 See Complaint in Case No. 20CIV01213 (San Mateo County Superior Court) (Feb. 26, 2020), at ¶¶ 3-4, 80, 89.
136 Complaint in Case No. 20CIV01213 (San Mateo County Superior Court) (Feb. 26, 2020), at ¶ 89.
137 Complaint in Case No. 20CIV01213 (San Mateo County Superior Court) (Feb. 26, 2020), at ¶¶ 90-92.
138 Complaint in Case No. 20CIV01213 (San Mateo County Superior Court) (Feb. 26, 2020), at ¶¶ 93-152.
139 Complaint in Case No. 20CIV01213 (San Mateo County Superior Court) (Feb. 26, 2020), at p. 60-61.

generally refrain from[140] marketing their products as recyclable and corrective advertising by the defendants.

Not long after Earth Island filed its complaint, the defendants removed the case to federal court on multiple grounds. Earth Island immediately filed a motion to remand the case to state court, similar to defendants' approach in climate cases.[141] Defendants argued plaintiff's state-law plastic pollution claims arise under federal common law because they seek to remediate plastic pollution in federal waters and seek damages done to such waters from transboundary plastic pollution. They further argued that the plaintiff's claims require the resolution of significant federal issues, and federal jurisdiction exists where state-law claims raise a substantial and actually disputed federal issue.[142] Defendants also argued for federal jurisdiction on the basis that the claims allege tort claims on federal waters and challenge marine plastic pollution on federal enclaves.[143] In February 2021, the U.S. District Court for the Northern District of California granted Earth Island's motion to remand, allowing the case to proceed to the merits in state court.[144] Citing several climate cases, the federal district court judge rejected the Earth Island Complaint defendants' argument that federal common law should displace Earth Island's state public nuisance claims and remanded the case to California state court.

The remand of the Earth Island Litigation to state court could set a precedent for other plaintiffs to file similar plastics-related claims in other state courts in the near future. Moreover, Earth Island's lawsuit bears a striking resemblance to a recent wave of climate change lawsuits states and local governments filed against fossil fuel companies alleging public nuisance and consumer protection claims in state court.[145] In those cases, defendants frequently removed the case to federal court where district

---

140 Complaint in Case No. 20CIV01213 (San Mateo County Superior Court) (Feb. 26, 2020), at p. 60-61.
141 Plaintiffs' Motion to Remand to the Superior Court of the State of California, Case No. 4:20-cv-02212-HSG (U.S. District Court for the Northern District of California, Oakland Division).
142 Defendants' Opposition to Motion to Remand, at 10, Case No. 4:20-cv-02212-HSG (U.S. District Court for the Northern District of California, Oakland Division).
143 Defendants' Opposition to Motion to Remand, at 10 Case No. 4:20-cv-02212-HSG (U.S. District Court for the Northern District of California, Oakland Division).
144 Order Granting Motion to Remand, Case No. 4:20-cv-02212-HSG (U.S. District Court for the Northern District of California, Oakland Division).
145 Keith Goldberg, *Big Oil Faces Tide of Government Climate Change Suits*, Law360 (Sept. 18, 2020), *see* https://www.law360.com/articles/1311199.

courts granted orders to remand the cases to state court.[146] While many of these cases have been remanded back to state court, one such case—*Mayor of Baltimore v. BP P.L.C,* 952 F.3d 452 (2020)—remains before the U.S. Supreme Court to resolve issues related to removal and remand at the time of this chapter.

Potential Defenses in Microplastics Litigation

Some threshold issues that could discourage plaintiffs from bringing microplastics claims are related to questions over who is responsible for microplastics pollution and whether microplastics exposure is even harmful to humans or the environment. Because of the similarities between the Earth Island plastic litigation and state-based climate cases, we discuss below some of the past legal issues that have shaped plaintiff's strategies in current climate cases.

Non-justiciable Political Question

Defendants in federal climate cases have had success in arguing that various claims of global scale present a "political" issue that is not appropriate for resolution by the courts. This argument is significantly aided by cases like the Ninth Circuit decision in *Kivalina v. ExxonMobil Corp.* and the Fifth Circuit decision in *Comer v. Murphy Oil*, both of which found that climate change issues presented a "political" question rather than one to be decided in the courts.

In addition, in *American Electric Power v. Connecticut*, another federal case, the Supreme Court addressed whether several states and three land trusts could maintain federal common law public nuisance claims against five carbon dioxide emitters operating fossil fuel fired power plants in several states, whose collective operations contributed 25% of emissions from the domestic electric power sector.[147] The plaintiffs alleged defendants' contributions to climate change created a "substantial and unreasonable interference with public rights" in violation of federal interstate common law, or in the state tort law, and sought a decree setting carbon

---

146 *See, e.g., Chevron Corp. v. County of San Mateo*, No. 20-884 (U.S. Dec. 30, 2020); *Shell Oil Products Co. v. Rhode Island*, No. 20-900 (U.S. Dec. 30, 2020); *Suncor Energy (U.S.A.) Inc. v. Board of County Commissioners of Boulder County*, No. 20-783 (U.S. Dec. 4, 2020).
147 *Am. Elec. Power Co. v. Connecticut*, 564 U.S. 410, 415 (2011) (hereinafter "*AEP*").

dioxide emissions for each defendant.[148] The federal district court held the claims should be dismissed because they presented a non-justiciable political question, and the Second Circuit reversed, holding the claims were not barred by the political question doctrine and that plaintiffs had met the Article III standing requirements. The U.S. Supreme Court reversed the Second Circuit's ruling and held that because other precedent made clear that carbon dioxide emissions qualify as air pollution regulated under the federal CAA, that the CAA displaces any federal common law right to seek abatement for carbon dioxide emissions from power plants.[149] The Court reasoned that because CAA "speaks directly" to carbon dioxide emissions from power plants, the federal statute displaces federal common law claims seeking to prescribe an abatement order.[150] The *AEP* Court's decision not to address state-based common law climate claims left the door open for plaintiffs to bring lawsuits under state law for the localized effects of climate change in instances where federal statute does not preempt state claims.[151] Relying in part on *AEP,* the district court judge in the Earth Island case found that federal common law provides no basis for removal of state public nuisance claims.[152]

Successful defenses to federal climate claims in the past may explain the recent wave of climate cases filed in state court, and defendants' subsequent efforts to remove the cases to federal court. The Earth Island parties notably followed a similar litigation path.

Removal

Recently, jurisdictional challenges in bringing state-based public nuisance and consumer fraud claims took center stage as energy company defendants sought to remove these lawsuits to federal court. Most notably, the Ninth and Fourth Circuits found defendants' removal of state climate claims to federal court to be improper.[153] At the vanguard of energy companies' defense has been the notion that climate change cases "have sweeping implications for national energy policy, national security, foreign

---

148 *AEP*, 564 U.S. at 415-418.

149 *AEP*, 564 U.S. at 424.

150 *AEP*, 564 U.S. at 424.

151 The Court observed, "the availability *vel non* of a state lawsuit depends, *inter alia*, on the preemptive effect of the federal Act," *AEP*, 564 U.S. at 429.

152 *Earth Island Inst. v. Crystal Geyser Water Co.*, Case No. 20-cv-02212-HSG (N.D. Cal. Feb. 23, 2021), Order Granting Motion to Remand, at 8.

153 *City of Oakland v. BP PLC*, 960 F.3d 570 (2020); *Cnty. of San Mateo v. Chevron Corp.*, 960 F.3d 586 (2020); *Mayor of Baltimore v. BP P.L.C.*, 952 F.3d 452 (2020).

policy, and other uniquely federal interests," and should therefore be in federal court.[154] Federal circuit courts have largely rejected these arguments for removal.

During the first half of 2020, the Ninth Circuit issued in a pair of opinions finding that local governments' complaints brought against fossil fuel company defendants in *City of Oakland v. BP p.l.c.* ("*City of Oakland*") and *County of San Mateo v. Chevron Corp.* ("*County of San Mateo*") could be heard in state court.

In *Oakland*, the district court had ruled previously that the cases should be removed because it had federal-question jurisdiction, reasoning that the cities' public nuisance claim raised issues relating to "interstate and international disputes implicating the conflicting rights of States or ... relations with foreign nations," which had to be resolved pursuant to a uniform federal standard.[155] The Ninth Circuit, however, said the cities' state nuisance claims did not require resolution of a substantial question of federal law" and the claims did not require interpretation of a federal statute or challenge a federal statute's constitutionality.[156] The Ninth Circuit acknowledged "[t]he question whether the energy companies can be held liable for public nuisance based on production and promotion of the use of fossil fuels and be required to spend billions of dollars on abatement is no doubt an important policy question."[157] However, it asserted such a question "does not raise a substantial question of federal law for the purpose of determining whether there is jurisdiction under [federal law]."[158] In *City of Oakland*, the Ninth Circuit vacated the district court's ruling and remanded with instructions for the court to consider whether an alternative basis for federal jurisdiction exists.

In *County of San Mateo* the Plaintiffs brought not only public and private nuisance claims, but also failure to warn, product defect, and negligence common law claims, all in state court. Again, the case was removed to federal court and the Plaintiffs filed a motion to remand. Unlike in *City of Oakland*, the federal district court in this case granted the Plaintiff's motion for remand, finding no substantial federal issue was

---

154 Kieth Goldberg, *Justices Will Review Baltimore Climate Case Remand*, Law360 (Oct. 2, 2020) https://www.law360.com/articles/1316241/justices-will-review-baltimore-climate-case-remand.
155 *City of Oakland*, 960 F.3d at 576.
156 *City of Oakland*, 960 F.3d at 580.
157 *City of Oakland*, 960 F.3d at 581.
158 *City of Oakland*, 960 F.3d at 581.

raised to invoke federal jurisdiction. In this circumstance, the Ninth Circuit, citing 28 U.S.C. 1447(d), determined that the federal statute prohibited it from reviewing a granted motion to remand unless the grounds for removal was either the specifically listed federal officer removal statute (28 U.S.C. 1442), or the civil rights removal statute (28 U.S.C. 1443). Because the Defendants' had listed federal officer removal as a ground for removal, the Ninth Circuit considered that basis for removal and found the Defendants did not establish federal officer jurisdiction. Because it lacked jurisdiction to review other grounds for removal, it dismissed the remainder of the Defendant's appeal. Thereafter, the Ninth Circuit denied Defendant's petition for rehearing before a larger en banc panel of judges. Then the Ninth Circuit issued a stay the mandate to remand pending a petition to the U.S. Supreme Court for review, which were filed in December 2020.

In *Mayor of Baltimore v. BP P.L.C.*, the Fourth Circuit also considered whether removal of the city of Baltimore's lawsuit against fossil fuel producing defendants was appropriate, in this instance determining whether under the federal officer removal statute[159] a state-based climate lawsuit should be removed to federal court.[160] Defendants asserted eight grounds for removal to the federal court, four of which relied on federal-question jurisdiction.[161] The district court rejected all eight grounds for removal, and the Fourth Circuit held that only the federal officer statute was an appealable basis for removal.[162] The Fourth Circuit rejected the defendants' arguments that their federal government contracts and offshore drilling leases provided adequate basis for federal officer removal and affirmed the lower court's decision to remand the case to state court.[163] Thereafter, the *Mayor of Baltimore* defendants sought U.S. Supreme Court review.

In October 2020, the U.S. Supreme Court granted the *Mayor of Baltimore* defendants' request for review[164] of the Fourth Circuit's decision to remand the suit to state court. Specifically, the Court Supreme Court will consider whether the statutory provision prescribing the scope of appellate

---

159 The Federal Officer Removal Statute is codified as 28 United States Code § 1442.

160 952 F.3d 452 (2020).

161 952 F.3d at 458.

162 The federal officer statute authorizes removal of state court actions filed against "any officer of the United States or of any agency thereof … " 952 F.3d at 461 *citing* 28 U.S.C. § 1442(a)(1). The basic purpose of the federal officer statute is to protect against the interference with federal operations. *Id.*

163 *Mayor of Baltimore*, 952 F.3d at 457.

164 *See* https://www.scotusblog.com/case-files/cases/bp-p-l-c-v-mayor-and-city-council-of-baltimore/.

review of remand orders "permits a court of appeals to review any issue encompassed in a district court's order remanding a removed case to state court where the removing defendant premised removal in part on the federal-officer removal statute."[165] The Supreme Court's decision in *Mayor of Baltimore* could impact the future direction of climate cases.

The outcome of these climate suits may serve as an indicator of future of plastics and microplastics litigation. Indeed, in its remand order the district court in the Earth Island litigation noted that "[t]he Ninth Circuit has recently confirmed in *City of Oakland* that it is not enough for the state law claim to "implicate[] a variety of 'federal interests,' including energy policy, national security, and foreign policy."[166]

Consumer Protection Claims

As climate and plastic lawsuits alleging consumer protection claims ultimately play out in state court, there are many additional avenues to potentially challenge consumer protection claims. For instance, conclusory allegations about false advertising and its purported materiality to consumer purchasing decisions can be challenged by consumer survey evidence, demonstrating that consumers purchase products because of the contents within their containers, rather than representations on the containers about their recyclability. *Cf. Picus v. Wal-Mart Stores, Inc.*, 256 F.R.D. 651, 658-659 (D. Nev. 2009). ("[M]any consumers purchasing Ol' Roy pet food may not have seen the 'Made in the USA' label. For those consumers, reliance cannot be established. For consumers who did see the label, they may or may not have relied upon the representation that the product was made in the U.S. In fact, the choice to purchase Ol' Roy products could be based on a variety of factors unrelated to the 'Made in the USA' label, such as price, convenience, or a pet's preference for the product.")

Conclusion

Microplastics and plastic marine debris are distinct but related issues. Both contribute to global plastic pollution, but the range of scientific and

---

165 *See* http://climatecasechart.com/case/mayor-city-council-of-baltimore-v-bp-plc/.
166 Order Granting Motion to Remand, Case No. 4:20-cv-02212-HSG (U.S. District Court for the Northern District of California, Oakland Division) (*Citing City of Oakland*, 960 F.3d at 580-581).

regulatory issues associated with microplastics clearly distinguish them from larger plastic trash. While microplastics are understood to be ubiquitous, the effects of their exposure to living organisms require development of new information. The scientific community recognizes the existing information gaps associated with microplastics and is exhaustively undertaking to develop tools and studies to bolster knowledge surrounding microplastics exposure.

Concurrent with the scientific community's increased attention on developing methods to sample microplastics and test the effects of their exposure to organisms, governments and regulators are discerning how to deal with broader plastic waste issues. While governments recognize microplastics as a potential problem, they lack the capacity to effectively address potential microplastics problems absent better testing and research to truly understand the scope of the problem. Moreover, without more precise definitions of microplastics effective regulation may prove difficult, especially for secondary microplastics. Efforts to regulate plastic waste, including microplastics, are likely to create pressure on the plastic production industry, as well as the wastewater treatment industry and water providers, as environmentalists and governments respond to global plastic issues related to marine debris and plastic waste management challenges.

Thus far, plastics litigation is limited. Environmental plaintiffs have had some success seeking to enforce the CWA against plastic production facilities and to compel EPA to fulfill its obligations under the federal statute. The Earth Island Complaint seeking to hold food and beverage companies responsible for plastic waste is an ongoing notable legal effort to hold just a handful of companies accountable for this global issue. In many ways the Earth Island plastics litigation follows the approach of states' and local governments' climate change lawsuits filed in state court. The remand of the Earth Island case to state court, as well as the remand of similarly styled climate cases, could pave the way for future plastics lawsuits honing in on state-based common law claims to deal with localized plastics and microplastics issues.

Environmental Degradation: Waste Disposal and Management in Kuwait

Ralph Palliam & Sara Al-Othman
American University of Kuwait, Kuwait

Introduction

Nature is an important resource. The negative consequences of its use and abuse should be successfully controlled and resolved through proper oversight. Should nature serve to sustain civilization, a utilitarian approach is required and a deeper understanding of human relationship to nature is necessary. Environmental problems can only be solved by individuals who are required to make value judgments that go beyond narrowly conceived human concerns. Findings suggest that humans produce more than a billion tons of garbage a year, which is either incinerated, buried exported or recycled. Waste in Kuwait has reached an epidemic proportion. Notwithstanding this, there is a growing concern about the threats posed by these environmental issues throughout the world. Newton's Third Law of Motion states that for every action (force) there is an equal and opposite reaction. Though not limited to physics alone, this can be metaphorically demonstrated in the case of Kuwait. The country is blessed with an abundance of wealth from the oil sector which endorses a conduct of high mass consumption. The equal and opposite reaction in this case is the high level of wastage emanating from rapacious consumption and inefficient production. Studies into the acute effects of air pollution on mortality contend that there is limited research in Kuwait on the health burden from exposure to pollution. The records of health effects of pollution in arid areas, where sand dust is the primary particulate pollution source, are not precisely provided. Consistent with the resource curse hypothesis, a culture of waste concomitant with wealth could very well make one to become insensitive to individuals and families that are suffering from hunger and malnutrition. Kuwait has identified sustainability as a key driver of its 2035 Vision. Therefore, addressing wastage in all its forms is critical for Kuwait's sociopolitical legitimacy, economic reputation, and ecological performance. Garbage accumulation in Kuwait is perhaps a manifestation of the gross wastage of water and energy. Consequently, curbing the culture of waste is further exacerbated by the benevolence of Kuwait's leadership. The purpose of this chapter is to identify waste management techniques, highlight the consequences of the current system waste management, and finally formalize an environment management system that is consistent with best practices. This entails the engagement of civil society and the public authority in a holistic fashion.

The demand for growth and exponential production are exhausting the natural world. The pandemic provides an opportunity to reflect on habits of energy use, consumption, and production. Presenting to the World Bank a report on harnessing the potential for green growth in Kuwait, Al Ahmad et al.[1] suggest that the environmental degradation arising from these economic activities and the corresponding environmental impact associated with the production and consumption of oil and gas products are expansive. The economic activities associated with what is considered primary energy and raw material sources entail the discharge of toxic and non-toxic waste generated during the extraction, refinement, and transportation. The industry sector's buildup of volatile organic compounds of nitrogen and sulfur and devastating spillovers have polluted the atmosphere, water, and soil to a point that is detrimental to life. Global climate warming, ocean acidification, and sea level upsurge are altered by the sector's emissions of greenhouse gases. Kuwait is identified as one of the wealthiest countries in the world due to the revenues generated from the oil sector. Invariably, the promotion of responsible economic growth while reducing harmful air pollution in this sector is paramount. Achilleos et al.[2] contend that the use of a wide range of operations and equipment is a significant source of emissions of methane, a potent greenhouse gas that has twenty-five times greater impact on global warming than that of carbon dioxide. The sector is the largest industrial source of emissions of volatile organic compounds. This group of chemicals contributes to the formation of smog and other air toxic pollutants. The exposure to ground-level ozone and air toxins is linked to a wide range of debilitating health effects. However, no established data are accessible to provide measures that address environmental degradation, and research in this area is scant. It is not surprising that

---

1   Al Hamad, M., Marwan, D., Samia, D., and Tom, R. (2013) *Harnessing the Potential for Green Growth in Kuwait*, No. 106 World Bank MENA learning and Knowledge, http://documents1.worldbank.org/curated/en/392351468089124747/pdf/837210BRI0 Box30ge0note0series0QN106.pdf.

2   Achilleos, S., Al-Ozairi, E., Alahmad, B., Garshick, E., Neophytou, A.M., Bouhamra, W., Yassin, M.F. Koutrakis, P. (2019) *Acute Effects of Air Pollution on Mortality: A 17-Year Analysis in Kuwait,* Environ. Int. 2019, 126, 476-483.

citizens of Kuwait, a predominantly Islamic country, have come to enjoy high standards of living. Teachings across the spectrum of religion encourage the conservation of the environment because it is the only resource of life. Islam too has a rich tradition of environmental protection and conservation of natural resources, and therefore, a call for an effective and comprehensive solution to environmental challenges is consistent with the studies of religion, science, economics, and public policy. A consistent stewardship over the environment, across international boundaries, would create an awareness and develop an esprit de corps in the promotion of the quality of all forms of life. The recent pandemic has revealed this. Rapacious and high mass consumption has become the norm both on a personal level and on a large-scale industrial level. Achilleos et al.[3] further identify Kuwait as a small country that measures 17,818 km². It is located at the tip of the Persian Gulf, between Saudi Arabia and Iraq. Al-Dousari and Al-Awadhi[4] point out that most of the country is covered by the Arabian Desert and is surrounded by five major dust sources (southwestern desert of Iraq, the Mesopotamian Flood Plain in Iraq, northeastern desert of Saudi Arabia, drain marshes area in southern Iraq, and dry marshes and abandoned farms in Iran). For this reason, Al-Enezi et al.[5] argue that dust storms are a significant source of pollution in the area. Landfills in the country occupy approximately 18 km². The landfills vary in their levels of depth ranging from 3 to 30 m and are scattered across the country. Operational difficulties and proximity to residential areas often lead to the closing of landfills before reaching capacity. This poses enormous challenges particularly when one considers the size of the country. The landfills are used indiscriminately for several types of wastes that include those from household, municipal waste, industrial, and construction waste, among others. The waste management system in Kuwait is highly flawed due to inadequate policy, untrained personnel, lack of urgency on the part of authorities to act, and large unmanaged volumes of overcrowding landfills. Perhaps a lack of knowledge and care of the environmental damage caused by waste are major reasons for the burgeoning problem. The improper

3 Achilleos, S., Al-Ozairi, E., Alahmad, B., Garshick, E., Neophytou, A.M., Bouhamra, W., Yassin, M.F. Koutrakis, P. (2019) *Acute Effects of Air Pollution on Mortality: A 17-Year Analysis in Kuwait,* Environ. Int. 2019, 126, 476-483.
4 Al-Dousari, A.M., Al-Awadhi J. (2012) *Dust Fallout in Northern Kuwait, Major Sources and Characteristics,* Kuwait J. Sci 39, 171-187.
5 Al-Enezi, E., Al-Dousari, A., Al-Shammari, F. (2014) *Modeling Adsorption of Inorganic Phosphorus on Dust Fallout in Kuwait Bay*', J. Eng. Res., 2(2).

disposal methods have led to consequences such as spontaneous fires, emission of toxic fluids and gases, and a climate for breeding pathogens.[6]

Environmental Concerns in Context

Hertsgaard[7] expresses concern at the declining health of the environment and investigated the escalating crisis by embarking on an odyssey that spanned nineteen countries. He reports the environmental predicament through the eyes of the people who live through this decline and provides solutions to the essential question: Is the future of the human species at risk? The poorer nations are identified as the most vulnerable. Alolayan et al.[8] present data that suggests an application of cost-effective emission controls and development of forward-looking environmental health policies have the potential to significantly reduce emissions, population exposures to and the burden of mortality and morbidity from pollution. The Kuwait Direct Investment Promotion Authority recognizes that Kuwait has the highest rate of municipal waste generation of 1.4 kg/day per capita in the Gulf Cooperation Council (GCC) region. Some of the factors responsible for the high waste generation include the high growth in the construction and energy sectors, increase in population, and rapid urbanization. By 2019 the annual solid waste generation reached more than 17.1 million tons. Kuwait is also expected to generate 14.6 million tons of inorganic waste per annum, primarily construction waste. Organic wastes such as household and agricultural waste are expected to amount to another 1.8 million tons per annum.[9] The overdependence on one type of waste management method is ill suitable and not desirable due to the negative outcomes. Moving forward, Kuwait is advised to review alternate advanced waste management approaches and consider one of the concepts of "hierarchy of waste management" proposed by the UN Centre for Regional

6 Zafar, S. (2017) *The Menace of Landfills in Kuwait*, retrieved Apr. 24, 2020, from https://www.ecomena.org/landfills-kuwait/.

7 Hertsgaard, M. (1999) Earth Odyssey: Around the World in Search of Our Environmental Future, Broadway Books.

8 Alolayan, M.A., Brown, K.W., Evans, J.S., Bouhamra, W.S., Koutrakis, P. (2012) *Source Apportionment of Fine Particles in Kuwait City*, Sci. Total Environ., 448, 14-25. DOI: 10.1016/j.scitotenv.2012.11.090.

9 KDIPA (2016) *A Guide for Investment Opportunities in Kuwait*, retrieved 2020, from https://e.kdipa.gov.kw/main/KDIPA-Investment-Guide-2016.pdf.

Development. The accruing benefits of introducing into solid waste management the 3Rs (Reduce, Reuse, and Recycle) could result in zero waste. Plans to achieve zero waste are being prepared in several municipalities throughout the world.

A closer examination of the Gulf will reveal how Kuwait a piece of haven is harmed environmentally by carelessness which is overlooked by the authorities and of least concern to its growing youth population. The Gulf is contaminated with different kinds of pollutants and toxic materials that include plastic, garbage, metal, rubber, and sewage that have detrimental effect on the marine life. Toxins in the form of mercury and other dangerous substances have exceeded normal levels allowed by the World Health Organization. The impact on ecology and on climate changes cannot be overemphasized. The Environment Studies Unit at the Ministry of Health provides evidence that Kuwait's shoreline is polluted with waste pumped from sewage plants. Untreated and contaminated sewage waters in the form of bacteria, fungi, worms, and viruses pose severe health risks.

Environmentalists conclude that environmental degradation results not only from a lack of government intervention but also from a lack of social cohesiveness in addressing environmental issues. A compendium of literature suggests that addressing environmentally relevant issues provides opportunities for achieving a level of sustainability while simultaneously reducing environmentally degrading economic behaviors. The United Nations and the World Resources Institute contend that, despite extensive economic growth and increases in the quality of life over the last century, concern remains that the era of industrialization has had substantial negative effects on the natural environment and that these effects diminish the vitality and sustainability of our economic systems. In addition to the localized problems of air pollution, surface-water degradation, and toxic wastes in groundwater, recent scientific discoveries have revealed global effects such as ozone depletion, climate change, and the worldwide destruction of ocean fisheries. The long-term economic impacts of these effects will be quite substantial as a large portion of the world's economic output is dependent upon the viability of natural systems. The State of Kuwait's Second National Communication Submitted to the United Nations Framework Convention on Climate Change points out susceptible and compromising issues that the country faces and provides several vulnerability indices to this effect.

The negative consequences of the use and abuse of nature is a result of uncontrolled and proper oversight. Should nature serve to sustain civilization, a utilitarian approach is required and a deeper understanding of human relationship to nature is necessary. Environmental problems can only be solved by individuals who are required to make value judgments that go beyond narrowly conceived human concerns.

Ecological Risk Management

If one accepts the unprecedented anecdotal evidence and number of hypotheses relative to the risks to Kuwait's ecological environment, the efficacy and the sustainability of its ecological risk management systems are in question and present apparent shortcomings particularly when ecological risks are rampant. The scourges of various financial, economic, social, political, ecological, and environmental crises in the region have made it agonizingly clear that waste management system in its current form is not tenable in Kuwait. The disappointments associated with non-governmental environmental leaders predicate an urgency to responsibly diffuse best practices of waste production across the region. For decades life scientists have repeatedly speculated the potential environmental risks will result in diminishing supplies of many of the key natural resources of the planet because of rapacious consumption and poor waste management systems in place. Consequently, the longevity of all forms of civilization is at risk. To address the defining ecological and environmental realities of Kuwait, there requires a constellation of forces that include important stakeholders: government and nongovernment associations; businesses; producers; householders and consumers to propose and address a knowledge ecology framework for sustainability. The potential for all stakeholders to inculcate a more positive impact on ecological and environmental protection has never been greater, and therefore, the need has arisen for stakeholders particularly multinational corporations to harness all forms of knowledge for common good. To merely report financials that have positive impact on economic, social, and political environment has proven to be inadequate. Stakeholders are required to do more and should be mandated to operate sustainably, meeting the needs of the present generation without compromising the ability of future generations to meet their needs. To this end, a waste and ecological risk management, together with a knowledge ecology framework for sustainability of people, profit and planet, should consider how stakeholders' interest can be configured to embed environmental planetary footprints in their decisions that have become the foremost challenge of this century. The concerns of environmentalists over Kuwait's waste management must be addressed.

The destruction of cultural and biological diversity predicates that decision-making should ideally focus upon anthropogenic issues related to people, planet, and profit. Within this context corporations finding themselves challenged by ecological risks are in a very precarious position because of the varied values and concerns of different stakeholders. Integrating sustainability into their strategy requires stakeholders to engage meaningfully into ecological resource preservation and social equity within the confines of economic prosperity. The degree to which the world ecology has deteriorated because of corporate activities is startling and is in essence a major cause for concern. Integrating a risk management system is an essential prerequisite to address this concern. Notwithstanding that society and ecology actively shape each other within the context of time, space, and nature, corporations, as juristic individuals and natural persons, are collectively mandated to address ecological risks.

When economies address their economic wealth, growth, and prosperity, it would be critical to consider and report on a host of ecological issues that range from geographic space and climate change to animal, vegetation, and people. The ongoing pursuit of revenue toward an economy's self-actualization is geared toward satisfying the personal needs of constituencies at times at the expense of the ecology. A deep ecology movement within an economy entails a meaningful relationship with ecopsychology and ecocriticism that entail what Naess[10] identifies as "ecosophy," defined as a philosophy of ecological harmony or equilibrium. A philosophy as a kind of *sophia* (or) wisdom is openly normative; it contains norms, rules, postulates, value priority announcements, and hypotheses concerning the situation in the universe.

One of the challenges that face humanity is to meet the growing demands of the present generation without compromising the ability of the next generations to meet the growth of their own demands. Questions relating to the ability of the human community to feed its own offspring are being addressed by eco-philosophers. Consequently, corporations and governments, as major stakeholders, are being called upon to take responsibility for the ways their operations impact societies and the natural environment. Consequently, from an anthropocentric and a biocentric perspective, more ecological concerns need to be formulated and linked to areas of public and corporate policy.

10 Naess, A., (2005) Selected Works of Arne Naess (10 vols., Drengson, Alan R., ed.), Springer.

Sources of Pollution

The pollution of the atmosphere (air), water (lakes, rivers, and ocean), and soil (land) has reached catastrophic proportions due to multiple sources of pollution. The literature provides several sources of pollution to Kuwait's air, water, and soil. Notwithstanding these sources, the carelessness of human beings in the form of action and non-action can be attributed as the single most important source of pollution and environmental deterioration. The critical levels of wastage are a result of human beings, who, in turn, are implicated for the presence of contaminants in the atmosphere, soil, and water are alarming. It is not uncommon to see garbage flung out of moving cars and then picked up by a large contingency of street cleaners employed specifically for this purpose. Human beings' rapacious consumption is undeniably a major contributory factor. The inability of the authorities with vested powers to curb high levels of pollution can also be philosophically attributed as a source of the problems of pollution. Legal measures to curb corporate waste disposal conduct are to be promulgated with immediate effect.

Kuwait's demand for pollution control equipment is expected to increase in the next few years due to the newness of the market and the steadily increasing environmental awareness in the country. Worldwide trends are gradually moving toward an environmentally sustainable direction. Furthermore, the excellent relations between Kuwait and the United States and the similarity of their environmental standards and specifications indicate future growth of the U.S. share of this market in Kuwait. Despite the establishment of the Environmental Public Authority in 1996, as a result of increasing concern over these problems, the incidence of pollution has continued unabated. Dredging and land-filling operations, coastal engineering works and mining, industrial effluents, oil extraction, sewage discharges from beach houses, urban and agricultural drainage, hot water discharges from desalination plants, marine transportation, terminal operations, tanker loading and ballasting operations, dumping of domestic waste on shorelines and seas and overexploitation of fisheries are environmental concerns that require immediate attention and action.

Decomposition of Waste Material

The Peace Corps is a service opportunity for motivated change-makers. These volunteers immerse themselves in a community abroad, working side by side with local leaders to tackle the most pressing challenges. In addressing the challenges of wastage, they identify the decomposition time of everyday waste items. A glimpse at the decomposition time of waste materials is frightening and should send worrisome signals to controllers and agents of environmental protection. The waste materials are used in countless other products worldwide and once disposed overburden the earth. Technological advancement has enabled the production of some materials that can withstand extreme temperatures, durable to various conditions and powerful enough to defy the biological process of waste breakdown. According to Narayan (2006),[11] the harmful impacts of non-biodegradable products include the emission of toxic pollutants due to changes in the chemical composition of the material as a result of contact with air, light, or water exposure over time. Concerns arise when toxins and chemicals reach water supplies or into food increasing the health risks of all forms lives. These health risks include cancer, insulin resistance, and conception-related problems. Another issue is referred to as outgassing which means plastic is melted through constant exposure to heat or extreme sunlight experienced in countries like Kuwait. Melted plastic transmits these biochemical reactions in the atmosphere thereby polluting the air supply.[12]

Environmental Impact of Solid Waste Landfilling

Landfilling is the most used method for solid waste disposal, and which is one of the sources of pollution that include gas and leachate. The environmental concerns extend to include groundwater pollution, air pollution with impact on climate through methane emission and potential health hazards. For the disposal of solid waste, modern landfills ought to be well engineered and managed and monitored in accordance with laws. These must be designed in such a way to protect the environment from contaminants, which may be present in the waste stream. Landfills are not to be built in environmentally sensitive areas. Health hazards related to waste pollutants and proximity to landfills is not to be taken for granted. According to findings, gases emitted from landfill sites consist primarily of

---

11 Narayan R. (2006) Biobased and Biodegradable Polymer Materials: Rationale, Drivers, and Technology Exemplars, American Chemical Society Symposium Ser., 939, Chapter 18, p. 282.

12 Paventi, J. (Aug. 14, 2017) *The Effects of Non Biodegradable Products*, retrieved Apr. 22, 2020, from https://www.livestrong.com/article/151703-the-advantages-of-biodegradable-products/.

methane and carbon dioxide, with other gases such as hydrogen sulfide and mercury vapor being emitted at low concentrations, and a mixture of other volatile organic compounds. Landfills also discharge contaminated waste liquids, metals, and air pollution and combustion products. A primary concern is the emission of known or suspected carcinogens or teratogens such as arsenic, nickel, chromium, benzene, vinyl chloride, dioxins, poly-cyclic aromatic hydrocarbons, and animal vectors such as seagulls, flies, and rats.

The top ten pollutants regarded as having the greatest potential impact on human health include cadmium, mercury, arsenic, chromium, nickel, dioxins, polychlorinated biphenyls (PCBs), polycyclic aromatic hydrocarbons (PAHs), particulate matter (PM10), and sulfur dioxide (SO2). Microbial pathogens also pose a threat. Cadmium, arsenic, chromium, nickel, dioxins, and PAHs are linked to cancer. Other toxins are potentially harmful to the central nervous system, liver, kidneys, heart, lungs, skin, and reproduction. Chemicals such as dioxins and organochlorines have been associated with affecting the endocrine system and reproduction. Other factors to be considered include exposure length and intensity, susceptibility to diseases (immunity), and proximity to landfills.

Reproduction health complications in relation to landfill sites is an area commonly researched. Findings show that there is a correlation between landfill proximity and low birth weight, fetal and infant mortality, and birth defects. Research on the Love Canal landfill site shows that there is an increase in low birth weight in that area. Another research in New Jersey shows that those living within a radius of 1 km to the Lipari landfill also had noticeable patterns in low birth weights. It is noteworthy that the research in New Jersey was done in the years 1971-1975, a time of heavy pollution and streams including leachate. Research on a landfill site managed poorly in California revealed trends in low birth weights as well. A study conducted in Great Britain in the years 1982-1997 showed a correlation between living within 2 km to a landfill and increased risks of neural tube defects, malformations of the cardiac septa, chromosomal abnormalities, and abnormalities of arteries and veins. The increase is correlated with the time of operations and post-operations rather than pre-opening the landfill sites. Other researchers hypothesized that landfill sites are correlated with cancer mortality rates, respiratory problems, skin; eyes; nose irritations, gastrointestinal problems, fatigue, headaches, allergies, and even psychological problems. Two studies in the U.S. found that there is an increase in cancer in areas with poorly managed landfills, particularly gastrointestinal, esophageal, stomach, colon, and rectal cancer.[13]

Workers handling waste are prone to various health risks as the nature of their jobs increases the time and proximity around waste materials and a wide range of harmful chemicals and bacteria. A study conducted in Chandigarh, India showed that 12.3% of street sweepers, 17% of rag pickers, 17.3% of waste collectors, and 17.6% of waste processors experienced respiratory related problems. Another study in Calcutta showed that 71% of waste collectors experienced respiratory problems. Furthermore, more than 90% of those working in waste management related jobs reported allergies. The lack of protective gear increases the risk of injuries. Incidences of vomiting and body aches were also reported.[14]

Marine Life in Kuwait

Human existence is dependent on waterways such as oceans, gulf, lakes, and rivers. These waterways have been used to facilitate production, as a waste dump, for recreational activities (such as individuals who have picnics by the seaside and leave waste behind), for economic opportunities and transportation purposes. However, it is these very activities that affect marine life. What is done to the land is done to the water. Marine life is one of the aspects negatively affected by improper waste management in Kuwait. One of the countries geographically located along the Persian Gulf also known as the Arabian Gulf Sea is Kuwait. The countries surrounding the sea engage in the production of fertilizers, chemical products, petrochemicals, minerals, and plastic products. The manufacturing of such products endangers marine life as waste products such as heavy metals, oil and petroleum-based compounds, nutrients, and halogenated organics are dumped into the sea as wastewater. Sewages receive secondary or tertiary treatments before discharge; however, other channels making their way into the water are not as controlled or monitored. Water sources susceptible to human caused interruptions increase the chance of harmful algal blooms (HABs) spreading which increases the likelihood of toxins transferring

---

13 Rushton, L. (Dec. 01, 2003) *Health Hazards and Waste Management*, British Medical Bull., Oxford Academic, retrieved 2018, from https://academic.oup.com/bmb/article/68/1/183/421368.

14 Ravindra, K., Kaur, K., and Mor, S. (2016) *Occupational Exposure to the Municipal Solid Waste Workers in Chandigarh, India.* Waste Management and Research, 34(11), 1192-1195. doi:10.1177/0734242x16665913.

onto the food chain or creating a high level of biomass inhibiting required light penetration. Kuwait Bay during August-September 2001 experienced a bloom of the species Ceratium furca which caused a decrease in penned and wild fish. One of the possible contributing factors leading to this increase is the elevated nutrient levels from sewage units discharge.[15]

Marine life is further threatened by oil spills. The largest oil spill in history occurred in 1991 as a result of the war between Iraq and Kuwait when the Iraqi troops set fire to desert oil wells and opened valves on pipes causing leaks. Between 5-10 million barrels of oil spilled into the Persian Gulf causing serious damage to wildlife. It is estimated that 30,000 water birds were killed by the incident; fish eggs and larvae also suffered. Consequently, some bird species breeding success was reduced by 50% after the incident.[16] The most recent oil spill incident occurred in 2017 in Al-Zour. The spill clearly stained the beach with black streaks; however, the origin of the spill according to sources remained ambiguous. Boats and crews placed booms into the water to try to cleanup the spill ("Kuwait Battles," 2017).[17] Loose regulations and supervisions of oil fields piping systems are intolerable; one mistake can result in the endangerment of several species, water pollution, and waste of oil resources. Several preventative contingency plans must be actively in place 24/7 to prevent spillage in the first place.

Recommendation

Pollution has profound population health effects. Creating an awareness of health risks associated with waste is primarily the route to follow. A holistic approach to waste management needs to be implemented. Proper waste

---

15 Sale, P., Feary, D., Burt, J., Bauman, A., Cavalcante, G., Drouillard, K., Van Lavieren, H. (2011) *The Growing Need for Sustainable Ecological Management of Marine Communities of the Persian Gulf.* Ambio, 40(1), 4-17, retrieved from http://www.jstor.org.ezp. auk.edu.kw/stable/41417242.

16 Tutton, M. (2010) *Lessons Learned from the Largest Oil Spill in History,* retrieved from http://edition.cnn.com/2010/WORLD/meast/06/04/kuwait.oil.spill/index.html.

17 CBC News, *Kuwait Battles Oil Spill in Persian Gulf Waters* (Aug. 13, 2017), retrieved from http://www.cbc.ca/news/world/kuwait-battles-oil-spill-in-persian-gulf-waters-1.42457020.

management strategies and recycling laws, together with available facilities that encourage these, increase the likelihood of recycling.[18] To ease recycling, government-corporate support is required by building the local recycling facilities. Once awareness is established, the primary idea for Kuwait is to launch recycling campaigns, educating individuals from a young age on the methods to combat wastage. Educational institutions are expected to make a conscientious effort to propagate knowledge and to contribute sustainable principles of responsible education. The worldwide trends in environmental awareness are increasing gradually. By taking proper initiatives, Kuwait has the potential to become an environmental leader in the Gulf region.

There must be an immediate rethinking on curtailing landfills through recycling initiatives, reducing mass wastage, and reusing waste material. Commonly used materials in production facilities and construction sites that include metals, plastic, concrete, wood, paper, cardboard, cement in large volumes have contributed to the deterioration of the environment. Depositing these waste materials into landfills is an inefficient approach. Identifying opportunities to reproduce the materials into other useful raw materials to develop infrastructure may be a better alternative. The South African initiative to reuse plastic pellets into road construction materials may be an option. Further research and development into these types of alternative uses are necessary. Any support toward environmentally friendly large-scale recycling companies dealing with petrochemicals, construction waste, and hazardous waste should be encouraged.

The implementation of laws that promote a clean environment is also paramount. Strict adherence to environmental protection and management would go a long way in curbing waste. Waste in Kuwait is expected to grow in the upcoming years. Governmental intervention and citizens' cooperation are essential for waste reduction and efficient waste management initiatives to succeed. The vision for change requires a movement toward reducing wastage, reusing and recycling as the new norms in both households and industries. The construction sector whose waste constitutes a large volume would need to be part of the solution. It is not possible to experience sustained prosperity by compromising the environment. When correspondingly environmentally friendly initiatives are put into practices, sustainable prosperity will be attained. Both natural and human ecosystems throughout the world are increasingly impacted by natural hazards as

18 Viscusi, W., Huber, J., and Bell, J. (2011) *Promoting Recycling: Private Values, Social Norms, and Economic Incentives*, Am. Econ. Rev., 101(3), 65-70, retrieved from http://www.jstor.org.ezp.auk.edu.kw/stable/29783716.

a consequence of global environmental changes. Notwithstanding this, the threats also reflect an interaction between social and ecological systems. To this end, an effective ecological disaster risk management system requires increasing community capacity to mitigate against the potential hazards. One of the reasons for the widespread ineffectiveness in the preparedness of authorities has been the absence of environment-community interactions and the knowledge of their impact. Kuwait requires a holistic ecological risk management and capacity-building model to address waste management. This holistic model necessitates a four-phase plan as follows:

(1) *Phase One*: Identify the problem and provide a clear definition of pollution within the Kuwaiti context.
(2) *Phase Two*: Create an awareness of the pollution challenge. Impact creation using the media.
(3) *Phase Three*: Identify stakeholders and create focus groups.
(4) *Phase Four*: Implement a plan of action based on a holistic stakeholder model.

Nature is an important resource. The negative consequences of its use and abuse should be successfully controlled and resolved through proper oversight. Should nature serve to sustain civilization, a utilitarian approach is required, and a deeper understanding of human relationship to nature is necessary. Environmental problems can only be solved by individuals who are required to make value judgments that go beyond narrowly conceived human concerns. In so doing, attempts should be made to develop and accept a more systematic and scholarly version of biocentric ethics and respect for nature.

Conclusion

The adage: "cleanliness is next to godliness" is both the abstract state of being clean and free from impurities. In Islam, individuals are responsible for any damage done on earth. Consequently, the environment should be protected, and its natural resources must be conserved. Solid wastes are the discarded leftovers of our advanced consumer society. The growing mountain of garbage represents not only an attitude of indifference toward valuable natural resources but also a serious economic and public health problem. The process of achieving and maintaining a state free from litter and garbage is a major challenge in Kuwait. Over the years, individuals have recorded in the form of photographic images the environmental deterioration in Kuwait. Should the situation go unchecked, Kuwait will face a major catastrophe. Cleanliness is an endowment that one generation hands over to the next. This is yet to be seen in Kuwait. The garbage that accumulates because of inappropriate practices by mindless individuals ought to be a major cause for concern in Kuwait. Cleanliness in all forms has a social, economic, and political dimension. Embracing this model, this action-based applied research addressed the issues with environmental deterioration and cleanup. This chapter recommends a model that encompasses the engagement of a host of responsible stakeholders in environmental cleanup. The intention is to create an awareness of the problem, identify stakeholders, form focus groups, and ameliorate theory to several institutions in the private and public sectors. Disposing of waste in an environmentally friendly manner is crucial to the existence of Kuwait and Kuwaiti society.

Piecemeal attempts in the form of occasional beach cleanup initiatives are made by individuals or groups of individuals toward environmental cleanup. This must be applauded. However, what these individuals address are the symptoms and not the causes. The enormous government expenditure can be avoided if the causes are tackled with a sense of urgency. This chapter has articulated how a stakeholder model can help resolve the environmental problems of Kuwait and move in a direction toward the 2035 Kuwait vision.

Brazil's Comprehensive Regulations on Large Dams Safety

Leonardo Lamego
Partner at Azevedo Sette Advogados

Introduction

Dam failure or dam collapse is a catastrophic type of failure characterized by the sudden and uncontrolled release of impounded tailings, water, or waste.

Over the last decades there was a considerable occurrence of serious dam failures and accidents worldwide, including collapses of large dams,[1] many of them causing significant environmental harm, economic impacts and human victims.

In many jurisdictions—especially countries with considerable number of large dams, including mining tailings dams, such as Brazil, Canada, United States (U.S.), Chile and Australia—there are regulations in force establishing dam safety policies. Nevertheless, the number of accidents shows that legislation by itself does not prevent accidents with severe consequences from happening.[2]

---

1 A large dam is commonly defined as a dam with a height of 15 meters or greater from lowest foundation to crest or a dam between 5 meters and 15 meters impounding more than 3 million cubic meters (ICOLD—https://www.icold-cigb.org/GB/world_register/general_synthesis.asp, accessed on Apr. 20, 2020). Domestic legislation may establish different criteria. A large dam may serve different purposes such as hydropower energy, water reservoir, tailings dam, industrial waste, etc.

2 *World:* The exact number of accidents involving large dams and tailings dams is uncertain, and there is a high possibility of unregistered or uninformed accidents. Different sources provide different numbers. According to ICOLD: *"there have been around 300 reported accidents, although the overall failure rate of dams is around 1%, a time-related analysis shows that this has been reduced by a factor of four or more over the last forty years"* (https://www.icold-cigb.org/article/GB/dams/dams_safety/dams-safety-is-at-the-very-origin-of-the-foundation-of-icold-5, accessed on Apr. 20, 2020). Regarding "Tailings Dam Incidents," U.S. Committee on Large Dams—USCOLD, Denver, Colorado, ISBN 1-884575-03-X, 1994, makes a compilation and analysis of a total 185 tailings dam incidents. World Mine Tailings Failures.org (https://worldminetailingsfailures.org/) informs the occurrence of 236 dam failures between 1908-2017. The Minas Gerais State Environmental Secretary informed 119 tailings

The actual number of accidents may differ depending on the source and methodology applied, for example, the International Commission on Large Dams (ICOLD) informs that there have been around 300 reported severe accidents and the overall failure rate of large dams is around 1%.

Minas Gerais State, the largest ore producer in Brazil[3] and with a significant number of large dams (mining, industrial and hydropower), issued a report informing the occurrence of 119 large mining tailings dams' reported accidents worldwide between 1960 and 2019, summarized in Figure 8.1.

---

dams accidents between 1960 and 2019 (*see* Figure 8.1). Science Engineering & Sustainability, *Science Engineering & Sustainability: Dam Break Simulation with HEC-RAS: Chepete Proposed Dam*, retrieved Dec. 07, 2019, reports that more than 200 notable dam failures happened worldwide between the years 2000 and 2009.

U.S.: According to the Association of State Dam Safety Officials' assessment (https://damsafety.org/dam-failures, accessed on Apr. 20, 2020) from "*January 2005 through June 2013, state dam safety programs reported **173** dam failures and **587** 'incidents'—episodes that, without intervention, would likely have resulted in dam failure.*"

Brazil: According to the Brazilian National Water Agency's *RSB 2018* ("Large Dams Safety Report, 2018," available at http://www.snisb.gov.br/portal/snisb/relatorio-anual-de-seguranca-de-barragem/2018, accessed on Apr. 20, 2020), there are 17,604 registered large dams in Brazil whereas *68* are considered with severe structural problems. *Twenty-seven accidents* were reported between 2011 and 2018.

3   The States of Minas Gerais and Pará together represent more than 85% of the total Brazilian mineral production. States of Goiás and Bahia follow in third and fourth places, respectively.

Figure 8.1   Tailing Dams Accidents from 1960 to 2019

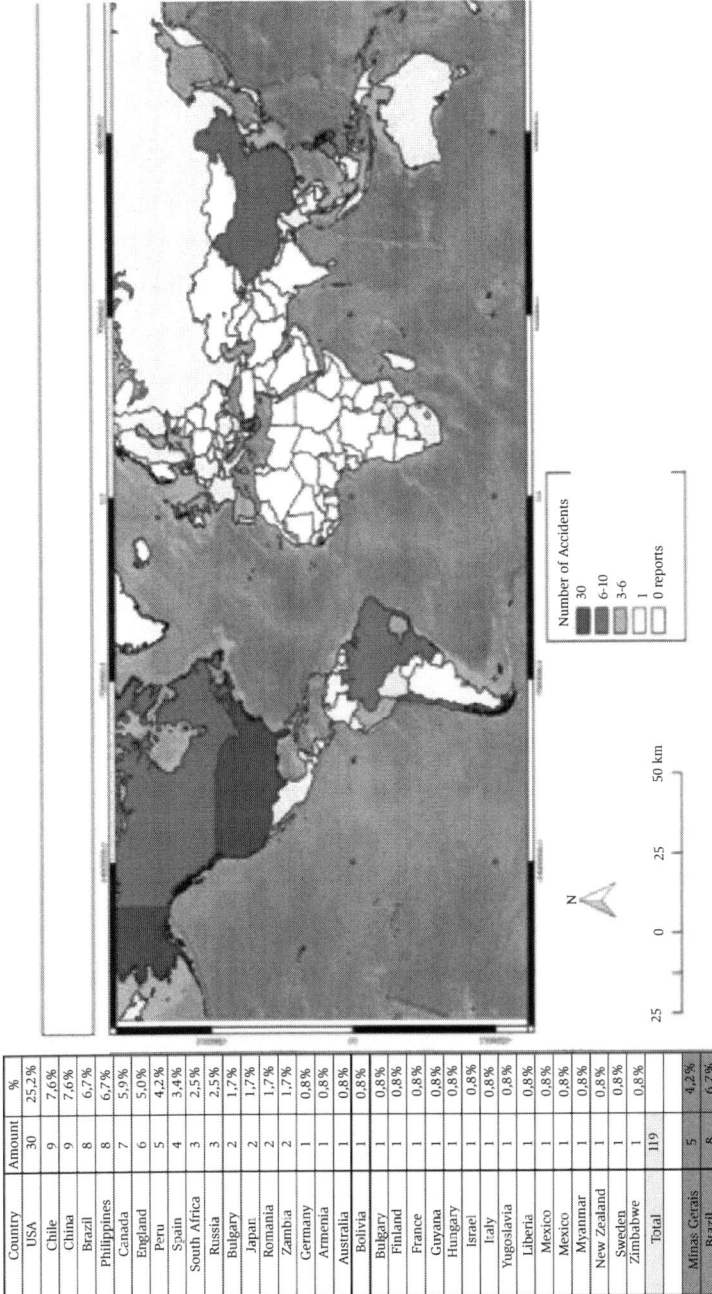

Number of Accidents
- 30
- 6-10
- 3-6
- 1
- 0 reports

N

25   0   25   50 km

Country	Amount	%
USA	30	25,2%
Chile	9	7,6%
China	9	7,6%
Brazil	8	6,7%
Philippines	8	6,7%
Canada	7	5,9%
England	6	5,0%
Peru	5	4,2%
Spain	4	3,4%
South Africa	3	2,5%
Russia	3	2,5%
Bulgary	2	1,7%
Japan	2	1,7%
Romania	2	1,7%
Zambia	2	1,7%
Germany	1	0,8%
Armenia	1	0,8%
Australia	1	0,8%
Bolivia	1	0,8%
Bulgary	1	0,8%
Finland	1	0,8%
France	1	0,8%
Guyana	1	0,8%
Hungary	1	0,8%
Israel	1	0,8%
Italy	1	0,8%
Yugoslavia	1	0,8%
Liberia	1	0,8%
Mexico	1	0,8%
Myanmar	1	0,8%
New Zealand	1	0,8%
Sweden	1	0,8%
Zimbabwe	1	0,8%
Total	119	
Minas Gerais	5	4,2%
Brazil	8	6,7%

The United Nations Environment Programme's (UNEP) assessments made in 2017[4] highlights that, although the number of dam failures has declined over many years, the number of serious failures has increased, despite advances in the engineering knowledge that could prevent them.

According to ICOLD, the main causes of tailings dams' failures are shown in Figure 8.2.

Figure 8.2   Causes of Tailing Dams Failures 1915-2016

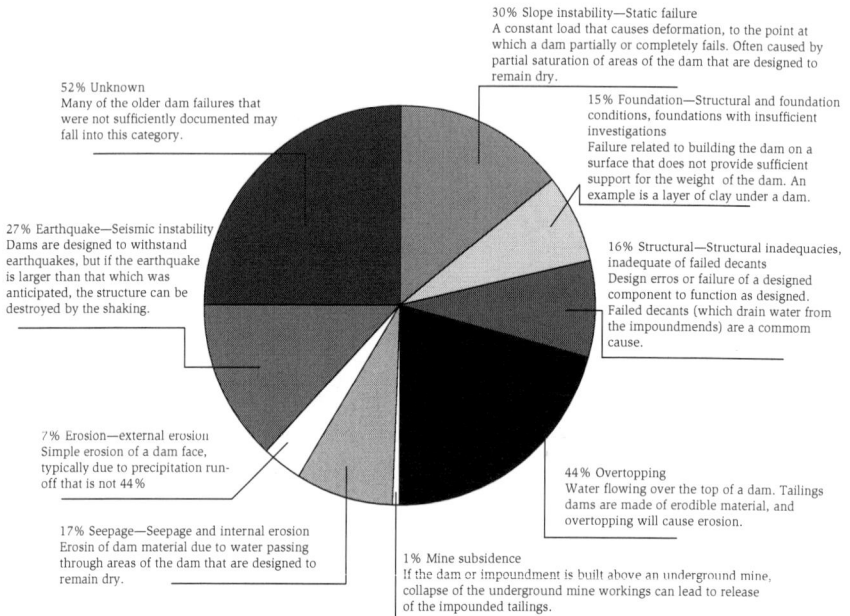

30% Slope instability—Static failure
A constant load that causes deformation, to the point at which a dam partially or completely fails. Often caused by partial saturation of areas of the dam that are designed to remain dry.

52% Unknown
Many of the older dam failures that were not sufficiently documented may fall into this category.

15% Foundation—Structural and foundation conditions, foundations with insufficient investigations
Failure related to building the dam on a surface that does not provide sufficient support for the weight of the dam. An example is a layer of clay under a dam.

27% Earthquake—Seismic instability
Dams are designed to withstand earthquakes, but if the earthquake is larger than that which was anticipated, the structure can be destroyed by the shaking.

16% Structural—Structural inadequacies, inadequate of failed decants
Design erros or failure of a designed component to function as designed. Failed decants (which drain water from the impoundmends) are a commom cause.

7% Erosion—external erosion
Simple erosion of a dam face, typically due to precipitation run-off that is not 44%

44% Overtopping
Water flowing over the top of a dam. Tailings dams are made of erodible material, and overtopping will cause erosion.

17% Seepage—Seepage and internal erosion
Erosin of dam material due to water passing through areas of the dam that are designed to remain dry.

1% Mine subsidence
If the dam or impoundment is built above an underground mine, collapse of the underground mine workings can lead to release of the impounded tailings.

Source: ICOLD 2001, Chambers 2017.

The United States Federal Emergency Management Agency (U.S. FEMA), which coordinates the U.S. federal government's role in preparing for, preventing, mitigating the effects of, responding to and recovering from all domestic disasters, whether natural or man-made, including acts of terror, also points out that dams usually fail for one or a combination of the following reasons:

 – *overtopping* caused by floods that exceed the capacity of the dam;
 – deliberate acts of *sabotage*;

---

4   Roche, C., Thygesen, K., Baker, E. (eds.), 2017, *Mine Tailings Storage: Safety Is No Accident,* A UNEP Rapid Response Assessment, United Nations Environment Programme and GRID-Arendal, Nairobi and Arendal, available at https://www.grida.no/publications/383.

- *structural failure* of materials used in dam construction;
- movement and/or *failure of the foundation* supporting the dam;
- settlement and cracking of concrete or embankment dams;
- *piping and internal erosion* of soil in embankment dams; and
- *inadequate maintenance and upkeep.*[5]

Based on those sources, it is possible to affirm that the main causes of large dams' failures may be summarized as being:
- design/project failure or its inadequacy;
- maintenance and upkeep failure; and
- force majeure.

In 2017, the United Nations Environmental Programme issued the assessment report, *Mine Tailings Storage: Safety Is No Accident, 2017*, recommending an approach to tailing dams placing safety first by making environmental and human safety a priority in management actions and on-the-ground operations, according to which regulators, industry and society should adopt a zero-failure objective. According to this assessment, measures and regulations should include, among other, encouragement to *reduce waste generation*; innovate in the *reuse and recycling of mine tailings*; development of *technological solutions to eliminate the main causes of failures*; expand regulations to include *monitoring, independent monitoring and enforcement; financial and criminal sanctions for noncompliance; avoid/ban dam construction methods known to be high risk*; enforce *mandatory financial securities* among other recommendations.

Brazil, having over 17,604 registered dams[6] and as a relevant global player in mineral production, was no exception to this risk scenario; but until the year 2002, it had almost no legislation on dam safety, and there were no laws requiring any of the practices and recommendations above-mentioned. From 2001 to 2019, six large tailings[7] dams collapsed, causing extensive environmental harm and victims.

More recently, two major tailings dams collapsed, one in 2015, Fundão Dam at Mariana City in the State of Minas Gerais, and in January 2019 in

---

5 https://www.fema.gov/why-dams-fail, accessed on Apr. 16, 2020.
6 National Water Agency ("ANA") *in* Relatório de Segurança de Barragens, 2018.
7 Macacos Tailings Dam, Nova Lima/MG 2001 (Upstream heightening method); Cataguases Dam, Cataguases/MG, 2003 (industrial waste dam); Tailings Dam Rio Pomba/ Cataguases, Miraí/MG 2007 (downstream method); Tailings dam Herculano, Itabirito/MG 2014 (upstream heightening method); Tailings dam Fundão and Santarém, Mariana/MG 2015 (upstream heightening method); Tailings Dam Feijão Mine, Brumadinho/MG, 2019 (upstream heightening method).

the city of Brumadinho, also in Minas Gerais, each of them causing significant social, economic and environmental harm and also human victims. Although Brazil already had some regulation on dam safety, including the Dam Safety National Policy (Federal Law 12,334/2010) and its regulation, its (in)efficiency was put to the test due to the successive accidents which revealed that there was room for regulatory, oversight and practices improvement.

In addition to the above-mentioned background, those recent accidents triggered the adoption of a series of additional policies, laws and measures aiming to avoid new accidents of that scale, set forth stricter rules and better address and regulate the response, recovery and liability in cases of environmental disasters.

In the months that followed the Córrego do Feijão Mine dam break (January 25, 2019), dozens of laws and regulations on dam safety and environmental protection were enacted at the federal and state levels[8] bringing significant modifications to the legal framework and establishing a new paradigm to large dams construction, operation and decommissioning. Although the new legal framework affects and regulates all large dams, the mining tailings dams were at the center of the concerns and are in the focus of the regulations, thus receiving special treatment and subject to additional precautionary and control measures.

Brazilian Regulations on Large Dams and Tailings Dams Safety

From 2000 to 2015: Setting a Legal Framework for the National Dam Safety Policy

Until the year 2000, Brazil and the main mining states had no law establishing safety policies specifically to large dams; thus, these structures were subject, essentially, to the same legal general framework applicable to other large structures/buildings and general regulations for mining,[9] energy, industrial waste and water supply activities, depending on the case.

---

8 Especially in the traditionally mining States, Minas Gerais and Pará.
9 For example, DNPM's Ordinance No. 237/2001 established on *NRM-18—Beneficiamento and NRM-19—Disposição de Estéril, Rejeitos e Produtos,* some

One aspect that draws up the attention is the fact that, despite Brazil's large number of dams[10] (mining, hydropower, industrial waste, water supply, etc.) and many relevant accidents in the past, prior to 2000, there was almost no legislation focused on dam safety and no national policy or official guidelines; whereas in other countries with relevant number of large dams (e.g., U.S., Finland, Canada and China), such legislation dates back to the 1970s and 1980s.[11]

It was only in 1999, that the Brazilian Committee on Dams published a Basic Guide on Dam Safety largely based on the Dam Safety Guidelines published by the Canadian Dam Association which was used as a general reference for dam owners and engineers in Brazil and was used as a base for the bill proposal which, in 2010, became the National Dam Safety Policy Act—NDSP.

It is worth mentioning that in Brazil, pursuant to Articles 23, 24 and 30 of the Brazilian Constitution, dam safety is considered a federal, state and also local matter; thus, the legislative branch of the three levels of government may legislate and regulate on this subject. To avoid overlapping and

---

general requirements related to dams safety are having a qualified professional responsible for the dam's design and its safety, periodic monitoring of water, groundwater and seepage, and also mandatory evacuation in cases of rupture or imminent risk of collapse.

10 The National Water Agency ("ANA") estimates the existence of more than 24,000 large dams in Brazil of which 17,604 are currently registered and classified pursuant to the NPDS and its regulations. ("Relatório de Segurança de Barragens 2018," available at https://www.ana.gov.br/noticias/ana-lanca-relatorio-de-seguranca-de-barragens-2018, on Jun. 1, 2020.)

11 Examples: *U.S.*: National Dam Safety Program Act (NDSPA), passed in 1972, revised in 1984, and incorporated as section 215 of the Water Resources Development Act of 1996, PL104-303, Oct. 12, 1996.
    Finland: 1984 Dam Safety Act (DSA); Dam Safety Decree 27.7.1984/574 (DSD); the 1985 Dam Safety Code of Practice (DSCP), which was last revised in 1997; and the Water Act of 19.5.1961/1264.
    In *Canada,* this is a state matter, and the provinces of Alberta, British Columbia, Ontario, and Quebec (Canada) have specific legislations; e.g., Alberta: Dam and Canal Safety Regulations of 1978, the Dam Safety Guidelines of 1975 and the 1995 Dams Safety Guidelines of the CDA.
    In *Australia,* it is mostly a state matter, and there is relevant legislation in New South Wales (Dams Safety Act (DSA)), Queensland (Water Resources Act of 1989), and Victoria (Water Act of 1989) also have specific legislation, in addition to the 1994 Australian National Committee on Large Dams (ANCOLD) Guidelines on Dam Safety Management.
    China: Reservoir Dam Safety Certification Regulations (Mar. 20, 1995); Hydropower Station Dam Safety Management Regulations (January 1997), Detailed Rules on Hydropower Station Dam Safety Inspection (August 1988) (*source*: Daniel Bradlow et al., "Regulatory Frameworks for dam Safety—A Comparative Study," The World Bank, Washington D.C.).

contradictory regulations, the Constitution sets forth that if there is a federal law setting forth the legal framework and the general rules applicable, the state and local legislation must be harmonic with the federal general rules.

Prior to 2010, in the absence of a framework federal law or even a state policy regarding dam safety, based on the environmental laws and general legal framework, the Minas Gerais State issued the Resolution SEMAD 99/2002, COPAM's Ordinance 62/2002 and, later, the COPAM's Ordinance 87/2005, that established the minimum safety requirements; mandatory registry, classification according to the dam-associated risks and size; procedures and requirements for implementation, operation, upkeep, care and maintenance and decommissioning; inspection and oversight; mandatory periodic auditing procedures and evacuation measures. The above-mentioned regulations may be considered the first Brazilian set of environmental and safety rules that took a systematic approach to dam's safety issues and established the basic policies, requirements and guidelines aiming to control, monitor and reduce associated risks (social, environmental and economic) and foster safer practices. Moreover, the state authorities were clearly starting to demand from the authorities and entrepreneurs a harder look at how large dams are designed, build, operated, monitored, maintained and decommissioned.

However, a turning point for the legal initiative was the occurrence of a severe accident in 2003 (Cataguases City, Minas Gerais State), when an industrial waste dam collapsed causing contamination of the *Pomba River* and *Paraíba do Sul* river, extensive environmental harm and interruption of the water supply of over 600,000 people. After that event, federal and state authorities enacted several laws and regulations establishing environmental and safety policies for large dams, worth mentioning the following:

(1) *Federal Law 12,334/2010* (Bill 1,181/2003)[12] establishes the *NDSP*The NDSP is the main law regarding this matter and sets forth important mechanisms and instruments, aligned with international recommendations, practices and guidelines, such as:

(a) a *National System of Large Dams Safety* ("SNISB," acronym in Portuguese), which shall gather, store and analyze information regarding dams under construction, operation, decommissioning and deactivated. Also, the information on SNISB is of public

---

12 The Bill 1,181/2003 expressly mentions the accident of Cataguases Dam as being the sort of severe risk that the lack of dam safety regulations and practices poses to society and to the environment.

access, and the parties responsible for the dams must keep the information up to date in the system.

  (b) *Dam Safety Plan ("DSP")* which must comprise, at least, the following information:

      (i) identification of the entrepreneur and responsible party;

     (ii) technical data regarding the implementation of the project, including, in the case of projects built after the enactment of this Law, the project "as built," as well as those projects necessary for the operation and maintenance;

    (iii) organizational structure and technical qualification of the professionals of the dam safety team;

    (iv) manuals of procedures for the safety inspections and monitoring and dam safety reports;

     (v) operational rule for the discharge devices of the dam;

    (vi) indication of the area surrounding the facilities and their respective accesses, to be protected from any permanent uses or occupations, except those essential to the maintenance and operation of the dam;

   (vii) *Emergency Action Plan (EAP)*;[13]

  (viii) *safety inspection reports*; and

    (ix) *periodic review* of the plans.

  (c) *Dam Safety Report.*

Pursuant to the NDSP, only large dams destined to the accumulation of water for any uses, final or temporary waste disposal and the accumulation or impoundment of industrial waste with at least one of the following characteristics are subject to this law and its regulations:

  (1) height of the embankment, counted from the lowest point of the foundation to the crest, greater than or equal to *15 m*;

  (2) total reservoir capacity greater than or equal to *3,000,000 m³*;

  (3) reservoir containing *hazardous waste* according to applicable technical standards; and

  (4) category of potential associated damage *("PAD" or the acronym in Portuguese DPA –Dano Potencial Associado), medium or high,* considering the economic, social, environmental or loss of human life potential impacts.

---

13 Not all dams are subject to this obligation, for example, large dams with low associated risks may be exempt.

The NDSP also indicated the authorities responsible for oversight and law enforcement. In sum, the law says that the inspection, oversight, regulation and enforcement of the dam safety national policy and its regulations, without hindering or limiting the oversight and inspections powers of the environmental agencies that are part of the National Environment System ("Sisnama"), shall be performed by:

(1) the agency, authority or governmental body that granted the water use permit;

(2) the entity that granted or authorized the use of the hydraulic potential ("ANEEL"), when it is a preponderant use for the purposes of hydroelectric generation;

(3) the entity granting mining rights ("ANM") for the purpose of final or temporary disposal of tailings; and

(4) the entity that provided the environmental license for installation and operation for the purpose of industrial waste disposal.

Such legal framework reiterated the overlapping power of authorities causing, to some extent, jurisdiction conflicts and uncertainty regarding law enforcement. In addition to this legal problem, as mentioned before, the matter may be regulated at the federal, state and local levels. Figure 8.3 illustrates the overlap of powers to inspect, regulate and enforce dam safety law and regulations.

Figure 8.3   Oversight and Enforcement Powers—Pursuant to the NDSP

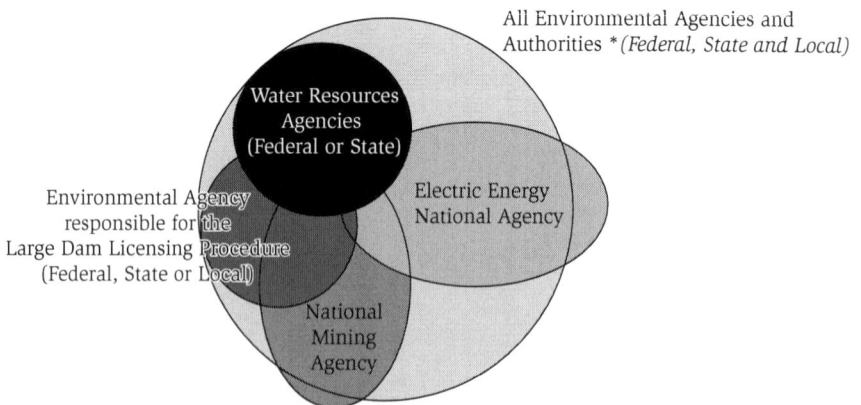

For example, a mining tailings dam licensed by a state environmental agency, using federal water resources (e.g., federal river) shall be subject to inspections and oversight not only from ANM, State Environmental Agency and National Water Agency, but also by any environmental agency or environmental authority (federal, state and local).

From one perspective, more public agents and authorities were inspecting and implementing law enforcement, raising more awareness of the issue. However, in the following years, there was some extensive debate and some relevant judicial litigation regarding the apparent overlap of legal capacities and dispute over which authority is mainly responsible and even liable for the approval of large dams and/or for the lack/omission in properly inspect such structures and enforcing the laws and regulations.

As mentioned above, Articles 23, 24 and 30 of the Federal Constitution only made this debate more complex because it establishes a shared capacity that may not be limited or excluded unless the Constitution itself is revised or amended.

To mitigate this problem, later legislation (e.g., Complementary Law 140/2011) aimed to organize and coordinate the actions of the actors and authorities that share the oversight and enforcement powers over the matter and also to clarify which aspect of the law should be assigned to which governmental body or authority.

After the enactment of the NDSP in 2010, many mechanisms, instruments and obligations established at that law remained ineffective (Safety Inspections, Dam Safety Reports, deadlines, etc.) until further regulation, which were gradually regulated at federal and state level. In this period between 2000 and 2015, it is worth to highlight the following regulations:

- *CNRH*[14] *Resolutions 142 and 143*, issued on July 10, 2012, establish general criteria for classification of dams by risk category, associated potential damage ("DPA") and their volume, in compliance with Article 7 of Law 12,334/2010.
- DNPM[15] *Ordinances 416/2012 and 526/2013*, which created the National Registry of Mining Dams and large dams associated with mining activities and established the mandatory *Mining Dam Safety Plan, Periodic Safety Review and Regular and Special Safety Inspections of Mining Dams*, also defines the minimum structure

---

14 CNRH is the acronym in Portuguese for "Conselho Nacional de Recursos Hídricos," the National Council for Water Resources.

15 DNPM is the acronym for "Departamento Nacional de Produção Mineral" (National Department for Mineral Production), which was substituted by the National Mining Agency—NMA.

and content of the *DSP* (acronym in Portuguese: "PAEBM") and its revisions.
  – Furthermore, these ordinances set forth the obligation to present a periodic *Stability Condition Declarations* ("DCE") for each dam under the company's responsibility, prepared by external auditors, co-singed by the company's CEO (or equivalent), certifying the structure safety and soundness according with the minimum safety factors required.
  – *ANEEL*[16] *Resolution 696/2015* regulates the Dam Safety Policies regarding hydroelectric power plant dams, establishes criteria for dam's classification, criteria for the formulation of Dam Safety Plans and requirements to carry out the Periodic Dam Safety Plan Review pursuant to NDSP.

By 2015, the new legal framework was established, and most of the dam safety basic mechanisms and obligations set forth thus far were in place. In a nutshell, by then, the main obligations could be summarized as being:
  – report and provide information to the public authorities;
  – periodically inspect the structures and certify its stability; and
  – prepare and update the emergency plans.

However, private and public sectors were still struggling to understand, assimilate and comply with all the recent laws and regulations, and to provide, process and systematically analyze the information to effectively address the safety issues. Moreover, some obligations were still within the legal deadline, thus, an evaluation regarding the effectiveness and the adequacy of the regulations would still be premature.

On November 5, 2015, another large tailings' dam collapse drew the nation's attention again to this issue and triggered social and political pressure to further regulate and set forth more strict and severe rules regarding dam safety and liabilities.

Brazilian States Join the Regulatory Effort

In 2015, the NDSP and its federal regulations were in place already setting the framework and the general rules regarding large dams' safety. Never-theless, after the collapse of Fundão Tailings Dam, states authorities were

---

16 ANEEL is the acronym for "Agência Nacional de Energia Elétrica," the Electric Energy National Agency.

prompted to enact several regulations on the matter, either to reinforce the federal rules or to add new or stricter requirements.

By 2017, all twenty-six Brazilian States, with very few exceptions, had issued specific legislation on large dam safety, as the table below illustrates:

State	Dam Safety Plan	Safety Inspection	Special Inspection	Safety Report	Emergency Plan
AC	Port. 07/2017	Port. 07/2017	Port. 07/2017	Port. 07/2017	Port. 07/2017
AL	Port. 492/2015	Port. 491/2015		Port. 492/2015	Port. 694/2016
AM	Port. 160/2016			Port. 160/2016	
AP					
BA	Port. 4672/2013	Port. 4672/2013		Port. 4672/2013	
CE	Port. 2747/SRH/CE/2017	Port. 2747/SRH/CE/2017	Port. 2747/SRH/CE/2017	Port. 2747/SRH/CE/2017	Port. 2747/SRH/CE/2017
DF					
ES		Res. 062/2017			
GO					
MA	Port. 132/2017	Port. 132/2017	Port. 132/2017	Port. 132/2017	Port. 132/2017
MG					
MS	Res. SE MADE 44/2016	Res. SE MADE 44/2016	Res. SE MADE 44/2016	Port. 576/2017	Port. 576/2017
MT	Res. 99/2017	Res. 99/2017	Res. 99/2017	Res. 99/2017	Res. 99/2017
PA					
PB	Res. 04/2016	Res. 03/2016	Res. 03/2016	Res. 04/2016	
PE	Res. 03/2017 DC	Res. 03/2017 DC	Res. 03/2017 DC	Res. 03/2017 DC	Res. 03/2017 DC
PI					

State	Dam Safety Plan	Safety Inspection	Special Inspection	Safety Report	Emergency Plan
PR	Port. 14/2014	Port. 15/2014		Port. 14/2014	
RJ					
RN	Port. 10/2017	Port. 10/2017	Port. 10/2017	Port. 10/2017	Port. 10/2017
RO	Port. 379/GAB/SEDAM	Port. 379/GAB/SEDAM	Port. 379/GAB/SEDAM	Port. 379/GAB/SEDAM	Port. 379/GAB/SEDAM
RR		IN 01/2017	IN 01/2017		
RS	Port. 136/2017			Port. 136/2017	
SC					
SE	Port. 58/2017	Port. 58/2017	Port. 58/2017	Port. 58/2017	Port. 58/2017
SP	DD 279/2015/C	DD 279/2015/C	DD 279/2015/C	DD 279/2015/C	
SP	Port. 3907/2015			Port. 3907/2015	
TO	Port. 483/2017	Port. 483/2017	Port. 483/2017	Port. 483/2017	Port. 483/2017
FED	Res. 236/2017	Res. 236/2017	Res. 236/2017	Res. 236/2017	Res. 236/2017

Source: Author's own work.

Besides the evident need to better address dam safety, the recent history of accidents brought awareness to another issue: the use of upstream heightening method to
build dams. One of the reasons was that among the seven most severe accidents—from the social and environmental perspective—involving large dams between 1980 and 2015, five dams used upstream heightening method.

However, from the technical perspective there was some argument about the use of upstream heightening as being a valid and safe method if properly designed and kept; the fact is that the upstream heightening was considered less safe compared to other methods such as downstream and centerline. Moreover, the public and regulators' opinion was set on to limit or even to ban this method and demand the use of safer technologies and alternatives.

Minas Gerais State, where most of the accidents and collapses happened, on January 21, 2016, promptly passed the State Law 21,972/2016 establishing that the executive branch should, by all means, act to foster and demand better and safer alternatives to avoid environmental harm and associated risks related to large dams and specially mining tailing dams. On May 2 of the same year, State Decree 46,993/2016 set forth precautionary measures until further regulations on the issue:

(a) extraordinary dam safety inspection of all dams built using upstream heightening method;
(b) immediate suspension of activities until safety standards are met; and
(c) suspension of all environmental licensing procedures related to large dam projects using the upstream heightening method.

The initiative in Minas Gerais set the stage for the definitive ban of upstream heightening method, at the federal level and in other States. Worldwide, among other countries with significant mining production, only Chile had banned this method thus far.

On May 17, 2017, the National Mining Agency approved the Ordinance 70,389/2017 regulating all instruments of the NDSP and consolidating the rules on the matter, regarding dams' structures associated to mining activities.

By the end of 2018, the NDSP and most of the legal framework regarding dam safety were enacted and entered into force in Brazil, and practically all Brazilian States had local rules in addition to the federal legal framework. Therefore, the Ordinance 70,389/2017 with other regulations gave full force to the NDSP, setting forth the detailed obligations and the deadlines to be complied with, under the penalties of the law.

Additional Precautionary Measures

In January 2019, another large mining tailings dams' collapse[17] with significant human victims triggered a series of additional measures and further regulations that brought stricter rules and a more comprehensive and precautionary approach over this matter.

The list below illustrates the volume of laws and regulations that were hastily enacted after January 2019, specifically related to dam safety, and focusing mainly on mining tailings dams and industrial waste dams:

- January 25, 2019—Minas Gerais State Decree NE No. 23/2019;
- January 25, 2019—Federal Decree No. 9,691/2019;
- January 28, 2019—Resolution of CASA CIVIL 1;
- January 28, 2019—Resolution of CASA CIVIL 2;
- January 28, 2019—Resolution of ANEEL ("Federal Electric Energy Agency") Cc/Cmsrd No. 2—institutes the Special Committee to prepare the bill proposal aiming to update and modernize the NDSP;
- January 29, 2019—SEMAD Resolution 2,762;
- January 30, 2019—SEMAD/FEAM Joint Resolution 2,765;
- January 31, 2019—Ordinance of the Ministry of Mining and Energy, No. 21—requests that all mining companies responsible for large dams provide updated information regarding safety policies and regulations compliance;
- January 31, 2019—Ordinance of CRBIO 151;
- February 8, 2019—Ordinance of "Secretaria de Geologia, Mineração e Transformação Mineral" No. 37—determines investigation procedures and intensifies inspections schedules regarding dam safety;
- February 15, 2019—ANM Resolution 4—bans the upstream heightening method for tailings dams and establishes a phase out of existing structures/projects using this method.
- February 19, 2019—CNRH Resolution 1;

---

17 Córrego do Feijão mine complex, mining tailings dam collapses at Brumadinho City, Minas Gerais.

- February 25, 2019—State Law (Minas Gerais) No. 23,291/2019 (the law commonly referred as "sea of mud nevermore");
- February 26, 2019—IGAM Ordinances 2 and 3;
- February 26, 2019—State Decree NE MG No. 176;
- March 21, 2019—Joint Resolution SEMAD/FEAM 2,784—bans upstream heightening method for large dams and sets forth a phase out for existing structures using this method;
- July 24, 2019—Joint Resolution Semad/Feam/Ief/Igam No. 2,827/2019;
- August 8, 2019—Resolution of ANM No. 13—establishes additional regulatory requirements to increase safety factors and assure tailings dams' stability/safety;
- August 26, 2019—SEMAD/Feam Joint Resolution No. 2,833, of August 26, 2019—requirements regarding inspections and conditions of stability certifications;
- August 27, 2019—Ordinance of MME ("Mining and Energy Ministry") 138—institutes the permanent technical committee on tailings dam's safety;
- December 19, 2019—Resolution of CNEN ("National Nuclear Energy Council") 257—establishes: (a) the registry of radioactive tailings dams; (b) the dam safety and management system; (c) the minimum technical requirements for safe operation; (d) minimum professional qualification and requirements for the people technically responsible for operation and providing information to the agency and (e) the structure and requirements for the dam safety and emergency plans;
- May 11, 2020—Resolution ANM No. 32, of May 11, 2020—owner/responsible for the dam must prepare the flood mapping studies to support the structure's classification regarding potential associated risk and to comply with other obligations related to the emergency action plan; and
- June 7, 2020—ANM Resolution No. 40/2020—requires that the mining dams have a safety monitoring system operating within 24 months.

This new set of rules added new instruments, obligations and deadlines for the public and private sectors aiming to avoid new accidents, among which:

- ban of upstream heightening method for large dams;
- a short phase out period to decommission existing structures using this method;

- increased safety factors to assure tailings dams stability/safety (from 1 to at least 1.3^{18}); and
- full-time automated monitoring and alert system.

It is worth to mention that none of these rules were preceded by a regulatory impact analysis,[19] thus some of the economic, environmental and social impacts, and the feasibility of the deadlines were not taken into consideration. High hierarchy public authorities even recognized that the regulations were issued as a prompt response to society and to address urgent matters; therefore, there could be room for adjustments, which indeed happened later.

After these new set of regulations issued in 2019, there are several new obligations, restrictions and deadlines whose timely fulfillment may be challenging and/or of significant economic impact for the companies, namely:

---

18 Pursuant Ordinance ANM 70.389/2017 and ABNT NBR 13028:2017.
19 The regulatory impact analysis only became mandatory after the Federal Law No. 13,874 passed in 2019 and its regulations Federal Decree 10,411 of Jun. 20, 2020.

June 17, 2019	*Install Alert System. For VG 1 and 2 (upstream heightening method), the alert system installation is due by April 30, 2019.*				
August 15, 2019	*Deactivate/remove installations, structures, buildings and services that may include human presence within the Self-Rescue Area (ZAS). *Deadline, postponed to October 12, 2019 (ANM Resolution 13/2019).*	*Conclude and submit to ANM the technical project for the decommission or decharacterization of tailings dams built or heightened by upstream or unknown method.*	Submit to ANM a new Plan of Economic Exploitation ("PAE") in face of the studies and technical projects determined by ANM's Ordinance #4/2019.	Conclude studies for the identification and implementation of solutions to reduce water contribution on active tailings dams, regardless of their method of construction. Identified solutions shall be implemented immediately after August 15, 2019.	Adequate tailings dams built or heightened by upstream method, active or inactive, to avoid water contribution from watershed and install, for such purpose, side channels or other technical solutions.

February 15, 2020	Conclude *reinforcement works for tailings dams built through downstream methods or conclude the construction of a new structure of contention with regard to tailings dams built through upstream or unknown method.*	Implement a *full-time monitoring system* on the tailings dams.
August 15, 2020	*Decommissioning or decharacterization of dams built for liquid effluents storage located immediately downstream to the tailings dams.*	

August 15, 2021	*Conclude the decommissioning or decharacterization of current inactive tailings dams, which were built or heightened by upstream or unknown method.*
August 15, 2023 *Deadline altered to* *September 15, 2022* *September 15, 2025* *September 15, 2027* *Depending on dam's size*	Conclude the decommissioning or decharacterization of active tailings dams, which were built or heightened by upstream or unknown method. Such tailings dams may remain active until August 15, 2021 upon the fulfillment of the conditions established by ANM Ordinance #4/2019.

Therefore, in addition to all safety requirements, since February 2020, all tailings dams classified with high DPA must have systems for automated monitoring in real time and full-time (24/7); thus any variation on its stability or safety may be identified earlier and should trigger the adoption of precautionary measures timely and accordingly with the emergency action plan submitted to the competent authority. It is likely that regulations will increase the number of dams to be monitored in real time in the upcoming years. Also, installations, structures, buildings and services that may include human presence within the Self-Rescue Area (ZAS—*zona de autossalvamento*)[20] must be removed or relocated to avoid any human presence in the areas of most risk, and emergency drills are to be performed periodically, to better prepare the responsible parties, affected communities and public authorities.

The new regulations also determine that the Declaration of Structure Stability ("DCE"—Declaração de Condição de Estabilidade, in Portuguese) must be signed by the: (i) technical responsible for report preparation and also (ii) individual with the highest authority in the hierarchy structure of the company, responsible for its direction, control or administration (e.g., CEO, Company President, etc.).

In regard to the environmental licensing procedures, the new legal paradigm sets forth the following scheme:

---

20 ZAS—The area downstream the dam that may be severely flooded (according to the flood mapping studies) and where there may not be sufficient time for evacuation or intervention, equivalent to 10 kilometer downstream or the extension of the inundation during the first 30 minutes, whichever is greater.

Aspect	Until December 2018	Current Legislation
Large Dams using upstream heightening method	Not forbidden	– Restriction forbids the licensing of upstream heightening method and the renewal of environmental licenses for such structures. – Phase out established. Existing structures must be decommissioned within legislation's deadlines.
All large dams *except for hydropower plants.*	Environmental Licensing Procedures would follow the general rule, which basically established the possibility of: – a *fast track* and simplified licensing procedure for small- and medium-sized dams or dam with small potential environmental impacts; – a *concomitant procedure*, consisting of a two-step licensing procedure (Preliminary+Installation License and Operation License); and	– All tailings dams are subject to EIA and public hearing. – Fast tracks or simplified procedures do not apply. – Burden to prove the nonexistence of technological alternative to the use of tailings dam (i.e., dry stacking). – Mandatory financial securities for decommissioning and accidents. – Independent monitoring of dam safety reports and peer review of projects and reports.

Aspect	Until December 2018	Current Legislation
	– a *full licensing procedure*, subject to Environmental Impact Assessment (EIA), Public Hearing and a three-step procedure (Preliminary License, Installation License and Operation License).	– Forbids the issuance of new licenses for dams if there is a community downstream within the self-rescue zone (SRZ). *(Licensing regulations and procedures may vary from State to State.)*
SRZ *except for hydropower plants.*	Did not forbid human activities, structure or occupation downstream.	Forbids human permanence, activities, structure or any occupation downstream. *(Not applicable to hydroelectric energy production dams.)*

Moreover, in case of noncompliance with such obligations, the responsible parties may be subject to the following penalties:

– *Fines*
- up to BRL 3,421.06 regarding the Mining Agency regulations, per infraction;
- up to BRL 1,288,809.19 regarding Environmental Law regulations, ordinary infractions;
- up to BRL 50,000,000.00 (federal environmental infraction and Pará State) or up to BRL 99,139,167.84 (Minas Gerais State Infraction) regarding Environmental Law regulations, in case of harm to the public health and society wellbeing and/or to the Economy of the State.

– *Suspension of activities* until obligations are complied with, especially if the company fails to timely remove structures, equipment and personal from the ZAS, lack of DCE (stability statement) or failure to adopt the required precautionary measures related to the dams safety.

- *Abrogation of the environmental license,* in cases of severe accidents, structure collapse, recidivism or severe violation with imminent risk or ongoing harm.
  - *Civil liabilities*—Legislation sets forth that civil liability is strict joint and several with inversed burden of proof. The party responsible for the large dam is liable and responsible to recover and indemnify all incurred costs and harms related to an accident.
  - *Criminal liabilities*—Federal Law 9,605/1998 (Environmental Crimes Act) sets forth a large list of crimes and felonies related to environmental infractions and accidents, such as: Article 54 (to cause pollution of any sort—fines, detention and imprisonment of up to five years); Article 60 (to perform activities with potential environmental risks without licenses or not complying with its conditions—fines or detention/imprisonment of up to six months); Article 69-A (to provide false relevant environmental information or to omit information in environmental processes—fines, detention and imprisonment of up to ten years).

Pursuant to the regulations abovementioned, companies and people responsible for large dams, and especially large mining tailings dams, must comply with a comprehensive set[21] of instruments, obligations, practices and mechanism aiming to improve control and prevent risks, that may summarized as:
- maintain *updated information* at dam's registry before the competent authority/agency;
- prepare and obtain the approval of *Dam Safety Plan* ("DSP") and *Emergency Action Plan (EAP)*;
- perform periodic *training and emergency/safety drills*;
- perform periodic and extraordinary/special *inspections* and file its reports at the governmental agency;
- Perform the *periodic review of plans* and reports;
- submit the *Dam Safety Report* to the public authority;
- if necessary, adopt *measures to increase safety factors* to assure tailings dams' stability/safety, pursuant to the new higher safety standard applicable;

---

21 Those are the main aspects; the list is not exhaustive, and the obligations, its deadlines and requirements may vary depending on the size, nature, and associated risk, and also on the state where the dam is located.

- implement and maintain full-time *automated monitoring and alert systems*;
- remove installations, structures, buildings and services that may include human presence within the *ZAS*;
- implementation of solutions to *reduce water contribution* on active tailings dams;
- *mandatory financial securities* for decommissioning and accidents;
- *independent monitoring/inspection* of dam safety reports and *peer review of projects and reports*; and
- *inform and alert any situation of noncompliance or imminent risk, triggering emergency plan actions.*

In addition, during the environmental licensing procedure for new large dams, its heightening or even license renewal, the environmental agency tends to take a hard look and be very thorough with these and other requirements and also to request evidence of the inexistence of better technological alternative to the use of tailings or industrial waste dam (e.g., dry stacking, recycling).

Therefore, it is possible to affirm that Brazil now counts with updated and comprehensive legislation on Large Dam Safety with a more precautionary and transparent approach, which has incorporated many of the international best practices and benchmarks and most of the recommendations provided on UNEP's *Mine Tailings Storage: Safety Is No Accident* (2017). That does not mean that Brazilian legislation is at state of the art, but rather that there has been a very significant evolution both in regulation and practices regarding dam safety, that may have a positive effect on risk prevention and mitigation in the coming years.

It is also worth mentioning that dam safety remains to be an international concern, and countries should address the issue to avoid unnecessary risks and harms. With that in mind, the UNEP, Principles for Responsible Investment (PRI) and International Council on Mining and Metals (ICMM) launched, on August 5, 2020, the Global Industry Standard on Tailings Management[22]—(GISTM or "Standard"), which also took in account the recent history and lessons learned in Brazil and proposes a joint effort to "*achieve the ultimate goal of zero harm to people and the environment with zero tolerance for human fatality.*" The Standard is composed of fifteen principles and seventy-seven auditable requirements

---

22 Available at https://globaltailingsreview.org/global-industry-standard/, accessed on Aug. 31, 2020.

subdivided into six topics: (1) affected communities; (2) integrated knowledge base; (3) design, construction, operation and monitoring of the tailings facility; (4) management and governance; (5) emergency response and long-term recovery and (6) public disclosure and access to information, providing relevant subsidies to improve companies' practices in addition to the laws and regulations applicable to the matter.

Conclusion

Undoubtedly, Brazil came a long way in dam safety regulations. From almost no regulation in the year 2000 to the current legal framework, relevant requirements were put in place in accordance with good practices and international benchmarks.

A prominent Brazilian poet once wrote that *"lilies do not spring from laws,"*[23] emphasizing that laws, by themselves, are not enough to solve problems in the real world. In this case, Brazil now counts on legislation aligned with international benchmarks and best practices, but to achieve effectiveness of dam safety laws it is also necessary a change of culture, to embody safety and precaution to the daily life, the adoption of better practices and the promotion of cycles of continued improvement, both in private and public sectors.

Of course, there is always room for regulatory and practices improvement. The best way to avoid risks is eliminating the source rather than to constantly control it. Reduction of waste generation, innovation in reuse and recycle of mine tailings, economically feasible dry staking, development of technological solutions to eliminate the main causes of failures and avoiding dam construction methods known to be high risk are key elements yet to be fully implemented.

---

23 Andrade, Carlos Drummond de, in the poem *Nosso Tempo* ("Our Time").

The Collapsing of the Earth's Lungs: Could "Third World Approaches to International Law" Breathe Air into the Amazonian Crisis?

Warona Jolomba
Transnational Law, LLM Alumna at King's College London

Introduction

This chapter will discuss the crisis of the Amazon rainforest and the extent to which the region can successfully stifle deforestation and limit climate change damage. In doing this, we will briefly delve into what has been occurring in the Amazon over the past few decades up to recently and assess how its containing countries are interacting with international environmental law (IEL). This will involve an examination of regional implementation strategies, a brief comparison between two Amazon countries, and a regional comparison between South America and Central America. After identifying any strengths and weaknesses in the Amazon region, we will turn to TWAIL (Third World Approaches to International Law) to see if there are any gaps that can be filled when looking for solutions for more effective climate change mitigation. This chapter will conclude that attempting to tackle a global issue demands global cooperation, but this should not necessarily come in the form of extraterritorial enforcement of international agreements; there should be a focus on regional cooperation and localized progress. This means that all countries cannot be held to the exact same standard when it comes to climate change, and TWAIL helps to contextualize climate change under a more historical and socioeconomic backdrop. TWAIL alone cannot save the Amazon, but it is worth a consideration in the grand scheme of IEL dialogue.

International Legal Developments Surrounding Amazon Protection

The Amazonian Crisis

The Amazon is given the title of the earth's lungs due to the immense volume of oxygen its trees provide the planet in exchange for carbon dioxide. It spans over 7 billion square kilometers across one continent, and its rainforest surpasses 5.5 million square kilometers.[1] However, extreme rates of deforestation have been occurring in the region since the mid-twentieth century. Motivations are linked to infrastructural development, such as the building of the Trans-Amazonian Highway.[2] It appears that the Amazon countries have been struggling to tackle the issues of climate change, especially concerning deforestation. Maria Tigre criticizes the Amazonian region's inability to implement policies that can help to aptly protect the heavily exploited rainforest; she states that though there is an institutional framework in place, it lags many paces behind.[3] The Amazon's ample freshwater supply is being affected by climate change, so water supply is a huge concern, as "transboundary watersheds are particularly vulnerable to increased disputes, and climate change may reduce the possibilities of cooperation between basin countries."[4] Brazil, Ecuador, Bolivia, Guyana, and Suriname have put emphasis on water sustainability through, *inter alia*, promotion of regional models for river-basin governance and community-based water management. The rainforest, however, was barely mentioned in these countries' national adaptation plans (NAPs).[5] Tigre argued that the difficulties in managing the water usage of

---

1 Brett Simpson, *International Involvement in Preservation of the Brazilian Amazon Rainforest: Context, Constraints and Scope* (2010) Asia Pacific Journal of Environmental Law, Vol. 13, Issue 1, Australian Centre for Climate and Environmental Law, 40.

2 Brett Simpson, *International Involvement in Preservation of the Brazilian Amazon Rainforest: Context, Constraints and Scope* (2010) Asia Pacific Journal of Environmental Law, Vol. 13, Issue 1, Australian Centre for Climate and Environmental Law, 41.

3 Maria Antonia Tigre, *Building a Regional Adaptation Strategy for Amazon Countries* (2019) Int Environ Agreements Vol. 19, Issue 4-5, Springer Netherlands, 422.

4 Maria Antonia Tigre, *Building a Regional Adaptation Strategy for Amazon Countries* (2019) Int Environ Agreements Vol. 19, Issue 4-5, Springer Netherlands, 415.

5 Maria Antonia Tigre, *Building a Regional Adaptation Strategy for Amazon Countries* (2019) Int Environ Agreements Vol. 19, Issue 4-5, Springer Netherlands, 415.

the second largest river in the world stem from it being shared by so many countries: "the level of complexity in transboundary basins is reinforced by the involvement of environmental, societal, and political factors, as well as the interconnection between and among systems."[6]

Along with deforestation comes endless violence against the Amazon's environmental human rights defenders (EDHRs); Latin America has been singled out as "the most dangerous region of the world for environmental human rights defenders," in which a multitude of human rights violations often occur by way of "violent attacks, torture, disappearances and killings."[7] A glaring example is the recent murder of indigenous defender, Paulo Paulino Guajajara, who was shot dead by illegal loggers in the Amazon.[8]

In 1998, the Amazon Cooperation Treaty Organization (ACTO) was created as a development of the 1978 Amazon Cooperation Treaty (ACT). It was an "international organization [advancing] political and diplomatic coordination between Amazon countries."[9] The Global Environment Facility (GEF) Project followed as a regional strategy tool was enacted to tackle climate change on a practical level. Focused mainly on water protection, it aimed to provide Amazon countries "with a set of tools to properly plan for climate adaptation."[10] However, even with this international framework, the Amazon has failed to find footing for protection, as the ACTO is in need of improvement in order for effective regional implementation of its policies.[11]

---

6 Maria Antonia Tigre, *Building a Regional Adaptation Strategy for Amazon Countries* (2019) Int Environ Agreements Vol. 19, Issue 4-5, Springer Netherlands, 417.

7 Article 19, *A Deadly Shade of Green Threats to Environmental Human Rights Defenders in Latin America* (2016), date accessed: Sept. 01, 2020, https://www.article19.org/data/files/Deadly_shade_of_green_A5_72pp_report_hires_PAGES_PDF.pdf.

8 BBC, Brazil: Amazon land defender killed by illegal loggers (2016), date accessed: Sept. 01, 2020, https://www.bbc.co.uk/news/world-latin-america-50278523.

9 Maria Antonia Tigre, *Building a Regional Adaptation Strategy for Amazon Countries* (2019) Int Environ Agreements, Vol. 19, Issue 4-5, Springer Netherlands, 416.

10 Maria Antonia Tigre, *Building a Regional Adaptation Strategy for Amazon Countries* (2019) Int Environ Agreements, Vol. 19, Issue 4-5, Springer Netherlands, 418; 419: "despite its intent to address water security concerns, the GEF Project failed to do so."

11 Maria Antonia Tigre, *Building a Regional Adaptation Strategy for Amazon Countries* (2019) Int Environ Agreements, Vol. 19, Issue 4-5, Springer Netherlands, 422.

Amazonian Countries' Contribution to IEL

The Paris Agreement

The Paris Agreement[12] was established in 2015, marking "a new era in climate negotiations, reinforcing environmental multilateralism."[13] It was the first legally binding piece of international legislation regarding climate change reduction, reached at the Twenty-First Conference of the Parties to the United Nations Framework Convention on Climate Change (UN-FCCC).[14] Politically, it is often used as a benchmark for assessing international cooperation of countries; the USA recently withdrew from the Agreement, which sparked political tension surrounding the leadership of the country. All parties that sign to it are required to implement NAPs and actions, which many have done so including some Amazonian countries like Brazil and Colombia.[15]

The Escazú Agreement

The Escazú Agreement[16] was created in 2018, complementing the 1998 Aarhus Convention,[17] which was sponsored by the UN Economic Commission of Europe. It is historic in being the first legal agreement to include an emphasis on protecting EDHRs,[18] and the first one to express the right to a healthy environment.[19] Andrés Liévano states that this Agreement matters, because it "seeks to give citizens more comprehensive access to

---

12 UNFCCC, Adoption of the Paris Agreement, decision 1/CP.21 (FCCC/CP/2015/10/Add.1) (2015), Bonn: United Nations Framework Convention on Climate Change Secretariat.

13 Maria Antonia Tigre, *Building a Regional Adaptation Strategy for Amazon Countries* (2019) Int Environ Agreements, Vol. 19, Issue 4-5, Springer Netherlands, 413.

14 Julia Dehm, *Carbon Colonialism or Climate Justice: Interrogating the International Climate Regime from a TWAIL Perspective* (2016) Windsor YB Access Just, Vol. 33, Issue 3, 130.

15 Maria Antonia Tigre, *Building a Regional Adaptation Strategy for Amazon Countries* (2019) Int Environ Agreements, Vol. 19, Issue 4-5, Springer Netherlands, 414.

16 Regional Agreement on Access to Information, Public Participation and Justice in Environmental Matters in Latin America and the Caribbean (Escazú Agreement) (Mar. 4, 2018) LC/CNP10.9/5.

17 Convention on Access to Information, Public Participation in Decision-Making and Access to Justice in Environmental Matters 1998.

18 Convention on Access to Information, Public Participation in Decision-Making and Access to Justice in Environmental Matters 1998, Article 9(2) and 9(3).

19 Convention on Access to Information, Public Participation in Decision-Making and Access to Justice in Environmental Matters 1998, Article 4(1).

information on environmental issues," as well as emphasizing the importance of environmental justice and the protection of human rights.[20] It also could help to spur on regional agreements in other parts of the developing world, as Lanalath De Silva points out.[21] However, Article 5 of the Agreement is an exemption clause that essentially gives countries discretion not to apply its Articles by way of their own domestic legislation, without defining these exceptions.[22] This therefore threatens its practical effectiveness.

Brazil Versus Colombia

In this section, we will briefly compare the effectiveness of two Amazon countries' climate change strategies.

There are nine South American countries that this biome covers. Brazil contains the majority of the Amazon, being deemed "the world's most biologically mega-diverse country."[23] Brazil came to make up half of the continent in the nineteenth century when the Spanish-speaking colonies were emancipated; Brazil redrew its borders using the international legal principle of *Uti Possidetis*, claiming as much of the Amazon as it could.[24] However, Brazil's infrastructural development has come at the rainforest's expense.

In 2002, Brazil signed a cooperation agreement with the World Wide Fund for Nature which established the Amazon Region Protected Areas Program. Bret Simpson observes this as potentially bridging the gap "left by the limited public international law instruments in this field […] giving practical effect to those […] that do exist."[25] Brazil's efforts can also be

20 Andrés Bermúdez Liévano, *What's the Latest with the Escazú Agreement?* (2019) Diálogo Chino, date accessed: Jan. 09, 2020, https://dialogochino.net/30927-whats-the-latest-with-the-escazu-agreement/.

21 Lanalath De Silva, *Escazú Agreement 2018: A Landmark for the LAC Region* (2018) Chinese Journal of Environmental Law, Vol. 2, Issue 1, Brill Nijhoff, 98.

22 Escazú Agreement Article 5(6): "Access to information may be refused in accordance with domestic legislation."

23 Brett Simpson, *International Involvement in Preservation of the Brazilian Amazon Rainforest: Context, Constraints and Scope* (2010) Asia Pacific Journal of Environmental Law, Vol. 13, Issue 1, Australian Centre for Climate and Environmental Law, 40.

24 Brett Simpson, *International Involvement in Preservation of the Brazilian Amazon Rainforest: Context, Constraints and Scope* (2010) Asia Pacific Journal of Environmental Law, Vol. 13, Issue 1, Australian Centre for Climate and Environmental Law, 42–43.

25 Brett Simpson, *International Involvement in Preservation of the Brazilian Amazon Rainforest: Context, Constraints and Scope* (2010) Asia Pacific Journal of Environmental Law, Vol. 13, Issue 1, Australian Centre for Climate and Environmental Law, 43.

seen as giving rise to the creation of the Reduced Emissions from Defor-estation and Degradation initiative, which emphasized the importance of forestry in the scheme of environmental law something that international legislations like the Kyoto Protocol[26] left out.[27]

However, since 2019 with the changing of governmental leadership in Brazil, it appears that the destruction of the rainforest has exponentially increased. William Carvalho and others observed that Jair Bolsonaro's successful campaign for presidency in 2018 also saw nearly a 50% increase in deforestation compared to the year before,[28] and that the administration has threatened to follow the USA's steps and leave the Paris Agreement, which would emancipate its obligations against deforestation.[29] This has transnational implications: in 2017, Norway cut half of its funding to the Amazon Fund as reaction to the rising deforestation rates and has since threatened to completely withdraw funding.[30]

Brazil has a notoriously lax legal system, which creates a "virtually endless succession of appeals," so if someone can afford to damage the environment, they will be able to, and "avoid punishment almost indefi-nitely."[31] In comparison, Colombia has been making waves in its judicial system in regard to environmental protection. There are three significant cases: the *Atrato River* case,[32] the *Barragán* case[33] and the *Pisba Paramo*

---

26 UNFCCC (1997) Kyoto Protocol to the United Nations Framework Convention on Climate Change adopted at COP3 in Kyoto, Japan, on Dec. 11, 1997.

27 UNFCCC (1997) Kyoto Protocol to the United Nations Framework Convention on Climate Change adopted at COP3 in Kyoto, Japan, on Dec. 11, 1997, 55.

28 William Carvalho et al., *Deforestation Control in the Brazilian Amazon: A Conserva-tion Struggle Being Lost as Agreements and Regulations Are Subverted and Bypassed* (2019) Perspectives in Ecology and Conservation, Associação Brasileira De Ciência Ecologica e Conservação, Vol. 17, Issue 3, 127.

29 William Carvalho et al., *Deforestation Control in the Brazilian Amazon: A Conserva-tion Struggle Being Lost as Agreements and Regulations Are Subverted and Bypassed* (2019) Perspectives in Ecology and Conservation, Associação Brasileira De Ciência Ecologica e Conservação, Vol. 17, Issue 3, 123.

30 William Carvalho et al., *Deforestation Control in the Brazilian Amazon: A Conserva-tion Struggle Being Lost as Agreements and Regulations Are Subverted and Bypassed* (2019) Perspectives in Ecology and Conservation, Associação Brasileira De Ciência Ecologica e Conservação, Vol. 17, Issue 3, 123.

31 William Carvalho et al., *Deforestation Control in the Brazilian Amazon: A Conserva-tion Struggle Being Lost as Agreements and Regulations Are Subverted and Bypassed* (2019) Perspectives in Ecology and Conservation, Associação Brasileira De Ciência Ecologica e Conservação, Vol. 17, Issue 3, 127.

32 Judgment T-622/16, Constitutional Court of Colombia (2016).

33 Judgment ST4360/2018, Constitutional Court of Colombia (2018).

appeal.[34] In these cases, the courts reasoned that nature itself deserves rights and protection, as well as the humans who would be most affected by environmental degradation. This is in stark contrast to Brazil's attitude to environmental protection. However, it is also understood that a solely eco-centric approach to the legal system could be "costly and difficult,"[35] so it all boils down to a cost-benefit analysis.

South America Versus Central America

On a larger regional scale, Amazonia can look to Central America (CA) for a more effective way of tackling climate change. CA has similar climate concerns to South America; however, they have much less of a carbon footprint and a lesser significant contribution to environmental damage.[36] Whereas South America only has the ACTO, CA has more nuanced regional development, with the Central American Integration System (Sistema de la Integración Centroamericana ((SICA)) and the Central American Commission on Environmental Development (Comisión Centroamericana de Ambiente y Desarrollo ((CCAD)). Tigre compares both regions, noting that CA "has progressed further toward a regional plan to tackle climate change," despite Amazonia having ties to an international organization, "which, however, still moves slowly toward achieving its goals."[37] She argues that the main problem is that there is not enough cooperation between the Amazonian countries for a regional strategy to succeed.[38]

34 Ximena Sierra Camargo, *The Ecocentric Turn of Environmental Justice in Colombia* (2019) King's Law Journal, Vol. 30, Issue 2, 230.
35 Ximena Sierra Camargo, *The Ecocentric Turn of Environmental Justice in Colombia* (2019) King's Law Journal, Vol. 30, Issue 2, 232.
36 Maria Antonia Tigre, *Building a Regional Adaptation Strategy for Amazon Countries* (2019) Int Environ Agreements, Vol. 19, Issue 4-5, Springer Netherlands, 419-420.
37 Maria Antonia Tigre, *Building a Regional Adaptation Strategy for Amazon Countries* (2019) Int Environ Agreements, Vol. 19, Issue 4-5, Springer Netherlands, 421.
38 Maria Antonia Tigre, *Building a Regional Adaptation Strategy for Amazon Countries* (2019) Int Environ Agreements, Vol. 19, Issue 4-5, Springer Netherlands, 422.

How Could TWAIL Affect Efforts to Protect the Earth's Lungs?

The Escazú Agreement was not only monumental for the reasons mentioned above; it was also borne out of developing countries' desire to denounce the Aarhus Convention's European roots and create a treaty specific to their needs.[39] Regarding Brazil, their apparent lack of cooperation regarding deforestation may stem from their upholding of *Uti Possidetis*, but it could also go deeper. Simpson noted that the issue stems from notions of sovereignty. He notes that it is:

> a key factor in Brazil's resistance to the assumption of international obligations in relation to deforestation or any other matter in which the international community could be seen to be impinging on Brazil's sole possession and ownership of ... its Amazon region.[40]

Simpson follows by noting that Brazil struggles with the idea of allowing foreign powers to have potential entitlement and governance over the Amazon,[41] and this affects their attitude to IEL. Brazil is considered a developing and third world country, with *inter alia*, a very low GDP and high mortality rates; it is also one of five fast-developing economies (BRICS).[42] Its extreme wealth and class inequality can be linked to colonialism and racism, as can its negligence of the indigenous population. In 1992, Brazil launched the Pilot Programme to Conserve the Brazilian Rainforests (the G7 Pilot Programme), in which Germany and other developed countries financially contributed; the main aim of the program was to help to protect indigenous Amazon land.[43] This can be contrasted with the current situation, where in November 2019, 300 indigenous

---

39 Lanalath De Silva, *Escazú Agreement 2018: A Landmark for the LAC Region* (2018) Chinese Journal of Environmental Law, Vol. 2, Issue 1, Brill Nijhoff, 94.

40 Brett Simpson, *International Involvement in Preservation of the Brazilian Amazon Rainforest: Context, Constraints and Scope* (2010) Asia Pacific Journal of Environmental Law, Vol. 13, Issue 1, Australian Centre for Climate and Environmental Law, 43.

41 Brett Simpson, *International Involvement in Preservation of the Brazilian Amazon Rainforest: Context, Constraints and Scope* (2010) Asia Pacific Journal of Environmental Law, Vol. 13, Issue 1, Australian Centre for Climate and Environmental Law, 43.

42 World Population Review, Third World Countries Population (2019), date accessed: Jan. 13, 2020, http://worldpopulationreview.com/countries/third-world-countries/.

43 World Population Review, Third World Countries Population (2019), date accessed: Jan. 13, 2020, http://worldpopulationreview.com/countries/third-world-countries/, 45.

groups teamed up with hundreds of European researchers and conservationists, penning a letter to the European Union asking that "Brazil protects indigenous and local communities, human rights and the environment, creating environmental criteria for traded commodities."[44] Though the G7 Programme was a success, it is important to note that it was only because Brazil wanted it to be. Simpson argues that it illustrated that Brazil's cooperation with IEL only worked if "the involvement was by way of substantial tangible support for action by Brazil itself."[45] If there is something to conclude here, it is that possibly looking at IEL through a developing country's lens may help to reduce the effects of climate change, and that is what TWAIL scholars aim to do.

Response to IEL

The Problem with IEL

According to James Gathii, TWAIL scholarship "provides a substantive critique of both the politics and the scholarship of international law, in addition to exploring the extent to which international law has legitimated global processes of marginalization and domination of the peoples of the third world."[46] He points to Karin Mickelson's work on the current development of IEL and how it often frames climate change as a result of developing countries' environmental damage. Modern notions of conservationism stem from the idea that non-Europeans are at fault for damaging the environment.[47] Therefore, there becomes a skewed image of the tampering with nature; European colonialism's historically much bigger contribution to climate change becomes downsized. It "erases hundreds of years of colonial rule under which economic power and ownership of vast vistas of territory was concentrated in a few countries over hundreds of

---

44 William Carvalho et al., *Deforestation Control in the Brazilian Amazon: A Conservation Struggle Being Lost as Agreements and Regulations Are Subverted and Bypassed* (2019) Perspectives in Ecology and Conservation, Associação Brasileira De Ciência Ecologica e Conservação, Vol. 17, Issue 3, 128.

45 World Population Review, Third World Countries Population (2019), date accessed: Jan. 13, 2020, http://worldpopulationreview.com/countries/third-world-countries/, 45.

46 James Thuo Gathii, *The Agenda of Third World Approaches to International Law* (2019) International Legal Theory: Foundations and Frontiers, edited by Jeffery Dunnoff and Mark Pollack, Cambridge University Press, 3.

47 Karin Mickelson, *South, North International Environmental Law, and International Environmental Lawyers*, (2000) Yearbook of Intl Env. Law, Vol. 11, 52, 60.

years."[48] According to TWAIL, IEL currently causes a bigger rift between developing and developed countries by determining who is to be held responsible for a global environmental travesty. This has, in turn, "produced backlash from northern industrial economies against developing country agendas."[49] For example, as mentioned above, the tensions between Norway and Brazil.

Carmen Gonzalez and Sumudu Atapattu have observed that the most developed countries are actually the most responsible for climate change damage, "accounting for 74 per cent of global economic activity since 1950, though such nations comprise only 18 per cent of the planet's population."[50] The North/South divide is seen as a blockade to IEL's effectiveness, due to the constant conflicts between developed and developing countries over how to establish international cooperation with environmental treaties and agreements.[51] Developing countries tend to suffer the most damage from climate change, so it is unfair to hold them to such an extremely high standard without allowing them the tools for economic national development and threatening them where they may fall short of their obligations. This is why treaties like the Escazú Agreement are a better step in the right direction, helping to create localized improvement of developing nations instead of holding them to a treaty penned by Northern countries. For example, the UNFCCC has been criticized for dismissing the primary cause of climate change, instead "threatening the livelihoods of those communities with limited responsibility for and high vulnerability to climate change," a term recently coined as "carbon colonialism."[52] There has also been pushback against international treaties such as the Kyoto

---

48 Karin Mickelson, *South, North International Environmental Law, and International Environmental Lawyers*, (2000) Yearbook of Intl Env. Law, Vol. 11, 52, 63.

49 James Thuo Gathii, *The Agenda of Third World Approaches to International Law* (2019) International Legal Theory: Foundations and Frontiers, edited by Jeffery Dunnoff and Mark Pollack, Cambridge University Press, 28.

50 Carmen G. Gonzalez and Sumudu Atapattu, *International Environmental Law, Environmental Justice, and the Global South* (2017) Transnat'l L & Contemp Probs, Vol. 26, Issue 2, 230.

51 Carmen G. Gonzalez and Sumudu Atapattu, *International Environmental Law, Environmental Justice, and the Global South* (2017) Transnat'l L & Contemp Probs, Vol. 26, Issue. 2, 231.

52 Julia Dehm, *Carbon Colonialism or Climate Justice: Interrogating the International Climate Regime from a TWAIL Perspective* (2016) Windsor YB Access Just, Vol. 33, Issue 3, 131.

Protocol and the use of its flexibility mechanisms, which include creating a carbon market that developing countries often struggle to benefit from.[53]

The questions then become, how do TWAIL scholars intend to tackle climate change issues? What are the criteria? Where does the burden of responsibility shift? How could this affect transnational relations between economically and culturally disparate nations?

Justice, Responsibility, and Rights

TWAIL scholars may often look at IEL through lenses of *justice*. Dehm states that "environmental justice is both a social movement and a framework through which to evaluate domestic and international laws, policies, and practices that have a disparate impact on vulnerable communities;"[54] Gonzalez and Atapattu argue that it can be a useful mechanism "for analyzing North-South environmental conflicts."[55] They also emphasis the importance of distributive, procedural, corrective, and social justice; for example, distributive justice focuses on the fact that the most affluent countries consume "roughly eighty percent of global economic output and generates over ninety percent of its hazardous waste, which is in turn often exported to the Global South;" procedural justice can help to highlight developed countries' dominance in the international sphere, dismissing the concerns of poorer countries.[56]

A good example of tackling distributive injustice is through the principle of common but differentiated responsibility (CBDR), which adds more nuance to the idea that every single country is equally at fault and therefore equally responsible for ending climate change. Dehm argues that differential treatment of countries should be contingent on their economic standing and the "historical responsibility of developed countries for

---

53 Julia Dehm, *Carbon Colonialism or Climate Justice: Interrogating the International Climate Regime from a TWAIL Perspective* (2016) Windsor YB Access Just, Vol. 33, Issue 3, 134.

54 Carmen G. Gonzalez and Sumudu Atapattu, *International Environmental Law, Environmental Justice, and the Global South* (2017) Transnat'l L & Contemp Probs, Vol. 26, Issue 2, 233.

55 Carmen G. Gonzalez and Sumudu Atapattu, *International Environmental Law, Environmental Justice, and the Global South* (2017) Transnat'l L & Contemp Probs, Vol. 26, Issue 2, 234-235.

56 Carmen G. Gonzalez and Sumudu Atapattu, *International Environmental Law, Environmental Justice, and the Global South* (2017) Transnat'l L & Contemp Probs, Vol. 26, Issue 2, 234.

climate change," thus helping to "ameliorate the North's unequal appro-
priation of atmospheric space."[57] Brazil has become somewhat indebted to
countries like Norway and Germany through their funding, and Dehm
argues that this worsens the North/South divide:

> countries in the South can be differently compelled to take action
> pursuant to a "common concern" if they are subject to conditionality
> through debt or in need of climate finance, than countries of the
> North who are providers of this finance.[58]

An argument against CBDR is that it could encourage complacency among
developing countries in regard to the mitigation of climate change. However, the author believes that it could create better international communication and cooperation, in terms of actually working exactly what needs to
be done where, as Dehm states: "transformation towards decarbonization
requires precisely different actions in different places, because social and
ecological changes unfold in contextual, situated and messy ways ... ."[59]

A TWAIL perspective may also shed light on a more human rights-
based angle to tackling deforestation. For example, Colombia's judicial
shift or the indigenous groups reaching out to Europe for human rights
protection. Gonzalez states that IEL lacks human rights mechanisms; it
forces victims of climate change to "[resort] to the human rights framework to seek redress."[60] It is important not to understate the value that
rights have in all of this; the amount of human lives lost, whether it be
through environmental danger or even human violence is something that
cannot go unaddressed, especially concerning the Amazon. Currently,
there is not a strong enough link between IEL and international human
rights law. Putting this focus on human rights could help to consider the
environment-based human rights violations that are constantly occurring
in developing countries. Dehm argues that a rights-based approach could

---

57 Julia Dehm, *Carbon Colonialism or Climate Justice: Interrogating the International Climate Regime from a TWAIL Perspective* (2016) 33 Windsor YB Access Just, Vol. 33, Issue 3, 141.
58 Julia Dehm, *Carbon Colonialism or Climate Justice: Interrogating the International Climate Regime from a TWAIL Perspective* (2016) Windsor YB Access Just, Vol. 33, Issue 3, 148.
59 Julia Dehm, *Carbon Colonialism or Climate Justice: Interrogating the International Climate Regime from a TWAIL Perspective* (2016) Windsor YB Access Just, Vol. 33, Issue 3, 150.
60 Carmen G. Gonzalez and Sumudu Atapattu *International Environmental Law, Environmental Justice, and the Global South* (2017) Transnat'l L & Contemp Probs, Vol. 26, Issue 2, 236.

help to mitigate some of the dominance that developed countries enforce through international law, but this would not necessarily stifle the growing global powers of the South, and that there would need to be an "understand-ing [of] how new forms of international authority over land are authorized by the climate regime."[61]

How Can the Amazon Be Saved?

A TWAIL perspective can introduce a different way of looking at the climate crisis, but what are more practical solutions that TWAIL thought could help to contribute toward?

A common conclusion is that the regional implementation of IEL needs to be much stronger. Tigre argues that "a regional component is essential for a multi-level approach, as actions from one country directly those that share this ecosystem."[62] This is evident for a biome like the Amazon that is shared by multiple countries in one continent. Simpson also argues for this, stating that it is important for strong cooperation between the Amazon countries that is "encouraged by functional national legal structures and by international support [and] … strong enforcement by the Brazilian au-thorities."[63] Dehm also argues the importance of building a jurisdictional foundation in order to customize local solutions to local environmental struggles as opposed to domineering international intervention.[64] As men-tioned before, Colombia is currently heading in that direction. Ultimately, there must be less rigidity in application of IEL in different contexts, and it should be much more open to constant adaptation and progression. Car-valho et al. suggest this, stating that "the legal structures, public policies and verification systems that underpin [deforestation regulations] must be constantly upgraded."[65] It can be very difficult to regulate an economically driven problem such as deforestation in the Amazon. However, if the

---

61 Julia Dehm, *Carbon Colonialism or Climate Justice: Interrogating the International Climate Regime from a TWAIL Perspective* (2016) Windsor YB Access Just, Vol. 33, Issue 3, 138.

62 Maria Antonia Tigre, *Building a Regional Adaptation Strategy for Amazon Countries* (2019) Int Environ Agreements, Vol. 19, Issue 4-5, Springer Netherlands, 413.

63 Brett Simpson, *International Involvement in Preservation of the Brazilian Amazon Rainforest: Context, Constraints and Scope* (2010) Asia Pacific Journal of Environ-mental Law, Vol. 13, Issue 1, Australian Centre for Climate and Environmental Law, 59.

64 Julia Dehm *Carbon Colonialism or Climate Justice: Interrogating the International Climate Regime from a TWAIL Perspective* (2016) Windsor YB Access Just, Vol. 33, Issue 3, 157.

65 William Carvalho et al., *Deforestation Control in the Brazilian Amazon: A Conserva-tion Struggle Being Lost as Agreements and Regulations Are Subverted and Bypassed*

current system of IEL is failing in Brazil, a country rich in biodiversity but not in GDP, it is important to continue to look at new ways to try and overcome this inequality and injustice.

Conclusion

There is no cut-and-dry answer to the title question. It is important to establish exactly what it takes to tackle global climate change. Climate change does not have one specific cause from one specific country, and it has clandestine roots in, transnationalism, globalization, capitalism, and growth in civilization. TWAIL arguments may not completely arrest the damage being done to the Amazon, but they could help to fill in gaps of thought that IEL often disregards the complex historical origins of climate change and socioeconomic disparities between countries. Focusing more on principles such as CBDR, rights-based approaches, and environmental justice may help to alleviate some of the tension and heated discussion surrounding Latin America's responsibility to reduce climate change. Ultimately, however, regional and local cooperation is the best step in the right direction in order to tackle the Amazonian crisis more efficiently.

(2019) Perspectives in Ecology and Conservation, Associação Brasileira De Ciência Ecologica e Conservação, Vol. 17, Issue 3, 128.